# Tamerlane

## The Ultimate Warrior

*Roy E. Stier*

**BookPartners, Inc.**
Wilsonville, Oregon

***BookPartners, Inc.***
P.O. Box 922
Wilsonville, Oregon 97070

*To my mother, nee Fern M. Cooley*
*who fell short of her 102nd birthday.*

# Acknowledgments

To the staff at the Santa Barbara Public Library for their professional help in source searches.

To the Archives Department at the University of Washington for their kind help.

To Dr. Muhammed Waley and his staff at the British Library for their many courtesies.

With special thanks to Marina Karpova for her many hours of help in research and translations, both here and in Russia.

# Table of Contents

*Reconstruction of Timur, 1941*

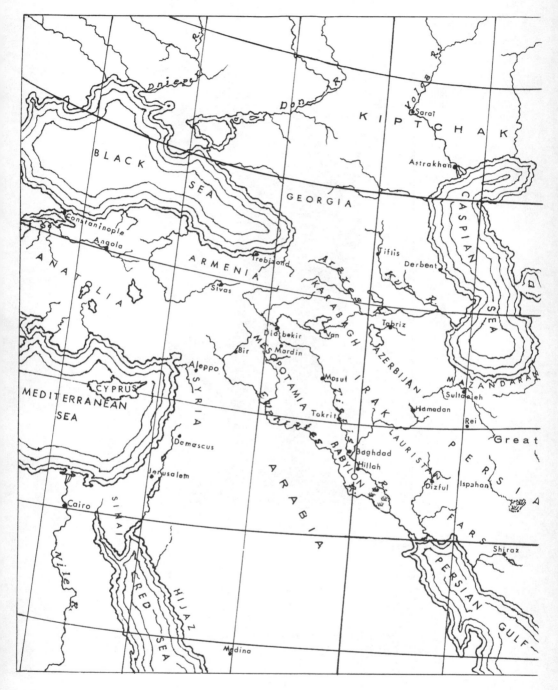

The Timurid Empire

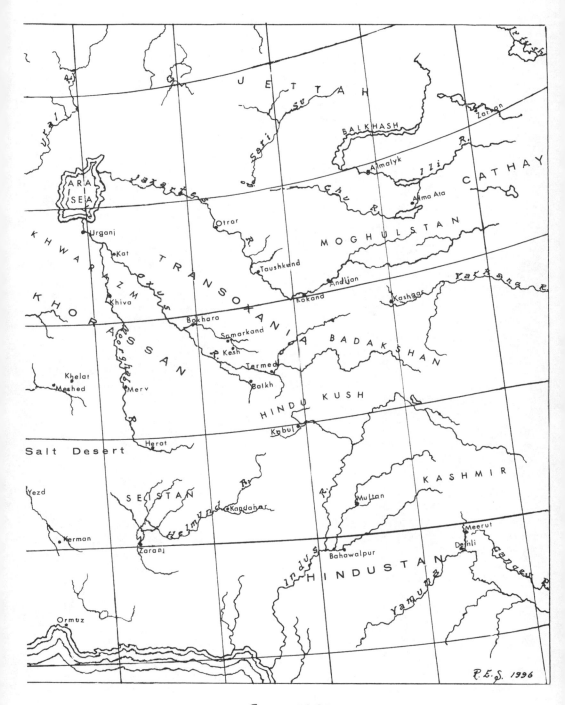

Circa 1405

# Prologue

I was drawn, as to a lodestone rock, to Samarkand, to the mausoleum of Gur Amir, to the great octagonal hall within. There, surrounded by wonder and mystique, under the biggest slab of jade in the world, lies the great warrior himself. Shafts of light through the high window openings do not penetrate the recesses of the majestic mausoleum and the sarcophagus cover of dark green jade appears nearly black.

The break in the stone that resulted from an aborted attempt by the Persian invader Nadir Shah to remove it in 1740 appears to have healed. The crippled body of the legendary conqueror lies beneath the floor in a sealed crypt. His last whispered words of, "Only a stone with my name on it," belies the grandeur within which he rests, after being spirited away in the dead of night, some 300 miles to his final resting place in his beloved Samarkand.

Tamerlane, as he was commonly known to the world, was part of the cosmos. We are also part of the cosmos, therefore, we are a part of Tamerlane.

# Introduction

An ancient book, *Predictions of the Stars*, foretells the birth of three great men who would succeed each other in power and influence:

"He who will be born during the ascent of Cancer, when the sun is in the first house of Capricorn and the moon is in the ninth house of Aquarius, and when the other seven planets will approach the ascending Cancer in Capricorn, he who will be born with such a lucky star shall be called Sakhibkiran.

"Therefore, God had created this world at such a time. At the will of the Master of the Worlds, every eight hundred years the planets come together in the house of Capricorn. The first man who will be born during such a time will declare himself God and will live for thirty-three years; the second, who will be born eight hundred years later, will declare himself half-God (God's messenger) and will live thirty years longer. The third will become Master of the World and will live several years longer than the second. And that number will be determined by adding the two figures of the age of the First One."

Alexander of Macedonia, commonly known as Alexander the Great, was born in 356 B.C. and lived for thirty-three years, conquering much of the known world. Approximately eight hundred years later, the prophet Mohammed declared himself God's messenger and lived sixty-three years.

Approximately eight hundred years later, four generations after Chinghis Khan* devastated central Asia, and forty-two years after his grandson, Khubilay Khan, passed from the scene, in a day when lesser khans fought among themselves for territory and power, the time was ripe for the advent of Sakhibkiran, who would be called the Master of the World.

In the fourteenth century, the villagers and tribal factions who lived in a small village called Sheri-Sebz, tucked away in a quiet valley in central Asia, had no idea of the extraordinary forces destined to follow the birth of an otherwise obscure child. In accordance with the ancient prophecy there arose from humble beginnings a challenger to the established military forces, whose amazing exploits would change the history of the ancient world. The scourge of his time, he remains today a shadowy figure, a tantalizing enigma only partly understood . History has passed him by without removing the shroud of mystery and intrigue that he left as a legacy.

He was born Timur Beg, but because he was lame through most of his life, he was given the name "Timurlene" by the historian Ajaib-al-Muklukat, thirty-five years after his death (*lene* means lame). His name was later Anglicized to Tamerlane, as he is now known.

The name Tamerlane normally evokes revulsion in those who have heard of him. But Tamerlane, or Timur, emerges from his place in history as a complex person with a reputation that crosses the spectrum from the devil incarnate to benefactor of millions. He became known as a great conqueror for his shrewdly cunning strategies and for his fearlessness in battle; for his ruthlessness with those who would resist him; and for his mercy to those who would submit and show him honor. He wrote in his memoirs about "the incalculable advantage which wisdom has over force, and with what small means the greatest designs may be accomplished."

Sir John Malcolm in his *History of Persia* says: "We find it difficult to pronounce whether this wonderful man had most art or

---

*etymological source in Persian was "Tshinghiz"

courage, or by which of these qualities he subdued the greatest number of his enemies. In the community to which he belonged, everything could be affected by a chief…who was popular with the soldiers of his army. To gain these was the great, the constant object of his life. He studied their characters, flattered their vanity, fed their avarice, generously rewarded their valor; and above all he was patient of their discontent, and ready to pardon even their crimes."

Through accounts of his deeds, as seen by his detractors and his admirers, we will try to capture the essence of his tumultuous life.

One of the scribes of his day, a captive known as "the Arab," who followed several of Tamerlane's campaigns, described him as tall and massive, with a high forehead. His skin was said to be lighter than many of his tribe and have a ruddy glow. He was heavy limbed, and had large shoulders and powerful hands. His beard was long, even for his time, and his voice deep and penetrating.

The historian Al Hacin adds that "Timur had a divine beauty in his eyes and their luster was oppressive to beholders. His hair was curly and fairly long, with a beauteous dusky brown or violet color."

In 1941, the partially mummified remains of Tamerlane were discovered and a group of     Russian scientists studied his corpse in detail. What emerged was a forensic view of a rugged individual with classic features.

Tamerlane's birthplace in Kesh lies in an area that was known as the Mawur-un-nehr, or "land beyond the river." The river is the Oxus, which rises in the mountainous area called the Pamir, a range of rugged peaks that forms the northern boundary of present-day Afghanistan.

The Mawur-un-nehr was roughly contained in the southern half of a larger area known as Transoxania, the land between the Jaxartes River (today's Syr Darya) to the north, and the Oxus River (today's Amu Darya) to the south. Both of these major waterways flow west to northwest and empty into the Aral Sea.

During Tamerlane's time it was advantageous to associate with the Mongol dynasty founded by Chaghatay, Chinghis Khan's second and favorite son. Certain favors and protection were given to those who became known as "Chaghatays." Most of the tribes and clans in Transoxania let it be known that they were members of this favored group, a distinction also claimed by Tamerlane's tribe, the Barlas.

At the time of Khubilay Khan's death in 1294, three cities dominated Transoxania in what is now Uzbekistan. Samarkand was destined to become the capital, with Bokhara and Taushkend as satellites. Samarkand rose from the ashes left in the wake of Chinghis Khan's invasion of 1220. An estimated three hundred thousand of its inhabitants were either killed or forced to flee into the tamarack and wormwood plains to the south. When Marco Polo arrived some fifty years later, however, he found Samarkand rebuilt into a "splendid city."

The dominant religion in the fourteenth century throughout central Asia was Islam, first introduced by the Persians and Turks during their migration period. Tamerlane's tribe, the Barlas, were members of a sect of Islam known as Sunni, and believed that Mohammed did not designate a successor.

The Barlas clan held land to the south and east of Samarkand in an area that was largely pastoral. Wealth was defined by the number of livestock and servants held by local chieftains. Although many servants were assigned the important responsibility of herding the valuable livestock, they were nonetheless considered just as lowly as other servants.

In Tamerlane's day, might made right. Perceived power and religious fervor often dictated how things were done. The law of the land was administered by a tribal and family code, with the blessing of the Islamic caliphate. Leaders, with a combination of religious justification and a high sense of personal purpose, often acted in self-serving ways. Tamerlane was certainly no exception.

Timur made decisions based on visions, which were accepted phenomena in his day. These visions profoundly affected his decisions and dictated a large part of his life style. As a conqueror, Timur knew no peer. At the height of his empire he governed or controlled more land than Chinghis Khan or Khubilay Khan. The scholar Clements R. Markham says that "Timur was no vulgar conqueror, no ordinary man; his history, as displayed both in his own writings, and in those of his biographers, proves that, if not in his acts, certainly in his thoughts and opinions, he was in advance of his age and country."

An inscription over the door of the Gur Amir, Tamerlane's mausoleum in Samarkand, denotes his reputation: "This is the resting place of the illustrious and merciful monarch, the most great sultan, the most mighty warrior, Lord Timur, conqueror of the earth."

What follows is a chronological account of the life and times of this legendary figure.

# 1

## The Formative Years

*Born in ash, a noble son,*
*The planets in conjunction:*
*Many pitfalls at each turn*
*Before you can a birthright earn.*

It was certainly a land in turmoil, a land of avarice and treachery. It was a time when neighbor distrusted neighbor and the clouds of uncertainty cast a pall over the uneasy alliance between Mongols and their unwilling vassals. This was Transoxania in the year 1336 when the prophecy of the ages was about to be fulfilled.

An ancient book called *Predictions of the Stars* became known to the Chaghatays and in particular the tribe in the southeast of Transoxania known as the Barlas. These early predictions were also printed in Sanskrit and called *Madzhmu Fi Akhram Annudzhnum*. In the text of that portion dealing with a remarkable revelation of clairvoyance we find this quotation: "He who will be born during the ascent of the Cancer, when the Sun in the first house of Capricorn and the Moon is in the ninth house of Aquarius, and when the other seven planets will approach the ascending Cancer in Capricorn, he who will be born with such a lucky star shall be called Sakhibkiran.

"Therefore, God had created this world at such a time. At the will of the Master of the Worlds, every 800 years the planets come together in the house of Capricorn. The first man, who will be born during such time, will declare himself God and will live for 33 years, the second who will be born 800 years later, will declare himself half-God (God's messenger) and will live thirty years longer. The third will become Master of the World and will live several years longer than the second. And that number will be determined by adding two figures of the age of the First One."

The interpretation from this ancient reading is quite apparent when we insert the great leaders in their respective time frames and age of their stay upon earth. They are:

- Alexander of Macedonia 356–323 B.C.
  (33 years)
- Prophet Muhammed circa 570–632 A.D. (approx. 63 years)
- Sakhibkiran (Timur) 1336–1405 A.D.
  (63 + 3 + 3 = 69 years)

Hadji Barlas, as chief of the Barlas tribe, became concerned about the prediction of the ancients when the local holy man had a vision that Sakhibkiran (born under a lucky star) was to be the issue of his brother's wife. He arranged for his brother Teraghay Nevian, to be sent on a hunting expedition, then for two warriors to be sent on a kidnapping mission to spirit away his wife. To his closest companions he declared that it was necessary to eliminate "he who would take the power away from me."

Hadji Barlas' wife, hearing of the plot, became alarmed with the planned treachery and sent a trusted servant to warn her sister-in-law. Takhina Khanum was immediately taken away to her brother's house in Sheri-Sebz where she was in hiding until the time to give birth.

At the onset of labor pains Takhina was taken to a peasant's house which was considered a safer location. There, a shallow pit filled with freshly prepared wood ash, was readied for the delivery. The ashes, soft and sterile, became part of the peasant ceremony which would guarantee a good omen for the newborn. Indeed, on the evening of the birth the heavens brought forth the predicted conjunction of the stars (actually the planets Jupiter and Venus).

The birth of the baby boy on April 9, 1336, year of the mouse on the Mongolian calendar, was declared to be a miracle by the family. It was the fulfillment of the local caliph, Shaikh Seid Amir Koulyall, in his pronouncement following the vision to accompany the conjunction of the "stars." Upon Teraghay's return from his obligatory hunting expedition he was assured that all was well as Hadji Barlas denied any threats to the newborn.

In the Mongolian calendar, having a twelve year cycle, the start of the annual season is in the spring. The symbolic years start with the mouse, then continue with the ox, tiger, hare, dragon, serpent, horse, sheep, ape, fowl, dog and pig. The persistent legend has it that the mouse crept up ahead of the camel and succeeded in getting first in the naming process, the camel then losing out entirely.

According to custom, the baby, after forty days, was dressed all in white and brought to the leading holy man for naming. At the time of the family arrival the holy man was reading from the 67th chapter of the Koran. Without hesitation he read aloud: "Are you sure that he who dwelleth in Heaven will not cause the earth to swallow you up? And behold, it shall shake." He turned to Teraghay and said: "We have just named your son Timur." (In the ancient tongue—Tamuru, or "it shall shake." Later the word "timur" refers to "made of iron.")

The official name given was Timur Beg, where the latter name means "noble." He was to carry other titles, however, Timur always held with the first pronunciation by the holy man. From the lineage of his famous ancestor Karacher Nevian who was the minister of the Chaghatay tribes stretching as far south as the Hindu Kush, the family had constantly embraced Islam.

From his birthplace near the village of Sheri-Sebz Timur was taken to the outskirts of Kesh where his father had an extensive herd of sheep, goats and cattle. Like his father before him, Teraghay preferred a more sedate life and eschewed the ministerial and administrative duties by delegating most of them to his relations. His home was rumored to be more of an encampment and quiet refuge for his reflections.

Although of noble lineage, Timur was brought up with people of the plains who taught him the rudiments of country life and of ultimate survival. It was during these formative years that he decided to become the protector of all life forms. This seems at extreme variance with his later development which more closely followed the legacy of his Mongol oriented ancestors. His first public appearance at age seven was occasioned by a holiday gathering of the Barlas clan at which time his uncle Hadji saw him for the first time while he was riding a small horse.

Soon after this Timur was foot racing with two other boys in a field when he soon outdistanced them. He later stated that he came upon an old man who he perceived to be a vision of one of the four Islamic immortal prophets—a khyzr. Timur was immediately arrested by his piercing black eyes as he asked the youth: "Where are your companions?" When Timur explained that he had left them far behind the old man proffered a prophecy: "You will never feel the defeat from anyone." To this Timur queried, "How do you know?" The vision replied: "Because you are the child of Allah. People will come to you and you will lead them. You will have power over many people and many countries." He also added: "When we meet again you will not be able to run as you have today, you will be limping." Timur was quite impressed and asked: "Who are you?" There was no answer to this as he was seen to mount his horse and slowly fade away. In the process he voiced the last words: "Alexander the Great is riding with you!" This incident was declared prophetic by his family and close friends; its implications dwelt with Timur the rest of his life.

The time had come to be sent to his grandfather's house for his education. The Atabegs (tutors and guardians) announced that this would take four or five years for the first stages. Teraghay, upon hearing this cried out, "Oh my God you wouldn't give me a warrior, you would give me a holy man. I need an heir, not an Imam." Here, Teraghay refers to the authority figures from the Shiite sect, very likely in a deprecating manner. In any event Timur remained with the Atabegs for elementary school training where the tutoring was very strict. The boys were beaten with sticks if they misbehaved. Much of the time was set aside for the study of the Koran and its teaching as it related to their coming manhood.

By the time Timur was nine years old he was gifted in the teachings from the holy book and would invariably sit by the side of the teachers in order to be closer to the source of wisdom. In his words: "I learned a fivefold prayer and became the most senior student in the school. At all gatherings I tried to sit next to the Ulems (teacher–monks). I sat with my knees on the ground. I was always respectful to the elderly."

Timur's play consisted of planning war games with his peers where he divided their numbers in half and declared himself the amir. It was about this time that his grandfather took him on an excursion to the suburbs of Karshi, to the ruins of Nakhsab and the place where Alexander the Great stayed during the winter of 329 to 328 B.C. Karshi was some 120 miles southeast of Samarkand and close to the Oxus River. It was sacked by Chinghis Khan in 1220 and never fully recovered. Timur reveled in the sites of several ancient shrines and imagined himself following the footsteps of Alexander.

During Timur's youthful years the reigning monarch of Transoxania was Kazan Sultan who had succeeded Muhammed Khan who had been assassinated after a short time on the throne in Samarkand. The only real challenge to Kazan Sultan was another descendent from Chinghis Khan, in the blood line known as the Chingisids, who had assembled an army near the town of Termed, south of the Oxus, and attacked Kazan's forces. Because of being forewarned by a scouting party, Kazan was able to defeat his foe who received an arrow in his eye and had to retreat to Karshi, thus ending the challenge to the khan for a time.

It was this warlord, Amir Kazaghan, that Timur came to admire as he fancied himself to eventually depose the ruling khan. While in Karshi he inquired about the whereabouts of the amir and made a pledge to himself that he would eventually seek him out. Kazan Sultan had made himself unpopular with the citizenry of southern Transoxania with his haughty and arrogant manner, however, it was his frequent executions of dissidents which ostracized him from the local tribal chiefs. Amir Kazaghan found it increasingly easy for him to recruit from the countryside and imperial army deserters.

During the winter of 1345–46 Kazan Sultan retired to Nakhsab where he suffered the loss of most of his livestock in the severest weather of the decade. His erstwhile enemy, Amir Kazaghan, took advantage of his handicap and mounted another attack. In the spring of 1346 he was able to defeat Kazan in an engagement where the khan of Transoxania was killed. The amir then followed up with a show of moderation as he refrained from sacking the ancient city Nakhsab and treated the khan's family with kindness.

In the succeeding years Amir Kazaghan first replaced the monarchy with another descendent of Chinghis Khan, Danishmundche, largely because he was affable and easily manipulated. This khan lasted only two years and was put to death by his rivals. The amir, still not wishing to take on the administrative duties himself, installed Bayan Khan, a respected member of the Chaghatays. He reigned for several years thereafter and proved to be a benevolent and compassionate ruler.

Meanwhile in Cathay, the warring grandirs descendent from Khubilay Khan were still disputing their various territories. When Pope Benuit XII travelled to the court of the northern Mongols he established a Christian mission in the principal city of the Jettah, Almalyk. The Jettah were a distinct group that separated themselves from the Chaghatays and often conducted raids on those tribal areas to the south of the Jaxartes River.

When Timur reached the age of twelve his father became worried about his upbringing and asked that he be returned from the holy order so that he could learn more about the sciences of his time nearer home. This new association with the somewhat nomadic families in the vicinity of Kesh impressed Timur with the need to prepare himself to become a warrior. From his memoirs he recalls that at this age there were many thoughts in his mind. He noted that:

"I fancied myself to have all the signs of greatness and wisdom, and whoever came to visit me I received with great hauteur and dignity."

Timur was fond of hunting quail and foxes with bow and arrow along with his three or four companions, also in setting up war games where he played at sieging cities. Said to be purposeful in all he did, even as a teenager he seldom laughed or engaged in small talk. One of his favorite pastimes was to charge his small horse while brandishing a tulwar* given to him by his father.

The newly installed Khan, Bayan, invited Timur's father to attend a koureltay (a formal military planning meeting) in Samarkand to insure that all the amirs and chieftains were pledged to his sovereignty. Timur, just turning fourteen years of age, was able to accompany his father. At this special meeting Timur was pitted against Hussein, grandson of Amir Kazaghan and three years older, in a wrestling match. After a considerable time with neither gaining an advantage, the khan declared the contest a draw and presented gifts to both.

As a teenager Timur consorted with the sons of viziers. At one of these meetings he was said to quote his grandmother saying: "My grandmother, who is skilled in augury and divination saw in her sleep a vision, which she expounded as foreshadowing to her one among her sons and grandsons, who would conquer territories and bring men into subjugation and be Lord of the Stars and master of the kings of the age. And I am that man and now fit time is at hand and has come near. Pledge yourselves therefore, to be my back, arms, flank and never to desert me."

In the spring of 1351 Timur accompanied his father on a hunting expedition where he impressed him with the degree of maturity he had attained and also the extent of his ability as a horseman. It was then decided that his education in the arts of the plains people could be enhanced if he spent some time with the shepherds in their environment. For the next year and a half Timur lived with them and learned of their ways, returning back home a toughened veteran in the vicissitudes of nomadic life.

---

* a small Persian saber

Later that year Timur was pondering over his dreams which he interpreted as threatening to his development into manhood. On a hunting expedition he became separated from his companions and came upon a warrior near a river who had apparently been stalking him and was about to draw his bow. With quick reflexes Timur drew first and was able to kill his assailant. Later he confessed to his mother that he had been apprised of the plot preceding his birth and that this incident with the would-be assassin was very likely the work of his treacherous uncle, Hadji Barlas.

In the spring of 1352 Timur's father brought him to the house of Shaikh Seid Amir Koulyall, the local caliph who had earlier predicted greatness for him before his birth. On this occasion it was to affirm his destiny as it was perceived by signs and visions. The old holy man announced to his household that they were about to receive "he who would become ruler of the world."

In a solemn ceremony he presented seven pieces of bread to Timur, each on a portion of fleece—these represented the seven parts of the world he would later rule. Following this Timur was presented with 370 seeds and was asked to count them—these represented the number of descendants that would follow the great monarch. Finally he was presented with seventy raisins and again asked to count them—these represented the number of his family who would become rulers in their own right. Before dismissing Timur, he declared that his next task was to memorize the ninety nine names of Allah, after which he would receive a sign from God when to return.

Before he was 18 years of age Timur had an experience which nearly ended his promised life. While riding down a deer with companions in the winter he became separated and suddenly found himself in a deep gully. Unable to turn his horse in time he had to throw himself backward as the horse plunged downward and was disabled.

With a new mount supplied by his companions they all became lost in a blizzard as darkness was starting to close in. Just by chance they spotted what appeared to be black mounds in the hazy distance. It wasn't until Timur's horse neighed that he felt the presence of other horses and found that the black mounds were felt tents of nomads. They were at first taken for marauders as men and dogs started to attack. Timur called out that he was a Chaghatay and was able to halt them in their initial assault.

The guests were given hot broth and quilts for sleeping. In his memoirs Timur remembers that he was unable to sleep because of the fleas and chose to stay up and tend the fire, telling tales of his ancestors until the break of day. Years later Timur sent gifts to this tribe as a way of thanking them for his timely rescue.

Timur, having come of age in 1356, was given many of his father's possessions in a special family ceremony. Most of the livestock which were pastured in the valley of their tribal lands, together with considerable personal property reverted to Timur. His father also conferred the title of amir to his son to be consummated at a later date when it could be earned. The ceremony was followed with the traditional invocation regarding his obligation to the prophet: "I would not have thee depart from the path of the law of God, where the messenger is Muhammed. Be strengthened by the four pillars of the law: prayer, fasting, pilgrimage and alms."

Soon after this Timur received another visionary experience from the old man with the piercing black eyes. His white bearded patron was quick to inquire if Timur had mastered the art of prayer to Allah and was able to name the ninety nine appellations to his God. When assured that he could indeed do this, the old man intoned a prayer and declared that the young man was ready to return to his holy leader and announce himself ready for the initiation rite. Before Timur could engage him further in conversation the old man slowly faded away and the vision was over.

Teraghay, having been apprised of the vision that the old khizr had foreseen, brought his son once more to the holy man's presence. The shaikh was greatly pleased with the manner in which his charge could repeat the ninety nine names of Allah without hesitation, but particularly that they were recited in the order presented by Shaikh Seid. Timur's grandfather was insistent that he next be apprenticed as a dervish for a period of one year.

Dervishes belonged to a sort of mystical order that were part of the Islamic faith. They originally were wanderers and even beggars, however, in Timur's time they were an established part of the monastery hierarchy. Timur was subsequently sent to a monastery in the eastern Khorassan, that part of Persia near the border of Afghanistan. While there he was befriended by a monk some years his senior, Kabul Shah. They conversed as much about world affairs as the teachings from the Koran. It was evident that Timur was restless to assert himself into what he perceived as his destiny, the military service.

By the time the year was up, Timur was languishing in the monk-style existence and decided to seek out the great Amir Kazaghan to fulfill his aspirations. When it came time to leave the monastery he was not sure just where to seek out his selected mentor. It was not unusual for the Chaghatays to travel over seventy five miles a day, carrying only a small sword and light hunting bow. Except for a bag of grain they carried no provisions, using the countryside as a means of forage.

Striking out to the north Timur came upon an Arab caravan and identified himself as the son of Teraghay Nevian. To his amazement he was informed that the Amir Kazaghan had asked to meet with him. Timur hurried to his encampment which he found in the forests just north of the Oxus River. The excitement that stirred within him was hard to contain as he wished to present a more composed figure.

As the only son of a Barlas chieftain Timur had been known to the plains people as a person to reckon with. It was his lordly sense of purpose, however, which had attracted the amir to ask for his presence. Upon entering the amir's pavilion he was greeted warmly and invited to join in with the Kazaghan army. To Timur's delight he was offered a force of some two thousand warriors to augment his own small band of followers.

Soon after joining the army of the amir a scout brought news to the encampment that some raiders had crossed over the Moorghab River near the city of Merv (in the Khorassan province of Persia) and had driven off many of the amir's horses.

This incident led to Timur's first assignment as a warrior chieftain.

Timur left in hot pursuit with a contingent of two hundred of the fastest horsemen, given the order to retrieve the horses and disperse the raiders to whatever extent he could. When the amir's new commander caught up with the retreating warriors he found them to be Persian raiders as they immediately divided up into two groups to better protect their plunder.

Timur's warriors urged him to attack that portion which consisted of the baggage train so that they could reclaim their property. In his first logistic decision Timur decided to attack the protecting party of warriors instead, saying that if they could be defeated, the others would flee for their lives.

As predicted, the outmatched Persians were routed in a battle where Timur charged at them in full gallop, thus dividing the defenders. Being outflanked, they were easily beaten back with the few survivors leaving the field in full flight. The baggage train, together with the missing horses, was brought back to the amir in triumph.

Kazaghan was very pleased with the initial exploit of his protege and presented him with his own bow and case as a trophy. The amir also noted that Timur was not a direct descendent of the Chinghis Khan, or Chingisid, blood line, yet was still in the forefront for certain favors that could come his way in the future. In particular, it was hinted that there was a potential post to the south where the city of Kabul was still ruled by the Chinghis and Khubilay lineage.

The precise time of Timur's marriage to Narmish Agha in the fall of 1355 has not been documented. As the daughter of Amir Bayan Selduz from the area bordering the province of Khwarazm, it was declared a good match as favorable omens were forthcoming from the holy men to this nineteen year old Chaghatay chieftain. The celebration following the ceremony was cut short when a letter arrived from Amir Kazaghan summoning the bridegroom to return in order to lead a force against Amir Hussein who was threatening Karshi. This was the same Hussein who Timur had fought to a draw in the wrestling match back when he was just fourteen years old.

Hussein, although the grandson of Amir Kazaghan, had broken away from the family after being officially made an amir. He had visions of grandeur and was in the process of establishing a foothold in eastern Khorassan.

Timur was outfitted with supplies and a group of fast horsemen to pursue Hussein and put an end to the plundering of the countryside. His plotted course was to outflank his adversary and hold back the reserves until a propitious moment. As a result of superior logistics and the element of surprise Timur was able to drive Hussein back to his stronghold at Balkh. This city had been built on the southern tributary of the Oxus and its fortifications were still intact after several earlier invasions.

To the northeast of Transoxania, the province of Moghulstan had been, for the most part, left unravaged by the warring factions of the Mongols. The country of the Jettah to the west was engaged in sorties across the Jaxartes to northern Transoxania, and the vicinity of the Tien Shen mountains to the south discouraged penetration from the province of Badakshan, on the upper reaches of the Oxus.

From Moghulstan came Amir Daoud, a leader of chieftains who had accumulated enormous power in his homeland. His marriage to Timur's sister, Kutluk Turkhan Agha, was the beginning of a long lasting friendship with his brother-in-law. In later years Amir Daoud was to develop a particular fondness for Timur and became one of his most trusted companions as well as consistent commanders.

Once again Amir Hussein was able to marshal his forces and was threatening to overrun part of the eastern Khorassan. Amir Kazaghan called a council of war to plan a counter move. It was at the gathering of commanders that Timur offered a plan to confront Hussein where Kazaghan's army could pick the time and place. It was structured around a downhill attack at a location and time when the sun would be in the enemy's face.

When the battle was joined this strategy was indeed a decisive factor, but Timur further pleased his lord by charging to the rear of Hussein's army with three hundred of his best horsemen to attack from that point, a move which decimated a number of the enemy and caused the remainder to flee for the security of Balkh.

Complaints had been received by Amir Kazaghan that the ruler of Herat, the largest city in the southern Khorassan, was oppressing his people and terrorizing his detractors. Malik Hussein Ghoury was able to deter any action by Kazaghan for some time as the amir felt that the petitioners did not represent the citizenry. Meanwhile his army was poised to attack the malik if it became necessary.

Timur advised Amir Kazaghan that having assembled his army for the relief of Herat, he should not procrastinate further but press the attack. Timur was given one thousand horsemen and nearly as many infantry to carry out the rescue of the citizens of the city. From a nearby hillside Timur surveyed the intended field of battle, following up the next day by attacking with his back to the sun.

Timur used a tactic that was to become his favorite ploy— he engaged the foe with a center charge and held his flanking sections until hand to hand fighting ensued. The malik's army was deployed behind a low wall. Although driven back, the Herat army was able to regroup and turn back the warriors of Timur at the city walls. Nearly a month of siege would follow before the exhausted city defenders were forced to surrender. The city gates were thrown open and Malik Hussein Ghoury delivered himself to Timur's encampment.

Kazaghan received the malik as a conquered friend but banned him from returning to the city as he placed his grandson in the governor's throne. Timur told some of his closest friends that he toyed with the idea of asking for the governorship but realized that he did not have sufficient support from the commanders.

Amir Kazaghan retired to his home in the countryside between Samarkand and Kesh, at a place where he could anticipate any moves the Mongols to the north might make. Timur continued to excel in leadership and he became bold enough to ask the amir for leadership of the scattered Barlas clan, the title once held by his father. The amir demurred at this request and offered the following counsel: "You must yet wait awhile longer. It will be thine some time or other."

In a move to placate Timur, Kazaghan decided that he should have a second wife and that he would offer his favorite grand-daughter who was only fifteen years old at the time. She was known to be of great beauty and handled herself with the grace of one considerably older. This marriage would be a means of preserving the blood line of the Chaghatays as well as the remnants of the Chingisids. Teen age wives were commonplace at that time and considered a desirable choice.

The wedding of Timur Beg and Abjaz Turkhan Agha was consummated in late 1355. Her common name was known as Aljai (the lord's lady). According to the scribes who were present the bride was prepared in a traditional manner for her wedding day. This consisted of bathing in rose water, followed by a hair cleansing in sesame oil and hot milk to produce the desired luster. The description of her wedding gown included a robe of silver whose train was handled by maids of her household.

Toward the conclusion of the wedding ceremony the amir presented gifts to the attending courtiers as well as to the groom. It was an occasion to drink heavily and recount old victories on the battlefield. At the end of the day, according to custom, Timur entered on a white Arabian horse and carried his bride off to his own pavilion .

Chaghatay wives traditionally did not remain in the home with servants and engage in weaving tapestry, but usually accompanied their husbands in the field. Aljai had just come down from the north where she was known as the princess of the Jalayr clan and was well versed in horsemanship and the hardships of camp life. The Jalayrs were once the leading family in Persia after the waning of the Mongol influence. They had been displaced by the Turkomans and continued to thrive, principally in the mountainous province of Badakshan to the northeast of Samarkand, and in pockets as far west as Armenia.

The newly wedded couple settled into a wing of the family house in Samarkand with carpets, silver and tapestry that had been taken during raiding expeditions. Timur's father, having retired from nearly all activities, settled upon his son most of the remaining cattle, horses, and camels, to accompany the balance of the family range lands. Timur's first wife, Narmish Agha, is little heard from for awhile as she is settled in another wing of the family house.

Soon after the marriage vows were exchanged Timur's mother died suddenly from a heart attack. In his memoirs he says: "I was for some time very melancholy and gave up my ambitious intentions." Once again we see reflections of Timur's inner thoughts where he becomes introspective for a short period of time. It was the influence of his mentor Amir Kazaghan which rekindled within him once again the innate ambitions of grandeur. At age twenty-one Timur became a Chaghatay chieftain as he inherited all of the remainder of the family property, including servants and courtiers.

While the army was engaged in the Khorassan with bands of marauders, back in Samarkand Timur's first born proved to be a son, from the union with his first wife Narmish Agha. He was named Jahanghir, freely translated to mean "world gripper." A festival to celebrate the birth brought most of the clan chieftains to the scene. Noticeably absent was Timur's taciturn uncle, Hadji Barlas.

For some time the Barlas tribes were discontent with their place in the Chaghatay hierarchy. Storm clouds were beginning to form as they became increasingly restless to assert their identity in a more overt fashion. Many of the subchiefs were in favor of putting to death the captured malik of Herat as a matter of revenge. In order to assert his authority, Amir Kazaghan released his prisoner at the River Oxus. Timur was evidently not a part of the plot when Barlas tribesmen ran down and beheaded the fleeing Malik Hussein Ghoury as a means of satisfying their code of honor.

Timur was still twenty-one years of age when his second son was born to his wife Aljai. There was no time to celebrate in ceremony since a plot had been discovered to assassinate Amir Kazaghan where Timur's quick response was successful in foiling the attempt.

In gratitude the amir granted the government of Shuburkan, a city nearly halfway between Balkh and Merv, to Timur. Before taking charge at his new post he rushed to the side of his wife Aljai to rejoice at the good fortune to have a second heir. The couple decided on a traditional naming of the infant—he was called Omar Shaikh, a name which carried the connotation of a noble person coupled with reference to a holy person. This was a time of relative tranquility as Timur basked in the pleasures of newly found fatherhood.

# 2

# The Mongol Invasion

*You'll lose the help of Kazaghan*
*And flee for life to Tokharistan;*
*But intrigue then will serve you well*
*From Mongol prince to infidel.*

Timur has often been touted as the embodiment of Chinghis Khan from a direct blood line. It is quite clear that this was not the case as the lineage study proves otherwise. Tracing five generations back in the Nevian family line we can see how this might have been misconstrued. Timur's distant direct relative Abual Atrak (father of the Turks) was both a forbear of the Nevian family and of Temugin, later Chinghis Khan—the former branch being distinctly Mongol through marriage.

In the ceremony to formalize his emergence into manhood, Timur was presented to Shaikh Abu Beker whom he considered the "polestar of religion." The holy man bound around the waist of Timur his own shawl-girdle, then placed the shaikh's cap on his head. A presentation was made later in the form of a carnelian ring which bore the engraving of Rasty va Rusty (righteousness and salvation). The shaikh once again referred to the prophecy given to him earlier as he predicted: "The aurora of your good fortune will shortly dawn...." Timur later made the ring into his imperial seal.

In the spring of 1357 Timur accompanied Kazaghan to the northern part of Transoxania all the way to the Jaxartes River on a combination sortie and hunting expedition. Being in enemy territory those in the party had dressed themselves in travelling gear over a suit of light mail in the event they were to run into an ambush. On the return to the vicinity of Samarkand Timur was notified that he was to be elevated to the governorship of a part of eastern Khorassan. His territory would include several cities, including Herat, on the upper reaches of the Moorghab River.

Installed in his new station, Timur started a training program for his warriors. He began the process by dividing his assigned troops into tens, hundreds, finally thousands, in the manner of the Mongol military order. His projected plan was to head a well trained army to eventually capture Samarkand and much of Transoxania as well.

This fond hope was suddenly drained from him as he received word that his mentor, Amir Kazaghan, had been treacherously assassinated while on a hunting expedition in the western part of Badakshan, in an area called Kunduz. Clad only in light gear, the amir and his party were ambushed by his own son-in-law, Kutlug Timur, and his father. Evidently prompted by revenge, the pair were set to expiate the removal of the father who had been the governor of Andijan, a primary city in southern Moghulstan. Amir Kazaghan had been informed about misdeeds of Kutlug's father.

Timur recovered the body of his revered patron and saw to it that the remains were "purified" and buried at his palace headquarters in Suly Sarai, south of Samarkand. Further intrigue came to light when it was discovered that Amir Kazaghan's eldest son, Abd Allah, had been apprised of the plot and was to be installed as vizier in the new government of Transoxania for his part in the treachery. As vizier, Abd Allah was to have charge of all tax collection, dispersal of funds and paymaster for the army.

This triumvirate of father, son, and brother-in-law proved to be short lived as Timur and the remainder of Amir Kazaghan's family vowed to avenge his untimely death. Timur first enlisted the help of his father-in-law Bayan Selduz, and gave him the fortress of

Shadman to seal the deal. Even his treacherous uncle, Hadji Barlas, was induced to join the revolt, and to insure success, a goodly number of Samarkand citizens were recruited as well.

Kutlug Timur and his father were driven into hiding where a search party discovered them in the mountainous region of the upper Oxus River. There, all of the renegade party met death and the relatives of Kazaghan reveled in the act of hacking Kutlug to little pieces. As to Abd Allah, he proved to be miserly and soundly hated, ending up in exile south of the Oxus where he died within the year.

For a time Timur, his uncle Hadji, and Bayan Selduz ruled the southern portion of Transoxania and the cities of Samarkand and Bokhara. The first crack in this shaky partnership came when Bayan, addicted to excessive drinking, succeeded in bringing about his premature death. This presented a new problem how to divide the properties of this departed Jalayr prince, a problem which further alienated Timur from his uncle. Timur's wish to divide the wealth among tribal relatives was negated by Hadji Barlas as he planned to inherit it all by default at a later time. In any event Hadji emerged as the more powerful of the two and took over most of the governmental duties.

Leaving much of the dispositions in a sort of limbo, Timur turned his attentions in another direction—a policy of divide and conquer. He sought the help of petty princes throughout Transoxania with letters of entreaty to join him in the sharing of government. This ploy worked to perfection as the princes were all unaware of the inclusion of others. In Timur's words: "Each of them bound themselves with the girdle of fealty to me." Timur then implored Elchi Bugha, the successor of Bayan Selduz in the city of Balkh, to respond to a rumored complaint from the inhabitants of Badakshan.

With promises of land annexation Elchi Bugha marched from Balkh to attack the eastern province, his heart filled with the spirit of a redeemer and local hero. Timur's ally of the moment was Hadji Ayzdy, from a neighboring tribe, who was requested to move into the vacuum at Balkh. He fell prey to the returning Elchi Bugha who found out about the ruse before actually entering Badakshan. He and his outmanned army sought refuge with Timur, now rejoicing in the weakening process he had set in motion which affected both armies.

Before Timur could follow up with his next move a family member arrived to announce the death of his father. Fearing for the safety of his wives and sons if he further exposed himself in intrigue, he provided for their safety and hurried to Kesh. There, he spent a disconsolate time in arranging for Teraghay's burial and taking over the few properties still held by him. In the later years of his father's life he had led a Spartan existence, largely in the company of his favorite holy men and scholars.

While still in the vicinity of Kesh, Timur was brought word of the incursions into northeast Transoxania by the reigning ruler of the province of Jettah, Tugluk Khan. The Jetes controlled a large territory in what used to be part of old Tatary, with their capital city Almalyk located on the Ili River. The river rose in western Cathay and flowed first westerly, then northerly to empty into a long, narrow lake called the Balkhash.

Emboldened by the chaotic conditions around Samarkand after the departure of the last titular head, Bayan Selduz, the khan penetrated well into Moghulstan, subduing the local amirs as he went. These successes sent him back to his homeland to organize a larger army for the purpose of returning to wrest control of Transoxania from the Mongols.

Hadji Barlas' control of Samarkand was waning as competing tribes were threatening to revolt and depose him. Becoming desperate, he called for a gathering of tribes considered somewhat loyal to him. At this special meeting, or koureltay, he was greeted with a great deal of suspicion and failed to raise an army sufficient to fend off a possible attack. He appealed to Timur for help in withdrawing to Herat if his position became untenable.

It was the Sarbadars, a race that once thrived in the Khorassan, who were actively challenging the Chaghatays. Having moved northward into Samarkand and Bokhara these Sarbadars (meaning "head to the gibbet") had become dominant in several fields, so much so that they were destined to be banished by Timur some years later.

This internal dissension caught the ear of Tugluk Khan as he decided that the time to invade Transoxania proper was as hand. His powerful army headed southwest, bypassing the subjugated Jalayrs as he went. Those tribes in that portion known as the Mawurunnehr were directly in his path. Timur received a warning from Amir Daoud, his sister's husband, that Tugluk had already captured Khojend, just south of the Jaxartes River, and was approaching with 100,000 seasoned warriors.

Just two days march from Samarkand, Timur entered the city where he was greeted by the populace and given the ceremonial keys to the city. With only a token force at his disposal he decided to consult with the spiritual leader Shaikh Tai-badi whether to remain in the area or flee to another country. The shaikh advised him to go to Badakshan and try to assimilate the population peacefully. With his close followers reduced to a mere 65, he decided that there must be a wiser course.

Once again, Timur the tactician, made a move in his best interest. He considered what he was about to do not as capitulation, but a realization that the Mongols were about to reassert their ancient claim to the territory. Although a great deal of plundering would be involved, his small home valley could be spared with a show of bravado.

Timur's wives and sons were sent to the protection of Aljai's brother, Amir Hussein, who had regrouped some followers and was encamped on the lower slopes of the hills near Kabul. Meanwhile Timur's warriors, now numbering only in the hundreds, withdrew into his own territory where he let it be known that he was, indeed, a direct descendent of Chinghis Khan.

There was a considerable exodus from Samarkand and Kesh as many were fleeing for their lives. Some of these came to Timur to pledge support, bringing gifts and asking for whatever protection he could offer. They were summarily turned away as fair weather friends who could not be sustained during normal times.

At the approach of Tugluk's army Hadji Barlas, together with a number of loyal followers, fled southward into the Khorassan. Bayazid Jalayr had been temporarily spared and the pretender to the throne of Samarkand was nowhere to be found. The three major amirs were biding their time in hopes of returning at a later date in possible triumph.

During Timur's youth Samarkand was vulnerable to invasion because there were no protective city walls or fortress enclaves. In 1337, the Sarbadars left in large numbers from the Khorassan and were able to establish themselves as the selfstyled defenders of the city against the sporadic invasions of the Mongols or Jettah. Made up from a nucleus of craftsman, shop keepers, and educators, they formed a dynasty with a succession of chiefs who were selected on the basis of their perceived strength.

At the time of the invasion by Tugluk Khan the leader was Ali Muayyad, and when confronted with the vicissitudes of preparing for war, came up wanting. In a hastily called meeting he asked: "Who amongst you will lead the defense of Islam?" When he was greeted with silence the burden of leadership fell to the main population of Samarkand. It was a lowly cotton cleaner by the name of Abu Bakr who eventually girded himself with weaponry and stepped into the role of commander. Later, this same Abu Bakr was to become a close companion to Timur.

Wherever possible the streets of Samarkand were barricaded and chains strung across the narrow sections. The approaching section of the army under Ilyas Khoja, son of Tugluk Timur, was anxious to distinguish their young leader. The Mongol horsemen were allowed to enter into the city but then were attacked on the flanks as the columns became more attenuated.

A fierce battle ensued where boys as young as twelve years were pressed into service. It was largely the archers who were ensconced in niches above street level who turned the tide and forced the attackers to withdraw. There followed a siege which forced the city dwellers to endure hardships which they were not accustomed to experience. For a time the bickering was threatening to undermine their efforts.

Providence was in store for the besieged Samarkanders as an epidemic was raging in the mounts of the Mongol Jetes. They had always depended heavily on their horses. When sickness claimed up to three fourths of their cavalry stock, the tables turned in favor of the defending foot warriors. Ilyas Khoja and his reduced army were forced to retreat in confusion back to the north and the main army commanded by the khan himself.

A group of mullahs from the mosques, also hearing about the plague, had teamed up with the people of Bokhara to help in the disposition of the retreating Jetes. Before Timur could take advantage of this good fortune his nemesis, Amir Hussein, entered Samarkand and the people, in an ecstatic mood, welcomed him as a conqueror. Although Timur had at least an equal claim to the throne, tradition dictated that neither was completely qualified to rule.

It was decided finally to install a puppet ruler who was in the line of ascension as a member of the Mongol blood line. Timur and his brother-in-law agreed upon one Kabil Shah, a member of the Chingisid family who they considered weak enough to control. He became the khan but opted soon after to give himself the title of emperor. This, neither warlord opposed, as it played into their hands for future negotiations with the other rulers.

All of this was short lived as the main army of the Mongols was once again on the move. This time there was no organized resistance ready to sacrifice body and soul for a lost cause. Arriving without serious incident in Samarkand, the invaders were surprised to find an undisturbed chieftain inviting them to his home as guests. Timur was holding his composure under trying circumstances as he called for a great feast to wine and dine the Mongol officer corps. After a number of gifts were presented he announced his intention to present himself at the court of the great khan.

Despairing of the khan's intention to ravage that part of Transoxania known as the Mawurunnehr, Timur tells of his intrigue as follows: "I deemed it necessary that I should first go unto them, and deceive them by presents and excite their avarice by temptations, that they might withdraw their hands from defoliating and ravaging the kingdom of Mawurunnehr, and from slaughtering the inhabitants thereof, until I should go and see Tugluk Timur Khan."

It was at this time that Timur demonstrated his adeptness at misdirection. He sent an envoy with a letter to the khan naming him as lord of Badakshan, Kashgar, and Transoxania, an inheritance directly from Chinghis Khan because of blood line. He further pledged complete devotion to him and offered many gifts in the course of adherence to the Mongol cause.

From Timur's memoirs came the khan's reply: "...It was once demanded of the fourth Khulleefeh, if the canopy of heaven were a bow, and if mankind were the mark for those arrows; and if almighty God were the unerring archer; to whom could the sons of Adam flee for protection?...thus it is thy duty to flee unto Tugluk Timur, and to take from his hand the bow and arrows of wrath."

Upon receiving this answer which he took to be particularly inviting, Timur describes his reaction as: "I became strong of heart and I saw Tugluk Khan." When the Timur cavalcade arrived in full court dress they found the khan in his encampment on the road between Samarkand and Kesh. He was seated on his traditional white felt matting and received Timur with a great deal of suspicion. Upon reciting the Mongol greeting and showing fearlessness, Timur's overture seemed to be working favorably on Tugluk. After emptying his treasury with more gifts, his demeanor and supplication carried the day.

It seemed that Timur had truly penetrated the Mongol mind with daring and warrior association. He was able to consolidate his place with the new regime. In contrast with Hadji Barlas' demeanor, his regal bearing won the confidence of the khan's top officers. Timur was given leave to return to his own valley where he could protect his home and possessions from any marauding band.

The commission given to Timur was his most triumphant of the entire intrigue as he notes: "...And he gave unto me the government of Mawurunnehr, and in this manner he wrote a commission and an agreement; and he restored unto me the Touman* of Amir Kurrauchaur Nouyaun in that kingdom; and I became the ruler of all the kingdom of Mawurunnehr, even to the waters of the Jaxartes. And this action came to pass in the beginning of my

*10,000 fighting men

fortune and power. And I found by experience that one skillful plan can perform the service of 100,000 warriors."

News of Timur's success with the Mongols reached the retreat encampment of Hadji Barlas and Bayazid Jalayr. The two leaders decided to combine forces with the intent of eventually regaining their territorial losses. They plotted the demise of Timur, realizing that he not only represented a future threat, but could be characterized as a traitor to the Barlas tribe. Meanwhile, Tugluk had withdrawn to the east, leaving his government of Samarkand in the hands of his chieftains.

Later, Bayazid Jalayr regretted the plot and let this lapse in loyalty be known to Timur. On the other hand Hadji Barlas was determined to eventually carry out the removal of his nephew. With renewed soldiers and horsemen, he decided to move upon Samarkand to reestablish his rule.

Timur, having an added number of warriors, intercepted his uncle's army south of Samarkand but was unable to defeat him. This was largely due to a number of defectors in his army which had been approached by Hadji with promises of gifts and promotions. Timur was prompted to make a decision which he later was to regret.

From his memoirs we learn that: "This was the greatest error I committed during my whole reign, for the man was of vile disposition, proud and miserly, but I did not know then of his character." In any event, the plan to invade Badakshan was in motion with Amir Hussein invading from Kabul and Timur from Kesh. It is axiomatic to say that rulers by force must continually look over their shoulders to check for treachery. The success of the Badakshan campaign depended upon a court traitor Kai Kobad who had conspired to kill the monarch. He then went to seek the favor of Timur. This duplicity alarmed Timur to the extent that he had this Judas put to death. "Those that live by the sword...."

Before any real invasion was under way Tugluk Khan suddenly appeared with his Mongol horde in March of 1361—"like a stone dropping among birds." The khan was not to be diverted this time with any overtures of allegiance. His first act upon entering Transoxania was to put to death the pretender Bayazid Jalayr.

Hadji Barlas was able to escape to the south with a small party of his followers. He soon after was set upon by a band of thieves from Seistan and lost his life in the struggle to resist. Meanwhile Amir Hussein had already launched his bid to recapture part of the Chaghatay territory and ran into a large contingent of Jetes southeast of Samarkand.

The amir was soundly defeated and only escaped with a small band of followers into the mountains near Kabul. During this time the inactive Timur was still in the good graces of Tugluk Khan and remained encamped to the east of Samarkand.

Once more taking command of Samarkand, the khan placed his son Ilyas Khoja in charge, and one of his generals to back up the young ruler and fend off any raiders. Timur was then named prince of Samarkand to be the ceremonial head under the other two. Ilyas was given the title of Prince of Transoxania. Timur made a mild objection to his new post, thinking that he should be superior to the General Bikijuk*. He was reminded that the descendants of Chinghis Khan were destined to rule all of his country and that the Chaghatay should serve in whatever capacity needed. As Timur demurred, he placed in the back of his mind the long range plan for opportunity and power.

When the khan returned back to his homeland, Jete General Bikijuk took it upon himself to ravage all of Samarkand. Prince Ilyas had no military at his command other than the palace guard so he satisfied himself with a share of the plunder. Many of the children were sent off as slaves and the holy men of the mosque were largely dispersed.

Timur's message to the khan in protest to this marauding reached Tugluk only after his campaign had started to free the captives of Samarkand. These acts of mercy were interpreted as a rebellion, however, it was the death sentence imposed on seventy Seid slaves which nudged Timur into action. Before they could be

---

*Tugluk's most trusted general

put to the sword he arrived with his followers to rescue these adherents of Muhammed. When word of this incident reached the khan, Timur was branded a traitor.

Still engaged to the north, Tugluk had to act upon the word from his son and sent a message which was intercepted by Timur and read in part: "Timur has exalted the standard of rebellion...." The message included an order to seek out and put to the sword this traitor to the Mongol cause. Timur, not having any plausible way to return in the good graces of the great khan, set about to recruit the valiant youth from the Barlas tribes. He elicited the help of a holy man who issued a decree authorizing the expulsion of the Duzbuks who were the Mongol Jetes engaged in terrorizing the countryside.

The text of the edict was a follows: "According to the conduct and the example of the orthodox Khulleetehs (four ruling caliphs), the followers of Islam, the doctors, and the holy man, and the soldiers, and the subjects, seeing Him noble and worthy thereof, have nominated Amir Timur (the Polar star of dominion, or whom by the favor of God) to the empire; and with their wealth, and with their lives they will exert themselves in expelling and in driving out, and in extirpating and in destroying the tribe of Duzbuk, who have stretched forth the hand of cruelty and rapine over the families and over the wealth, and over the property and over the effects of the faithful."

With this blessing Timur announced that he was eager to exalt the standard of war and gathered his now increasing number of followers for the holy expulsion of the hated Jettahs. He turned away from the prospect of attacking Samarkand as the inhabitants could not be counted upon to rise up in unison. He chose to regroup in the safety of the hill country near Tokharistan* until he could assemble a more formidable army. This became his retreat out of necessity.

Hearing of this effort, Ilyas Khoja dispatched one of his governors, Tukkul Bahaudur, to attack Timur with one thousand horsemen. With only fifty men at first, later rein-

---

*a small province in the mountains above Termed

forced with less than one hundred others, Timur fought with such fury that he won a decisive battle and reduced his attackers to an ineffective force.

While Ilyas Khoja was thus engaged in conflict with Timur, General Bikijuk decided to engage in a life of debauchery. Sorting out four hundred of the most beautiful women he engaged in a near continuous orgy with the company of his senior officers. The citizens of Samarkand were outraged and vowed to avenge the exploitation of these women at a time when the tide of martial control would later turn. Timur would eventually be the benefactor from this turn of events.

In the struggle to fulfill a prophecy of grandeur, his latent qualities of leadership were to be suppressed and sorely tested. Timur's fortunes were destined to confound him, to place him in the most humbling predicaments.

# 3

## The Way Back

*The call to arms as you embark*
*Where errant arrows hit their mark.*
*The Seistan battle is well fought*
*But lameness makes it come to naught.*

Timur, now reduced to only a small number of followers, was obliged to stay in virtual exile for some months. He then moved his encampment westward by skirting along the northern part of the Hindu Kush to the northeastern part of the Khorassan in old Persia. There he met up once again with his unreliable brother-in-law Amir Hussein, an alliance built of necessity for both. It was a slow rebuilding process for them as their thoughts were always centered on the invasion of Transoxania to restore the Chaghatay monarchy.

By gaining an alliance with the malik of Herat, Timur was able to increase his prestige with this race, the Karts. Since 1245 when the mountain men from the area known as Ghur were able to hold off the Chingisid Mongols, their people were the rulers of Herat and the area south to the province of Seistan. As the Mongol influence was waning, that of the Karts was on the ascendancy.

In search of friendly territory, the next move was to the mountainous country to the east of Balkh, near where Amir Kazaghan had met his untimely death. There, Timur carefully put together a nucleus of over 150 horsemen, some of which were deserters from the Jetes, his normally Mongol protagonists, but largely from his own Barlas tribe.

During the month of March, 1361, Timur came upon two lions, one male and one female. Stopping long enough to stalk them he succeeded in killing both with his bow and arrows. The next day in a march over rugged hills the army found an ideal campsite on a hill above a clear water rivulet. Here, they remained for three days, hoping for news that Amir Hussein was to join them imminently.

Fourteen days later, while encamped in the valley of the Arsutt River, Timur went to the top of the hill on the Muhammedan sabbath to spend the entire night. It became a memorable one for him as he later relates to his scribe: "And on that night, which was a holy night, I kept watch; and then morning broke, I was employed in prayer. And after repeating the prayers prescribed by the law, I lifted up my hands in supplication. And in the midst of my supplication I wept; and I implored almighty God, that he would deliver me from that wandering life."

While still encamped near the Arsutt, several detachments were sent out to gain intelligence. After several days news came that a party of troops was advancing from Kumrud (near Kabul) with an apparent notion to attack. Placing himself on a hilltop, Timur was poised to advance in the middle section to confront the enemy when he recognized Shyr Behhram, one of his old followers who had left the army to go to Hindustan, then repented and begged for acceptance into the army.

Four more days passed after this incident before Amir Hussein arrived at the encampment. About the same time contact was made with the Jete forces where the commander was enticed to join up with the Chaghatays by promises of future rewards. He declined, saying that he owed allegiance to Ilyas Khoja because of favored treatment. Although rebuffed, Timur was heartened by the arrival of two hundred cavalry from Kandahar. There was some disturbing news, however, as intelligence reported that some twenty thousand Jetes were making their way southward from Samarkand and were nearing the Oxus River.

The uneasy truce between Timur and his brother-in-law was broken as quarreling broke out among their followers which resulted in the defection of many from both sides during the night. With a diminished force then evident, they were attacked by foothill tribesmen where both leaders lost heavily. The amir's horse was struck by an arrow and he had to quickly substitute it with his wife's mount.

Back in their encampment, they counted their losses and tried to regroup. Although Timur was still confident, Hussein felt that he was following a lost cause. When the sun rose on the next day Timur discovered that his brother-in-law had stealthily left camp under cover of darkness.

Undaunted, Timur was eager to prove himself under battle conditions. With just sixty warriors he moved to the north where his small band attacked the fort at Urjanj, near the city of Khiva, on the lower Oxus. Although he was nearly able to carry it off, he was forced to retire with heavy losses. The long march from the mountains to the south had fatigued the men and Timur was asking for a miracle to conquer such a well fortified stronghold. Now with only seven horsemen and three foot soldiers, he was forced to travel eastward to seek shelter in the desert of Khiva.

By any criteria this situation left him at the lowest ebb of his life. The little band of fugitives, now joined by Hussein at his sister's urging, wandered across the wastelands until they came to a well in the desert. A shepherd gave them some goat meat and they had to content themselves with being wanderers. Timur's second wife Aljai, still travelling with her husband, tried to cheer them up by saying: "Surely our fortunes are now arrived at the lowest point."

For a month they subsisted by scrounging for meager fare in the desert, once again deserted by Hussein. They lived for a time in a deserted village where they were discovered by a band of Turkomans led by Alibek Kurbani and two hundred warriors. Confined in an old cow barn infested by vermin and fleas, the unhappy couple and their few retainers still held hope of survival. What followed was sixty-two days of confinement where Timur and Aljai suffered daily indignities in their desert prison.

The term "Turkoman" appeared first in the eleventh century, A.D. Alexander the Great was said to have noticed their cattle brands and facial features while on expedition near the Jaxartes River. These nomadic people seemed to resemble the Turks and he coined the term that was to surface centuries later. Originally the Turkomans were made up of twenty-four tribes but later consolidation reduced this number considerably.

Those that came from Mongolia down to the region of the city of Kashgar, lying between Moghulstan and Badakshan, brought with them certain peculiar rites for their deceased. Statues were erected over the graves in numbers to match those that the interred had killed during their lifetime, believing that these images would become the servants of their kinfolks during an afterlife. In the ranks of the nobility the deceased would be buried sitting upright with their belongings arranged neatly beside them. This custom was later adopted by Timur and his followers for those of more noble lineage. It is interesting to note that no special ceremony was reported for women who had passed away.

As the Turkoman tribes migrated south and west they gradually absorbed Persia by the end of the twelfth century. The first proper dynasty, the Seldjuks, emerged as the ones who descended from Timur Yayligh to become known as the "men with the iron bows." Their earlier migration ranged only as far as the Great Desert in central Persia, while still retaining a preponderance of power centered near Bokhara in the heart of Transoxania.

The Chaghatays carried much of the Turkoman heritage with them, particularly in their spoken language—Turki–Mongol. Timur was familiar with their devotion to Islam, making use of this by impressing his guard with extensive knowledge of the teachings from the Koran. The Turkoman, Ali, was worn down by Timur's constant pious offerings, however, it was a particular story about Muhammed's cousin who was involved in an incident of mercy which finally brought him to declare: "I bow before the great master Timur and I will free you from prison when I can and all my life will be devoted to serving you."

Meanwhile Ilyas Khoja had learned of Timur's captivity and offered a reward of 300 camels to the person or persons who would deliver him back to Samarkand. The second, and older one of Timur's guards, fell under his spell also and agreed to deliver a message to the nearest dervish. This act was only consummated after Timur surrendered his personal belt which held a single precious ruby, an article that had been hidden from his captors.

With the help of both guards Timur, his wife and small retinue were spirited away in the night on horses provided by the dervish. They made their way to just north of the Oxus where Timur was united with many of his lost warriors. As the word was passed along to the countryside of Timur's presence, many more presented themselves to him and pledged their service. This became the turning point in the great conqueror's career—he was never again to want for followers.

By now it was autumn and the anticipated rainy season was near at hand. Aljai had been counseling Timur to seek out her brother again in order that their combined strength would serve them better in their quest to regain control of the Chaghatay tribes. She was left with the retainers to move at a slower pace as the long confinement had left her sickly. Timur's first thought was to seek out his two boys who had been secretly cared for by relatives.

There is no record of the whereabouts of Narmish Agha, Timur's first wife, but it would seem reasonable that she was under virtual house arrest and long separated from her son Jahanghir. In all of the voluminous records of Timur's life, in particular his memoirs, there is no mention of the disposition of his wives, except on those occasions where they played a large part in a particular incident.

As Timur circled ahead of his wife who was then confined to a horse litter, he was anxious to renew ties with his tribal associates. In a surreptitious manner he was able to pick up followers at every stop as he encamped near the Oxus to await the coming of his wife. He could not breathe easily until they had forded the river between sand bars and she was safely hidden in the area north of Balkh.

Timur then followed with one of the most daring plans of his lifetime. In the company of a small band of faithfuls he once again entered Samarkand and visited friends in secret, some in mosques and others in their own homes. For forty-eight days he risked being seen as he was staying with his elder sister, Turkan Agha. When he received a tip that he had been discovered, he managed a hasty exit at night, this time accompanied by a band of fifty companions.

A fairly sizeable group was to meet him at a prearranged place in an abandoned pasture near Kesh. The enlarged band then headed south where they were joined by Aljai who was saluted by the warriors as having taken a major part in the desert battles. It was a tortuous road that the Timur followers chose to follow, for hundreds of miles through the gathering snow, across the west end of the Hindu Kush, and finally to the outskirts of Kabul. There they were able to get fresh horses and supplies to follow the Kandahar trail.

Winding down toward the valley of the Helmund, they finally were able to join up with Amir Hussein's army. Timur was pleasantly surprised to see that his brother-in-law had amassed a number much greater than his own. They were poised to enter the province of Seistan where the land was rich and filled with sheep and horses. The area was watered largely by the Helmund River which rises in the Kandahar and flows into Lake Zarrah. This then was the setting for the eventual return to power for Timur and his loyalists.

Once again good fortune was at hand. An ambassador from a certain hill people of the Beloochee tribes was asking for help to combat a rebel group who had seized seven forts from them. The combined army was given gifts and promised more if the marauders could be driven out. Amir Hussein's thoughts had drifted beyond a simple rescue as he contemplated the opportunity to become lord of this rich Seistan Province.

Timur was happy to be in the saddle again and reveled in the storming of the rebel strongholds. Using his inherent sense of logistics, he planned several surprise attacks, now using rams, ladders and Greek fire*. The first one was attacked and taken in one night. Hussein took over the booty and appointed his own governor. At the second fort the defenders came out of the surrounding woods to fight, whereby Timur fashioned fascines as a shield to continue his advance. This moving wall so intimidated the defenders that they promptly surrendered.

The third fort was attacked once again at night because of its location in the middle of a sandy plain. Timur's warriors, armed only with bows and arrows, found just a token sentry system and overwhelmed the citadel by employing a number of rope ladders. True to form, Amir Hussein arrived after the fact and proceeded to usurp a share of the command.

The remaining four forts, alarmed by Timur's rapid successes, opted to hold out as best they could. By now the pillaging under the amir's orders was sending a signal to all the countryside that the basic plan was getting out of hand. They were having serious second thoughts about the eventual outcome from their call of assistance.

When the Seistan chief left in the middle of the night to join the rebel cause, the blame was placed on Timur for excesses in the planned conquest. He told his countrymen: "If Amir** Timur tarry in this country. the province of Seistan will pass out from our hands."

In a major skirmish where the defenders were attempting to break out of a Timur entrapment, the wily warrior suffered severe wounds. In his own words: "I saw I was without remedy and I advanced toward them, and gave them battle. And an arrow came and pierced my arm, and another arrow came upon my foot, but in the end I obtained the victory over them."

This incident became the vehicle for two stories which have been perpetuated by several historians. It was said that the great warrior was thrown to the ground by the force of arrows and he had to feign death when overrun by enemy troops. The attacking

---

* a naptha base mixture of firebrand
** the first reference to this title, not yet claimed

*Timur Sustains Wounds in the Seistan*

warriors then were said to mistake him for a deceased person and cut off two fingers of his right hand as a trophy. He then was purported to remain on the field until nightfall, regaining his feet and making his way back to camp on a captured horse.

The other story, also pure fiction, was widely distributed by Timur's detractor, Arabshah. This one has also been fairly widely distributed and has Timur receiving his debilitating wounds while stealing sheep when the owner came upon him in the process.

During the Russian investigation of 1941 (see Appendix A) where scientific experts examined the remains of Timur, it was discovered that the arrow wound in his right arm was actually nearer the elbow, resulting in a permanently bent condition. Timur's referral to the foot wound was apparently close to the ankle where articulation was hampered from tissue damage, causing a shortening of the appendage. Certainly impatience in the due process of healing exacerbated the conditions leading up to his permanent deformities.

Back in his tent during the recovery period Timur learned that the Seistans were thoroughly defeated. His wife Aljai and young son joined him while he was given an application of native herbs for his wounds.

Meanwhile Hussein had retired to a winter headquarters to plot his next move. Some historians have placed Timur near the Persian Gulf for his two months of convalescence, however, it is evident that this time was spent in and around Kurrumfeer, in the northern desert. Evidently it was Aljai who actually did spend some time in Gurmseer, but for the purpose of keeping out of harm's way.

Regaining strength in his right leg proved to be a taxing experience for Timur as he became overly restless. Each day he would exercise with a limping gait as he struggled to walk erect as before. He also fretted about having to adapt an awkward grip while using his bow hand. During this time of recovery Hussein, against the advice of Timur, decided to attack Kabul. His now reduced army met the Jetes who were guarding the city on its outskirts with a frontal attack. The amir was beaten back and the pursuing Jetes scattered his army into small bands while he was obliged to hide in the Hindu Kush.

Together with his companions, Timur returned to the Khorassan where, by prearrangement, he was joined by one hundred more. There were remnants of Amir Hussein's followers who also joined up with him. By late 1362 the word had gone out that Timur was recruiting. Some of his old companions teamed up with others who felt that their destiny was closely linked to their lord, who by now, was becoming somewhat of a legend.

Timur's spirits were on the rise in spite of difficulty in pulling a bowstring and handling the reins of his horse. Before starting northward in his campaign to retake Samarkand, he decreed that ten days of feasting and rejoicing must precede this incursion. Chaghatay ranks by now had swelled to something over three thousand, nearly all seasoned warriors.

An encampment near the upper Oxus was to become the setting for an amazing incident. Timur's army had been waiting in vain for some remaining Hussein volunteers. They had apparently been discovered by the Balkh protective garrison. What followed was taken from the memoirs and deserves to be given in its entirety:

"I had not yet rested from my devotions when a number of people appeared afar off; and they were passing along in a line with the hill. I mounted my horse and came behind them, that I might know their condition, and what men they were. They were in all, seventy horsemen; and I asked of them saying, 'Warriors, who are thee?' and they answered unto me. 'We are the servants of Amir Timur and we wander in search of him; but lo! we find him not.' And I said unto them, 'I also am one of the servants of the amir. How say ye, if I be your guide and conduct you unto him?' And one of them put horse to speed and went and carried news to the leaders, saying, 'We have found a guide who can lead us to Amir Timur!' The leaders drew back the reins of their horses and gave orders that I should appear before them. They were three troops; and the leader of the first troop was Toghluk Khajah Barlas; and the leader of the second troop was Amir Saif-ud-din; and the leader of the third troop was Toubuk Behauder."

"When their eyes fell upon me, they were overwhelmed with joy; and they alighted from their horses, and they came, and they kneeled, and they kissed my stirrup. I also alighted from my horse, and took each of them in my arms. And I put my turban on the head of Toghluk Khajah; and my girdle, which was very rich in jewels, and wrought with gold, I bound on the loins of Amir Saif-ud-din; and I clothed Toubuk Behauder with my cloak. And they wept; and I wept also. When the hour of prayer was arrived, we prayed together. And we mounted our horses, and came and alighted at my dwelling; and I collected my people together, and we made a feast."

From his newly found friends Timur learned that an army of many thousand Jetes were on their way down from Samarkand, plundering as they went. Sensing that this force was rapidly building resentment, it could be a source for rebuilding an increasing army. To this end Timur decided to cross the Oxus and carry out a daring plan.

The Jetes under General Bikijuk had spread their forces along the river to cover all of the possible fords, knowing that an attack could come at any of these points. They left a token force at the only bridge, content that no considerable force could break through at such an advantageous choke point.

The famous stone bridge, located near Munk, the largest city of Badakshan, spanned a deep gorge of the Oxus where the river was narrow and deep. After scouting this deployment, Timur decided upon one of his notable strategic moves, once more with a smaller force than his enemy. Under cover of darkness, and with only an infiltration column, he sneaked behind the Jete lines and spread out in thin deployment along the lower hillside to the north of the Oxus. Each of these small groups lit a number of campfires in turn, giving the impression of a sizeable army in an outflanking position.

Bikijuk took the bait and gave orders for his army to regroup by moving northwest in order to consolidate. The main army of Timur which had been arranged at strategic points, then crossed the river at the fords and attacked the flank of the Jetes in force.

Although the Mongols had retreated in confusion, they were not yet defeated. As expected, the Timur fortunes picked up considerably in the countryside as he made what restitution he could from captured Jete stores. The remnants of Bikijuk's army were systematically picked apart by the resurgent Chaghatay regulars, now considerably augmented by fresh volunteers.

Hearing of the retreat by his general, Ilyas Khoja was bent on revenge. He took what forces he still had and entered the village near Kesh where Timur had spent much of his youth. The Mongol invaders captured and beheaded all of the inhabitants, putting many of the heads on poles as a gesture of defiance.

When Timur discovered this display of sheer brutality he was both outraged and deeply saddened. His grief was deepened when he retrieved the head of the local holy man who had been his father's spiritual advisor. In later legend, holy man Khakull Paluan, was said to have carried his head in his hand and miraculously returned to the small mosque where he disappeared into the wall.

In actuality the head of the revered holy man was preserved and became a sacred object which Timur kept in his possession for the rest of his days. In later years the mosque crumbled to dust but was replaced by a well and shrine which marked the sacred spot where the holy man was elevated to sainthood.

Each day brought new victories for the Chaghatays. Before they could reach Samarkand Governor Ilyas Khoja fled to Almalyk on his way toward Cathay. It was the news that his father had died which sent him home in confusion to claim his father's throne. Bikijuk and two other Mongol generals were captured. Despite counsel by Amir Hussein to put them to death, Timur displayed his often belied compassion. He gave them horses and set them free to return to their traditional homeland, now leaderless with the passing of Tugluk Khan.

Taking the city of Samarkand was enhanced by a typical Timur ruse. Within sight of the city walls he scattered his troops in all directions where each group cut poplar branches for dragging at all angles behind the horses. The prodigious amount of dust gave not only the impression of an immense army, but that they were coming in from all sides.

The Jete garrison, completely demoralized, left in haste, thus sparing any siege with its attendant loss of life. Historians have noted this turn of events as having elevated Timur to legendary status as they have written: "The Lord Timur, always fortunate in war, in this year defeated an army by fire and captured a city by dust."

Amir Hussein, sensing that greatness was slipping from his grasp, exacted money and certain privileges from Timur. The latter, in return, forced him to swear allegiance. Once again Aljai came into play by stressing the importance of a family alliance. Her beliefs were described in the old texts in the following manner: "To their camp came the illustrious princess Aljai who nursed the sick lords."

Hussein had taken the fort of Kurshee, some seventy miles southwest of Samarkand, and Timur felt honor bound to regain this important post. Since he had only a small force at the time, he had to resort to a particular strategy. He and his followers concealed themselves near the banks of the Oxus and spread the rumor that he had fled to the Khorassan.

The ruse was taken as fact by the villagers in the area, yet as they were about to celebrate the news, Timur sprang from hiding for an easy victory. What followed after this was one of the many ad hoc victories which became part of the Timur mystique. He first selected 243 of his bravest warriors, then crossed the Oxus and advanced to the village of Sheerkund, after which he laid low for twenty-four hours.

From there he made a rapid advance on Kurshee, halting at a distance of three miles to construct ladders. Timur, with a band of forty, went ahead to reconnoiter. In the dark they reached the moat and crossed it within a hollow tree that had been used to conduct water. Timur, in the company of one companion, first tried the gate wheel which was locked, then found a vulnerable place on the wall which they noted before returning to the advance group. With ladders and grapples they followed Timur's route to the weak spot on the wall and proceeded to scale it.

Once within they stealthily fell upon the gate guard, and having dispatched him, opened the gates to the main force. With his small contingent together, they advanced with the sounding of kettle drums and trumpets blaring to emulate a large army. Most of the posts were found unattended as confusion reigned. By daylight it was too late for the defenders to regroup as they were defeated by penetration and division. Timur recalls in his memoirs that: "…the incalculable advantage which wisdom has over force, and with what small means the greatest designs may be accomplished."

Amir Hussein was not among the defenders as he was on a nearby foray at the time. Timur sent a note to his brother-in-law written in the Mongol language. It read: "Say, oh Zephyr, to that friend, the layer of snares of treachery; doth not the treachery return back to the doer of treachery?"

Timur felt the need of holy guidance as he traveled to the city of Khof, some eighty miles west of Herat. There, he visited the famous prophet, Shaikh Zein-u-din Bakr. During their conversation Timur asked: "Venerable master! Do you teach nothing to your kings concerning justice and equity and warn them not to turn to violence and tyranny?" The holy man's reply was: "We teach that in truth and for that reason we visit them; but they do not suffer themselves to be taught, and so we have appointed you Lord over them."

Zein-u-din, dressed in his white robes and voluminous turban, then dismissed him. Timur left the holy man with the exhilaration that comes from one who had been given the mantle of greatness. He contemplated the tortuous road he must follow to achieve all of his desires—it was a challenge he felt duty bound to seek.

# 4

# The Six Year Campaign

*No solace as you then conspire,*
*To fight the Battle of the Mire.*
*You rid the land of one Hussein*
*And expedite yourself to reign.*

The land of the Chaghatay had been traditional Mongol country from the time of Chinghis Khan. It was not surprising that pride overtook Ilyas Khoja as he became ruler of Moghulstan after his father's death. He rankled over his defeat as governor of Samarkand and was busily engaged in raising an army to return and remove the hated Chaghatay. In the spring of 1364 his advanced units were spotted as they crossed the Jaxartes and were heading southwest.

Although Timur realized his own forces were formidable, he also knew that the Jetes were well disciplined and had a large group of leather clad horsemen, therefore, he sent for the mountain Ghur clans of the Kart race to augment his own. He was able to amass a large contingent of eclectic races, all equipped in fine steel mesh Persian armor, pointed helmets, and iron maces.

From the Samarkand forces, including the Sarbadars, he outfitted his army with reinforced bows, scimitars, and tulwars (two-edged Persian swords). Their long spears were reinforced with a number of shorter ones equipped with a heavy knob at the butt for smashing through armor. It was obvious that Timur anticipated a great deal of hand to hand fighting.

As the defending force moved out of the city in April of 1365 they were greeted by heavy spring rains which bogged down their horses and soaked their garments. The coming confrontation would later be known as the "Battle of the Mire." The Mongols fared quite well with the heavy weather as they halted their march and dug ditches around the felt shelters to divert the water away. As a result, the mud and desolation definitely favored the attackers.

Hussein, being both confident and daring, made the first move as he crossed the Chirchik River (a tributary of the Jaxartes) to meet the army of Ilyas Khoja on a face to face basis. Timur followed as the right wing of the combined army and succeeded in driving the enemy back, but Hussein found himself overpowered and chose to retreat. As they retired to the base camp they left some 2,000 dead on the battlefield. For the first time in Timur's military career his warriors became disorganized. Bows had become useless when the battle became reduced to a force of steel upon steel.

It was only when Timur was able to kill the general who carried the Mongol standard that complete disaster was averted. Sensing that the Jetes were always disheartened by the loss of a standard, Timur ordered the sounding of his saddle drums and cymbals. This, coupled with the war cry of the Tatars "Darufar," dispersed many of the enemy arrayed against them to return across the Chirchik River.

Bringing up the reserve army was always a sign that the battle was not going well. When Ilyas Khoja called for them it gave heart to the Timur warriors. Unfortunately the Hussein part of the army fell back for regrouping and forced Timur to pull back also at day's end.

That night Timur was in a foul mood. He refused to receive Amir Hussein's messengers or to make any plans to include his brother-in-law. It was at this time that he swore never again to go into battle with Hussein as a joint commander. This promise he was to keep.

By morning the Mongols were forming to attack and Timur had no choice but to meet them without help from the other camp. Although his outnumbered warriors fought valiantly, they were steadily pushed back. This situation became more difficult as the daylight waned into darkness. Fateful decisions had to be made.

Hussein's officers appeared at the Timur encampment and offered a plea to retreat into the Hindu Kush. Timur was instantly enraged. This was a virtual long distance headlong flight to Afghanistan where the very name "kush" means death. He sent back the message: "Let your road be to Hindustan or to the seven hells. What is it to me?"

Hussein eventually did retreat all the way back to Shibartu, on the northern tributary of the Indus River. Timur found that he had no other option but to retire and allow Ilyas Khoja free passage through Transoxania. He chose to regroup at Balkh where he felt among friends. No longer a heat ridden valley of the southern tributary of the Oxus, its spring temperatures were pleasant. It was a place that Alexander called Bactria and where new shrines and mosques had sprung up since the devastation left by Chinghis Khan. Once again Timur started to recruit from the countryside where his reputation made it an easy task. His hopes became buoyant when word came from Samarkand that was of the most positive nature.

Ilyas Khoja, hearing of serious turmoil in his native Moghulstan, was hurrying back to assert his command. A new face had emerged in the person of Qamar-al-din, the brother of the most powerful Mongol leader who had died about the same time as Ilyas' father. The new force anticipated the return of the Jete khan and waylaid Ilyas long before he could cross the Jaxartes. Qamar-al-din then set about to eliminate all relatives of Tugluk in order to assure his continuation of dominance among the Jettah population.

This vacuum left in Samarkand was quickly filled by several lords who aspired to be governor. Amir Hussein, anxious to establish himself in a salutary position, charged the leaders with violence and treachery. Using his military might he was able to imprison several of these pretenders after tricking them to attend an organizational conference. Most of the ones who posed threats to the wicked amir were subsequently sent to the gallows. Timur arrived after the fact and was only able to save one prominent noble. Among the many who were executed appeared the name, Abu Bakr, the one who had organized the population for the original expulsion of Ilyas Khoja.

Timur was furious but realized that Hussein had already established his power base and chose to wait for an opportunity to present itself to intercede. When Hussein imposed levies on the people, particularly the Sarbadars, Timur nearly precipitated an outright revolt. Instead, he chose to endear himself to many of his followers by nearly emptying his own treasury funds to settle all the accounts he could.

As Timur was patiently building his strength and improving his image with mosque dignitaries and the urban population, Hussein felt deep resentment and vowed to reciprocate in his own style. Returning to his home stronghold of Balkh, he proceeded to build a strong citadel. This offended the aristocracy who had always deplored such singular acts of contrivance.

This was the signal for Timur to seek out the sedentary lords, chiefs, and nominal princes. With their help he was able to share the power and become once more a reluctant partner in the government of Samarkand. He called upon an old friend Amir Musa to help him counter the power move of Hussein by strengthening his own defenses, particularly in Karshi. Amir Musa, although offering a helping hand, was still holding a commission as commander in Hussein's army which he was reluctant to disavow. Timur had to content himself with the nominal help offered.

Once again it was the lot of Timur to endure dark days. While near his stronghold in Karshi a messenger brought news which he could not have anticipated. His faithful wife Aljai had died suddenly from an unknown sickness. With heavy heart he returned to bury her in the garden house which he kept in Samarkand. In his memoirs he repeated the epithet that he often used for an occasion like this: "Verily we belong to God, and to Him we shall return."

Young Jahanghir was able to fill the devotional need for his father who refused to give up his plans of conquest. Timur was a master at chess and used a special board with twice the number of squares and pieces, including such additions as camels, giraffes, sentries, siege engines and a wazir (minister). While playing at this game he fantasized battle plans to be used at a future time.

About this time (the exact date is not known) Narmish Agha, Timur's first wife, presented him with his third son. For a time this exulted Timur and he temporarily forsook his brooding about the static state of affairs. With the appropriate ceremony attended by a holy man, this third heir was named Miran Shah, again with reference to a noble birth.

These were trying times as Timur retained his own valley with its pastoral overtones, a means of communing with the years of his youth while despising the shared rule with Hussein. Most of the next year and a half (late 1366 to 1368) was spent outside of Samarkand for the purpose of gaining recognition and gathering followers. He often hearkened back to his days with Amir Kazaghan when he felt that nothing would stand in the way of his rapid rise to power.

Restless in his quest to raise more recruits for his eventual reclamation of power, Timur traveled to Tus in the northern Khorassan. There, among his own Turkoman-Mongol people he was able to raise a small army. This city, just a few miles east of the larger city of Nishapur, would seem an unlikely place to accomplish this, but he found that here, not far from the Great Desert, he had been regarded as a demigod. Tus was the center for the production of cooking pots, cereals, belts and cloaks—not the usual place for producing warriors.

His primary target at the time was his familiar place for regrouping—Karshi. It had been taken by Amir Musa soon after he had pledged to help in alleviating Amir Hussein's power. That Musa was serving both sides of the Timur–Hussein dispute never became a matter of doubt. Timur planned a night attack on the city fortress and easily subdued it. A counter move by Amir Musa was repulsed as it was an expected tactic.

Timur then spent the winter in Karshi and sent a noble to collect taxes in Bokhara, a city which had been pledged to him. It was actually five cities in one, built on small rises and surrounded by the Sughd River. It was considered a sister city to Samarkand which was upstream on the Sughd some 150 miles. At the time of upheaval in Transoxania the prison served as the treasury for the area.

Timur later learned that his emissary to Bokhara had joined Amir Hussein there instead of being the collector of taxes. Amir Musa also turned up in Bokhara where this treacherous pair set in motion a plot to entrap and destroy Timur. As often happens, the details of the plan leaked out and the informer was rewarded for his exposure of the two amirs.

Timur felt that his position in Karshi was untenable and hurriedly moved his small army to a small village called Makhan, just a few miles west from Merv in northeast Khorassan. There, he was joined by the loyal garrison which left Bokhara to bolster his forces. Hearing of the now formidable army arrayed against them, Amirs Hussein and Musa opted not to attack but to occupy Karshi instead.

It was not until the summer of 1367 when Timur allied himself with the Malik of Herat to supply a considerable number of Ghur warriors that the occupation of Karshi was lifted. The recovery was aided by subterfuge where Amir Musa was invited away from the fortress to attend a contrived wine feast. The depleted garrison was easily overcome in the dead of night.

Many of the inhabitants of Karshi immediately defected to Timur's command. The ancient city of Nakshab, later to be engulfed by Karshi ("palace" in Mongol), was the home of the famous veiled Prophet. Timur tarried at the place where the shrine of Mokanna was said to be. He was described as being of hideous countenance with the celebrated veil covering a distorted blind eye.

Holding sway back around 767 A.D., the prophet was able to enlist the protection of a sinister tribe which engaged in pillage and rapine under the prophet's benediction. Said to have mastered the secret arts and attained supernatural powers the old mystic told his followers: "I am your God and the God of all worlds: I name myself as my will...." His mystique and godliness lived after him as the inhabitants of Nakshab claimed that his presence permeated the shrine built for him after he threw himself into a fiery furnace.

At this time the army of Timur was further bolstered by the warriors of Badakshan who were tired of their tribal wars. They were entranced by the stories of survival he endured and labeled him a sort of quasi-immortal. Joined also by some of his amir friends, Timur was urged to move on Samarkand. While engaged in preliminary plans he learned that his nemesis, Amir Hussein, had taken Kesh and was heading for Samarkand also.

Temporarily Timur settled in the northern city of Taushkend where he was set to regroup for the long planned invasion of his homeland. Amir Hussein, sensing a serious threat, planned a preemptive strike and was able to engage Timur on a field of his choice and with superior forces. After several skirmishes Hussein was able to drive Timur back to his stronghold at Taushkend where he was obliged to spend the winter of 1367–68.

That winter Timur was engaged in active preparation for the campaign which was to follow. In the spring of 1368 he crossed the Oxus with only a vanguard of three hundred men. In a series of daring raids he was successful in cutting his rival army's ranks into two parts, forcing Hussein to rush aid to them. With the help of his newly acquired ally, Keikhosrv, from the house of Jalayr, he was able to defeat Hussein and drive him back well southward.

At this time Timur was put into an awkward situation. He had requested help from his erstwhile enemies, the Mongols, who responded with a positive agreement to help by supplying a sizeable army. Then, realizing that it was probably a trap where the Mongols would eventually send additional forces to dominate Transoxania once again, Timur demurred. In any event he had already intimidated Amir Hussein to the extent that he was being offered a peace agreement whereby Kesh would be returned to him and a pledge of cooperation for the return of their old army combination.

With the two powerful amirs once again united in an unnatural alliance, Timur was able to repulse the Karts of Herat when they raided the regions of Balkh and Shaburkan. Meanwhile

Hussein had set up headquarters at Kabul and announced that he wanted to take over Balkh for his personal fortress.

Timur was revulsed by this notion and in the end they agreed to build the fortress in Balkh as a joint effort. Timur was still Hussein's major rival and as such, was constantly a target for an opportunity to be placed in a subordinate position. Some of Timur's people were sent to Balkh by his brother-in-law and others who were in the nobility, now becoming increasingly alienated by the high handed methods employed. Defections were increasing, even among the amirs.

In 1368 Timur's fourth son was born at a time when he was playing chess. He had just made a move which the Persians called "Shah Rukh" (dealing with the rook piece) when the news came. He was always seeking a good omen and decided that his new son should bear the name of the chess move. Years later many wondered how this name came about as it defied custom, but it was the mother of this newborn who was the center of speculation. It has been fairly well documented that a concubine, Toghay Tarkan Agha, bore the child, yet it was expedient to name Timur's third wife, Quinchi Khanum (little lady) as the mother to further the cause of legitimacy.

More and more of the chiefs were now presenting themselves at Timur's court as his popularity increased. It was the Jalayrs, however, who managed to tip the scales in his favor which set the stage for the return to Samarkand. They were a people considered as much Mongol as Tatar, the same combination as Timur's son Jahanghir. It then seemed a propitious time to make a determined move on his brother-in-law for control of the Chaghatays.

In 1369 Timur left Kesh at the head of a considerable army and directed his men toward his rival at Balkh. While encamped near Termed he received a visit from Nur Sayid Baraka, a most distinguished descendent of the prophet, and one who had just been dismissed by Hussein.

Having been belittled and reduced in funds by the amir he appeared before Timur and presented him with a standard and kettle drum, announcing that success and victory would thereafter accompany him in all of his undertakings. Receiving this as an omen of some import, Timur restored the holy man's funds and bestowed upon him a place in his court. In future years Nur Sayid Baraka became an almost constant companion.

The advance contingent of Timur's army under Amir Shaikh Ali and Khatai Bahaudur met and defeated a detachment of Amir Hussein's army near the Oxus River but received severe losses in the encounter. With the main army under his command, Timur arrived on a hilltop in sight of Balkh and ready to commence the siege.

During the operations on the first day Omar Shaikh, Timur's second son and only thirteen years of age, received an arrow wound in his foot during a display of gallantry. He allowed the wound to be cauterized without any display of pain or impatience. By the third day of siege it was becoming apparent that disgrace and ruin were in store for Amir Hussein.

The embattled amir then sent repeated messages to Timur requesting that his life be spared and that he be allowed to pass through on his way to retirement in Mecca. Still fearing for his life, the amir crept out of the city during the night but discovered before dawn that he was still in the old city. He sought refuge in an old minaret where he chose to hide out until the following night.

Unfortunately for Hussein he was discovered by one of Timur's soldiers who was bribed by a handful of pearls to spare his life. The soldier then reported the incident to Timur who dispatched a group to capture the amir. Again alarmed, Hussein hid in a cavern but was captured and brought to Timur, who did indeed, grant him refuge to Mecca.

Historians differ as to what happened next but it was quite evident that Timur expressed the wish to honor his vow to spare his brother-in-law. The most persistent explanation is that Timur left the council to its own devices, thereby not being involved with the final decision of putting the amir to death. His two sons were soon to follow, also being burned in the funeral pyre. From his memoirs we learn that Timur states in a putative manner: "It was for him the hour and the place appointed, and no man may escape his fate."

It was at a time of meditation while in the desert that Timur once again received a vision from the holy man of his youth with the piercing black eyes. Among the revelations given to him was that, although each person is accompanied by two angels, he alone had four. The vision also admonished him not to bear arms against his own blood line, saying: "You must not spill the blood of your brother. He who lifts a weapon for this purpose violates his vow with God. Allah has a measure for every deed." As Timur answered: "I surrender all my deeds to Allah!" the apparition once again faded away.

It was now early in 1370 and Balkh had a particular interest for Timur because of its legendary history. It was called Bactria during the time of Alexander the Great, later sacked by Chinghis Khan. The Mongols destroyed all the icons of Islam and left it with a considerable amount of rubble. Timur considered it his lot to rebuild the city in a fashion closely resembling its original grandeur.

The fortress outside the city called Kal-ah-Hinduwan (castle of the Hindus) was to be restored as the residence of the governor. The surrounding lands yielded sesame, rice, almonds and raisins, as well as lead and arsenic from the nearby hills. As Timur tarried at Balkh, the time for choosing a new Prince of Transoxania was overdue. The law of succession was centered around the accepted practice of naming a person in direct lineage from Chinghis Khan.

In order to determine this fateful dispensation, Tatar heads and holy men from the borders of Hindustan to the northern steppes gathered. Timur removed himself from the council but his friends, particularly among the imams, carried the day for him. For the first time in one hundred forty years a non Mongol was named ruler of Tatary*, an honor presented to Timur on his 34th birthday.

Actually the rule of Islam was invoked. The holy men stated that: "It is contrary to the laws of Muhammed that his followers should be servants to you who are infidels." The Jalayrs consoled themselves by stating that Timur was indeed, really a direct descen-

---

* in actuality, only that portion known as Transoxania

dent of the great khan. One of the first acts by Timur after becoming ruler was to confer the government of Balkh on Murad, a son of one of the Barlas chieftains.

On the following day, the 26th of Ramadan, 1370, Timur's formal coronation took place. In his pavilion on the plains outside of Balkh, the red throne of Kazaghan had been placed as a symbol of the Mongol dynasty. Timur was dressed in his warrior costume, complete with sword belt, helmet and riding boots. Kabul Shah, the temporary puppet ruler of Samarkand was given a seat of honor along with Sayid Baraka and two other shaikhs.

Since Zain-ad-din was the titular head of Islam in the area, he gave the final benediction. He carried a copy of the Koran on which Timur swore his everlasting allegiance to Muhammed. In the final words of the coronation Zain-ad-din intoned: "It is the will of God that thou shouldst conquer; thou wilt grow in power, and Islam through thee." At that time Timur eschewed the title of prince or emperor to remain with his title of amir.

Timur's old friend Amir Daoud was given the government of Samarkand, together with the leadership of the council. The aging Amir Jaku, who was with him from his days in Seistan, was given the standard for the consolidated Chaghatay tribes. Timur placed a golden crown upon his own head and bound himself with the imperial girdle. Princes, amirs and other nobles presented him with many gifts, including precious stones and articles of gold and silver. He was declared Emperor of the Age and Sahib Keran (Lord of the Fortunate Conjunction).

It was the retribution which followed that gave credence to the cruelty mantle that accompanied the Timur mystique. Following a long adopted code of the Barlas tribes, the council decreed that the close followers of Amir Hussein were to be put to death. To act otherwise would have been looked upon as a sign of weakness and lack of resolution. It was the zeitgeist for fourteenth century Tatary.

Also the custom in the Mongol dynasties was for the new ruler to take over the household of the deposed or slain ruler. Mulkh Khanum (great lady), wife of Amir Hussein, was the daughter of the former Sultan Kahzan and a direct descendent of Chinghis Khan. She was one of great beauty and grace, thus making it an easy choice for Timur to take as his own.

This great lady proved to be a courtly and attendant wife to the great amir. She wielded a great deal of influence in his internal decisions and entered wholeheartedly in the rebuilding of Samarkand. She is also the source subject for several legends which are still part of the tales told about the life and times of Timur.

It was by marrying a princess of the Chingisid line that Timur was able to strengthen his legitimacy to the throne. His new father-in-law was the last Chaghatay Khan of Transoxania. Mulkh became his chief wife but bore him no surviving children.

Timur also kept three other wives of the late Hussein who did not play an important part in the court but sat in succession behind Mulkh. One of these wives, Ulus Agha, was the daughter of Bayan Selduz who held the partial leadership of Transoxania until deposed by Amir Hussein. The remaining wives of Hussein (there were four) were given to amirs whose favor Timur needed to curry.

In the days that followed the council of state functioned in several ways. Grants of land were made for charitable purposes and that the holy men might prosper. Certain favors were passed out to those whose loyalty had inspired Timur's ascendancy to the throne. It was at this time that the royal scribe (Timur was not known to write personally) revealed the beginnings of his memoirs and first indications of what would later become known as the "Institutes." Already Timur was beginning to be known as the monarch dedicated to brilliant organization and fairness.

Part of the need to restore order to what had been chaos for many years in Transoxania, was the invocation of the Turki–Tatar codes, particularly that of the Yasao in the Mongol doctrine. The latter largely formed the internal structure for the military forces. A banner of red carried on a long lance tipped with a horsetail became the official standard. From that time on Timur always had a large kettle drum slung to the saddle of each outrider.

The civil government was headed by a Divanbeghi (Lord High Chamberlain), assisted by an underling and four viziers. The viziers tended to taxes, customs, pay and provisioning of the troops, registry, statistics, and the expenses of the Imperial Court.

Timur was often compared to the lion for being stout hearted, and with iron for his physical strength. He adopted the lion and the sun for his crest. Later he was to add three circles to signify his lordship over three main countries of the world. Coins and all other official objects of this later era were stamped with the combination early crest and the three circles.

Notwithstanding the oaths of allegiance taken by the amirs, there were several trouble spots which had to be resolved before Timur could be in complete control, in point of fact as well as in the titular area. Years of insubordination weighed heavily upon the Jalayrs of northern Transoxania and Timur decided to move in an unprecedented way. He declared their military structure void and followed up after the year 1370 with parceling out officers and troops to the various amirs. The proud Jalayrs were never again to threaten the empire in concert although remnants did revolt from time to time.

As one of his important edicts Timur proclaimed Prince Suyurghatmish, from the line of Chingisids, as khan to act as the true puppet governor of Samarkand and Transoxania in replacement for the ceremonial leader and old friend, Amir Daoud. Kabul Shah, who was a supporter of Amir Hussein, was sent back to his homeland soon after the coronation ceremony had ended. The new khan was invited to accompany Timur on several expeditions but was never given any real clout in the command or council. This then, was the culmination of what history has labeled the "Six Year Campaign."

# 5

# The Period of Consolidation

*The revolt of Sufis breaks the peace*
*And Jettah probes refuse to cease;*
*Your eldest son engaged in strife;*
*The injury will end his life.*

Perhaps the greatest vision that Timur received in terms of his administration responsibilities occurred while he was on a pilgrimage going from Samarkand to Kesh. During prayer at the holy spring in Urgut, the last vision from the holy man who he formerly perceived as one of the four immortals, came to him.

Timur always maintained that the three rings so prominent in his seal were confirmed by this vision. The prophet, according to his memoirs, intoned that: "With Allah's blessings you will enter into Samarkand and the city will become the center of the world. There will be three rings shining above it to commemorate the three countries which will be united by your holy campaign. You are to drink the holy water and swear to maintain the promise to Allah that these countries shall not war against each other."

During this vision seven angels appeared behind the old man. He was admonished to plant one tree for the old khizr and one for each of the seven angels to pledge his continued faith in the holy quest which was his ordained destiny.

By 1370 the Jetes, now fearing overwhelming forces being arrayed against them, retreated back to their traditional homeland. The new governor of Jettah, Kebeck Timur, rebelled at being subservient and had to be subdued by an army sent from Samarkand. Timur, not satisfied with his general's campaign, decided to head a fresh invasion into Jete territory. He started for home with a great deal of plunder and a host of prisoners.

Returning to Samarkand was always in the heart of Timur. He had often dreamed of making this beautiful city the capital of the world. He built a special tomb for his father with an arched gold dome. In the garden where his wife had been laid to rest he erected an imposing structure with fountains and courtyard. It was finally completed in 1380 and became known as the Ak Sarai (white palace) where Timur often chose to spend the winters.

It was in Samarkand, back in 329 B.C. that Alexander the Great rested for some time. He remarked that it was even more beautiful than touted, where he enjoyed the fruits and melons, as well as the local wines. In one of his unseemly moments he killed his own General Cleitus, said to be a result of a drunken brawl. He later was plagued with guilt but overcame it when friends insisted that it was the result of the god of wine, Dionysus, identifying Cleitus as a sacrifice to this god.

Although it was a time of consolidation, most of Timur's attentions were diverted to the rebuilding of the city walls, the widening of streets and the restoration of mosques which had been so important in his youth. He then set about to change the drabness of dull clay brick to more use of blue tiles, coupled with more grandeur in featuring the colors white and gold together.

Early in his ascendancy to the throne Timur assembled, in the Mongol manner, a koureltay, or general meeting of all the principal chiefs. This included the military commanders of the Hazarehs (one thousand men) and the Toumans (ten thousand men). Timur announced the adoption of his personal seal which carried the two Persian words engraved on his ring: Rasty va Rusty (righteousness and salvation).

The period of anarchy that persisted for over ten years with the Chaghatays was over. Timur and Amir Hussein had together amassed most of the tribal units and now Timur fell heir to those of his former rival. Historians have universally accepted the term "Timurid" for the dynasty that commenced with the coronation of Timur in 1370. All of the empire that contributed to his army and administration were known by this name.

There were a few desertions from the great amir's rule. Foremost among them was Amir Musa who had always been closely allied with Amir Hussein. The spokesman for the Badakshan clans thought that the lands should have been divided in a "brotherly fashion," which was interpreted to mean each province as a separate entity to care for and defend itself.

Perhaps the biggest problem to overcome was the objection of the strongest chiefs who wished to have returned to the "old order of things;" the reign of the lineage from Chinghis Khan. They had suggested that Timur could then become chief deputy. It was a monk known to all as the "Father of Blessings" who rose to defend Timur and to turn the tide of dissention. He said: "It is contrary to the law of Muhammed that his followers should be servants of you who are infidels. As to Chinghis Khan, he was a dweller in the desert who by violence and the sword conquered the Muhammedans. Now, at this moment, the sword of Timur is not less than that of Chinghis Khan."

Still not ready to render subservience to the great amir were various tribes from the province of Badakshan. Lying just north of the Hindu Kush, they were rugged mountain men who resided in the eastern extension of the Pamir range, sometimes referred to as the "top of the world." Believing that this resistance was more from uncertainty than overtly hostile, Timur decided to lead a small army into the tortuous mountain passes to investigate.

On one occasion Timur and his old and trusted friend Elchi Bahaudur, spotted a fairly large band of warriors in the ravine below. Elchi, managing a flanking maneuver while riding carefully down, confronted the main body of Badakshanis in person, suddenly appearing in his colorful sable coat and scarlet girdle, ivory and gold sword still in its sheath. He shouted to them: "Hai, ye sons of many fathers, draw rein and look. That man up there is Lord Timur!"

The enemy warriors, first confounded, then intimidated by the presence of the great amir, dismounted and threw down their weapons. Timur and the rest of his men joined them in a bloodless victory. Elchi, with his plumed headgear and gilded boots became known as Elchi the Valiant and went on to become Timur's trusted devotee.

After acknowledging the acquiescence of the mountain men who had been subdued by a mere force of six hundred men, Timur developed a spirit of camaraderie and sportsmanship with these tribal defenders and suggested that they celebrate their new found alliance. The entire group trooped down into the valley villages where they sealed their agreement with several days of feasting.

During the visit by Johann Schiltberger (see chapter 16) he later writes that "This country called Walaschoen (Badakshan) has high mountains where many precious stones are found; but nobody can take them because of the serpents and wild beasts. When it rains, it is the torrent that brings them down, then come the experts who know them, and pick them out of the mud. There are also unicorns in those mountains."

According to historians, the unicorns alluded to were probably horses that were a strain left by Alexander which bore birth marks on their foreheads which resembled horn stumps. There were reports of remarkable finds of rubies and lapis lazuli in the mountains, however, but the few serpents and "furry" wild animals did not discourage the miners. Timur did not mention these in his memoirs but did note that his march back to Samarkand was one of festivity and contentment.

In 1372 rumors had arrived in Samarkand of raids by bands of Jetes to the north. Timur rode with his army to the plains east of the Aral Sea and beyond to the edge of the Gobi desert, then through the large expanse of what is now Kazakhstan. His statement for the need on this occasion to mount his saddle was: "Before, we stamped out the sparks of conflagration—now we have to put out the fire."

As the Jete clans retreated farther into the hills they had to abandon some of their frontier valleys as they finally settled in Almalyk. Their traditional citadel being so well fortified, Timur decided not to follow, but instead, sent two of his amirs to punish those who had served with Hussein and had been raiding the lands of the Tatars for years.

When the two amirs found the Jete pasture lands deserted, they abandoned the quest and headed homeward. As they were crossing the Jaxartes River they were met by a contingent like their own going north. When asked about their mission, they answered: "Verily, to find the Jete hordes you did not find." At first angry, the two amirs then contemplated the results of a fruitless return to Samarkand, then thought better of it and decided to accompany the second division of the army.

The combined armies had to winter over in this bleak area but when they returned to Samarkand the following spring, they brought news of sacking Jete villages and had in their company all of the cattle from their vanquished foe. As Timur praised them he carefully avoided saying anything about the aborted attempt by the two amirs.

Prince Kaikosru, a Persian noble of Timur's court, abandoned the army in the face of the enemy while serving in the desert of Khiva. The remaining warriors went on to defeat the Jetes, but during the battle, while swimming the river with his horse, Elchi Bahaudur (Elchi the Valiant) was drowned.

When Timur was told of the demise of his old friend he ordered the deserter hunted down as a matter of revenge. Prince Kaikosru was finally cornered and brought to trial at the court in Samarkand. The amirs and judges decreed death for his treachery, after which they were said to remark to the assembled court: "It is good to obey the lord—they lie who say otherwise."

It was late spring in the year 1372 when Timur's attention was directed to the province of Khwarazm, the home of the Sufis. Sultan Hussein had pledged his support to the regime in Samarkand and had been away on an inspection trip when he returned to find that his son Yussuf had been violating his household concubines. In the upheaval which followed Timur was obliged to take a large cavalry contingent to the north in order to stabilize the civil affairs in this portion of his empire.

The Oxus formed a delta in the Khwarazm before it emptied into the Aral Sea and a large swamp filled with reeds had to be channeled with ditches to irrigate the surrounding lands. To the north, all the way to the point of entry into the Aral Sea of the Jaxartes, lay the great desert of the Ghuzz Turkomans. Both of the great rivers froze over for two to four months each winter, and the waterways served as highways for transport of produce. The populace was obliged to dig wells through the ice in order to obtain drinking water and to service their cattle.

Just before departing from the Khwarazm Timur received a tribute from the Malik of Herat consisting of many costly gifts, including what was to become his famous charger Kungaglan (brown lad). His route lay close to Bokhara and across the desert by Kat, which he bypassed at this time. When arriving in Urganj he found the situation serious enough to place both the sultan and his son under restraints.

During his confinement the sultan suffered a serious illness and died, leaving the leadership in doubt. After pledging his alliance as the new Sufi head, Yussuf was released from bondage and attended the court in Samarkand where he was installed as the new sultan. He maintained peace with the court at first, then decided to raid the countryside claimed by the Chaghatay. Later in the year Timur was obliged to come to the aid of his own tribes and those of Khwarazm as well. The disciplined Timurids easily defeated the scattered bands of Sufis and drove them back to their homeland near Urganj.

The city of Kat (old name Akhsikat), some distance below Urganj on the east bank of the lower Oxus, was occupied by Timur's Khwarazm expedition before returning to Samarkand. Earlier it had been flooded and for some time the streets were used as latrines. There was a strong castle built with columns of black stone, located near the Friday mosque, which did not present any hostile response when asked to surrender. The area was famous for a particular variety of almond, largely because the husks could easily be removed. It was the mining industry, located in the nearby mountains, which interested Timur greatly. They yielded quantities of naptha which was necessary for the production of his "Greek fire."

When Yussuf once again raided the Chaghatays in 1373, he retired quickly upon being confronted by Timur. This time he apologized profusely and sent gifts along with a renewed pledge of friendship. Timur did not follow up on this affair as he was busy in another direction. He had conquered the rich Farghana valley between Andigan and Kashgar, then set up his son, Omar Shaikh, as governor with his own army.

Along with the continuation of the building process in Samarkand came a feeling of pride in the population. The city was now referred to as the Gok-kand (blue city), at that time surpassing the number of blue tiles found in Herat. Timur was becoming known as the "lord with the iron hand," and the people drew aside when he rode down the widened avenues on his long limbed charger Brown Lad, closely followed by his court retinue flashing crimson and silver.

From the several campaigns into Khwarazm and tributes proffered by Yussuf, abundant treasures were taken to Kesh, together with a number of artisans and craftsmen transplanted from the northern province. Timur built a palace to house these treasures, and as a commemorative to the victories, he spent the entire winter of 1372–73 in his native city.

In following an old Mongol custom, the women of the households, where the husbands had been slain in battle, found their way into residences of their conquerors. Mulkh Khanum, having the blood of Chinghis Khan in her veins, followed this custom. She was the mistress of an oversized household which she administered with honor and dignity. Her guidance of the young grandchildren was seen as important in their early maturation. On many occasions she was seen riding with Timur on hunting expeditions and on visits to nearby population centers.

During the first part of 1373 there were revolts in scattered parts of Transoxania, largely those of Jalayr and traditional Mongol

*Mulkh Khanum Rides with Timur*

extraction. Timur divided his army into several divisions to meet this threat of renegade amirs and chieftains. With superior forces at his disposal, the Timurids were able to defeat and break up all organized resistance in a matter of weeks.

To celebrate three years of peace and prosperity, a number of festive days were planned in the year 1374. Not only had the threat of invasion been stemmed but it was a time to prepare for the wedding of Timur's first son, Jahanghir, an arranged one, to the princess promised from the city of Urganj. Days of feasting and self congratulation brought forth much gift giving and drinking of the ceremonial wine, forbidden except on special occasions.

The gifts offered to Jahanghir were displayed in a special pavilion. In another pavilion gifts of gold, jewels, silver brocades and other precious items were displayed as a demonstration of affection from Amir Timur. In addition he supplied fine horses and women slaves for his new daughter-in-law.

As the sun was setting the scent of smoke from sandalwood and ambergris filled the air while lanterns were lit in acacia trees surrounding the pavilions. Timur was said to have strolled among the celebrating nobles to scatter gold and pearls in their turbans. His scribe noted that: "It was all surprising and no place for melancholy anywhere."

The dark-haired princess had the official name of Savin Beg, but commonly was known as Khan Zada (the khan's daughter). She was from the old kingdom (province) of Khwarazm which lay just south of the Aral Sea and to the west of the desert of Khiva. Her father, known by both as khan and prince, was born a Jalayr, but had inherited the title of Sufi. Although a titular appellation, it also applied to the residents of the capital city Urganj—they became known as Sufis.

This city of Urganj was built near the confluence of the Oxus and Moorghab Rivers where a large delta had formed through the centuries from continuous changes in the water courses. An immense dike that protected the low land was destroyed by the Mongols but long since repaired. The new capital of Urganj, having replaced the old one at Kat, was famous for its carvers of ivory and ebony, together with its many talented workers with wrought iron.

Khan Zada had been chosen by Timur because she was both from the lineage of the Jettah and the Jalayr. This formed a bond between the new dynasty of Timurids and Mongols which strengthened that which he enjoyed by claiming Mulkh Khanum as his wife. His belief that the Sufis would become his vassals was not to be borne out. Their fierce pride of inherited lineage, spawned in the dust of the centuries, would be reduced only by the will of the sword.

After the wedding celebration Timur turned his attention to his capital city. Samarkand had been unfortified since its conquest by Chinghis Khan. Work had started back in 1371 to rebuild the old walls and by the end of 1372 it had been encircled with five miles of wall, together with a deep ditch to discourage invaders. He also restored the Gok-Sarai, or Blue Palace, at one time more of a prison than a stronghold. Its restoration provided a treasury for much of the accumulated wealth and other objects ranging from weaponry to general supplies.

The beauty of Samarkand lay in its avenues of plane trees, its extensive orchards and mulberry groves. Numerous mosques and palace buildings furnished an ambience of pride and contentment. New construction featured the blue tile that had caught Timur's eye when he first visited Herat. The white and gold decor which decorated the buildings were complementary to the tile and gave an air of splendor.

The clicking of looms could be heard as many hands were busy in the manufacture of red cloth (cramoisy) which was in demand as an export to Europe. The population conversed on balconies and on benches near the garden areas, while silk robed nobles and colorful craftsmen roamed the flagstone streets. People thronged to greet Timur when he appeared on his horse in full uniform. He was dubbed the Lion and Conqueror, the Lord of Good Fortune.

Late in the year 1375 Timur put into action a plan to invade Moghulstan and drive the Jetes out of the area northwest of the Tien

Shan mountains. With only 40,000 warriors outfitted for winter he moved across the Kashgar River and set up an encampment in a secluded valley. During one of the worst winters in recent history he struck northward in a two pronged attack.

Half of the invading force was given to Jahanghir and sent toward the Ili River where it ran westward toward Alma Ata, accompanied by three trusted amirs. Timur headed toward Zaisan on a northeast tack. The Jetes were taken by surprise as the Timurids appeared suddenly to devastate their winter encampment.

In a hasty retreat, the Jetes left a great deal of booty behind, as Timur spent fifty-three days clearing up the remnants of the retreating warriors. Meanwhile Jahanghir was pursuing the elusive Qamar-al-din into the mountains and defeating his detachments one by one, finally capturing the khan's wife and daughter.

Timur had continued across the mountain pass and into the Arpa River valley. Upon meeting up with Jahanghir he selected the khan's daughter, Dilshad Agha, to be his eighth wife. The custom of multiple wives had been customary for generations, however, the law of Islam which dictated a limit of four was conveniently over-looked. It was a matter of prestige with Timur as he collected a veritable harem during his lifetime. Wives numbered five through seven were simply obscurely named without accompanying dates.

Sometime after separation from his father Jahanghir met with an accident while fording a swift stream in pursuit of a detachment of Jetes. Whether the accident which resulted in a severe back injury was particularly severe, or the accompanying thermal trauma from the freezing water was the greater cause, Jahanghir had to be taken back to Samarkand for treatment. His condition was not reported to Timur as life threatening, an opinion which he received as reassuring.

Timur then busied himself with plans to construct a string of fortresses on the northeastern front to protect against incursions from Jettah. On his way back toward his homeland he stopped in the city of Khojend, on the west bank of the Jaxartes River, where he met with several amirs who he perceived were forming a conspiracy. On this occasion he simply chose to leave and not confront the issue. There were more important problems on his mind at the time.

News of an uprising with the Jalayr leaders of Moghulstan had reached Timur at about the same time as he learned of trouble brewing in the province of Khwarazm. Normally he would have sent Jahanghir on one mission but his convalescence in Samarkand prevented this choice. He sent a division into Moghulstan and was about to head westward toward Khwarazm when another crisis was brought to his attention—the mongols under Urus Khan who was the leader of the Blue Horde had left their homeland and were on the attack.

An offshoot of the Golden Horde of Mongols, the Blue Horde came from the area of the Rivers Don and Volga to settle in the plains country north and east of the Aral Sea. From this part of Eastern Kiptchak or steppe country, they had launched an attack southward which had reached nearly to Samarkand before being turned back.

By the time Timur was able to regroup for a confrontation, the Mongol army under Urus Khan had crossed the Jaxartes and was seeking to team up with the Jalayrs. During the halfhearted pursuit northward once again, Timur and his nobles engaged in several hunting expeditions. The love of the chase was easily overcome by the lure of returning homeward; like a magnet, the Timurids were drawn to the "blue city" in what resembled a forced march.

At the outskirts of Samarkand the returning army was met by the elder Amir Saif-ud-din who had scattered dust on his black garments. This behavior portends bad news and Timur dismounted from his horse with heavy heart. "It concerns your son" offered the elder. "In his youth, before his strength was full, thy son is gone. Like a blown rose at the wind's touch, he is gone from thee."

Jahanghir's illness from the accident had not been reported as particularly alarming beforehand, but he had died just a few days before at the age of twenty. The advance party of the army all dismounted and entered the city in a solemn procession. That night the kettle drum which heralded Jahanghir's rank was brought to Timur and ceremoniously broken. This ritual was somewhat like a toast in times of heraldry—the glasses would be broken so that no lesser toast could be made with the same goblet.

In a typical Moslem–Mongol fashion the grave was dug to a man's height with a side compartment large enough so that the deceased could sit facing Mecca and meet the angels as they come to question him. Each of the three principal holy men performed the rites by throwing a handful of dirt on the grave as they invoked the three stages of life and death: 1. "Of this I have created you." 2. "Of this your body shall return to." and 3. "Of this I shall resurrect you."

Timur followed the mourning custom of drinking from a cup where dried apricots were turned to syrup from a previous evening's soaking. The normal period for mourning was prescribed by Mongol custom as twenty days. By necessity these days of mourning were often cut short in the old Tatar societies. In any event Khan Zada was with child and Timur's second grandson was born forty days after his father's death. The child was named Pir Muhammed; he was destined to outlive his older brother and also become a celebrated prince.

Apart from the normal mourning period, Timur remained unconsolable for many days. Jahanghir's tutor was so affected that he asked for release from his normal duties to make a pilgrimage to Mecca. Khan Zada was not seen in court after the loss of her husband and it was assumed that she was given to Miran Shah as the custom dictated in order to provide her with a household. She does not reappear in the unfolding story of Timur and his family until many years later, and in a most interesting way.

Within the month of the birth of Timur's second grandson he was mourning the death of his favorite niece, the daughter of his sister, Turkhan Agha. She had died as a teenager and was said to be:

> *"Slender as a cypress.*
> *Beautiful as the moon;*
> *As clever as Socrates."*

A tomb was built for her in the place where the mystical King Afrosieb was said to have landed on his snow leopard. To this day her two-story mausoleum in the Shah Zinda is the best preserved of all in the old city.

Timur was obliged to cut short his mourning for her in order to put down an uprising in Khwarazm, the continuation of the one that he was unable to attend to when the Blue Horde invaded. It was while so engaged that his old enemy, the Jete leader Qamar-al-din, decided to invade Farghana. This province was situated just south of the Jaxartes River in northwest Transoxania. It was well eastward of the Khiva Desert and into good pasture and orchard land.

As soon as he could disengage himself from the incidents in Khwarazm Timur turned eastward to meet the Jete threat in Farghana. Prompted by the arrival of the Timurids, Qamar-al-din predictably fell back across the Jaxartes to more familiar surroundings. When Timur followed he ran into an ambush. Ever alert, the advance unit quickly responded with a strategic withdrawal and a delaying action. In the main engagement which followed, Qamar-al-din was defeated and sustained a serious wound, still managing to escape. He was destined to continue to plague Timur for some years to come.

The stage was now set for Sakhibkiran (born under a lucky star), destined to become Master of the World, the child of Allah, Lord of the Grand Conjunction, to emerge as the largely unsung great conqueror whose amazing skills in logistics sometimes defied imagination.

# 6

## The Expansion Years

*Troubles brew near Aral Sea:*
*Your plan will lead to victory.*
*Reduce Herat while on your way*
*To spare Khelat its spiteful day.*

Not all uprisings were quelled by the ascendance of the new amir to the throne of Samarkand. The outlying tribes had long profited by spasmodic raids on Tatar territories and some of them refused allegiance. One, in particular, the Sufi of Khwarazm, referred to Timur's days as a fugitive and became defiant. In his words: "I have conquered Khwarazm and the desert of Khiva with the sword and only with the sword can it be won from me."

In the winter of 1376–77 Timur was holed up at Otrar waiting for the severity of the season to abate. He received news that Yussuf Sufi was laying claim to part of Transoxania, the eastern portion of the Khwarazm. He had sent a detachment of troops to plunder Bokhara. An envoy was immediately dispatched from Otrar to demand why the unprovoked incident was implemented.

For an answer the envoy was imprisoned and some time passed before the news reached Timur. This time the Amir of Transoxania sent an ordinary messenger with the text: "Yussuf Sufi must be aware that, both with respect to life and liberty, the person of an ambassador is to be considered strictly inviolable; neither is he ought obnoxious but to the unreserved communications of truth."

Once again Yussuf Sufi ignored Timur's entreaty and detained the messenger. He added to the indignity of the occasion by sending another detachment to Bokhara to seize and carry off a tribe of Turkomans with all their cattle. Shortly after receiving this news came an account of the chaos building in Persia after the death of Abu Saeid, the ruler of the important western part of the country. Several shahs were then reigning in that portion of Persia.

It was the spring of 1377 when Timur made his move to counter the insolence of Yussuf Sufi. His armies first marched upon Khiva without bringing up any battering rams or catapults. The Timurids filled the dry ditches around the walls with brush and mounted ladders to storm the city. The walls were soon breached and the small number of defenders were shortly thereafter over-whelmed.

Leaving a small detachment to administer Khiva and its environs, Timur then moved on to Urganj where Yussuf was preparing his defense. The city was built on a canal which was protected by an immense dike and four gates. It had to be rebuilt after the Mongol invasion when the city was completely flooded from the waters of the canal. During Timur's time it was once again a large city which was famous for its merchandise to outfit caravans and for shipping on the Aral Sea.

Upon arriving at the citadel which protected Urganj, the Timurid forces fanned out to completely surround the city walls. Using a tactic of attrition, Timur then sent small groups against the defenders at many places and at various times, day and night. While this was going on other detachments were sent into the countryside to destroy all provisions that might be brought to the aid of the Jalayrs.

After a number of days using this unorthodox type of siege, Timur received a message from Yussuf to ask how long he proposed to make the Musulmans* suffer in a quarrel which only concerned two individuals. According to the memoirs the note read:

* term for Muslim used by the Mongols, Jalayrs, etc.

"Why destroy so many of our followers? Let thou and I decide our quarrel with no man's hand between us. Let him be victor upon whose hand blood runs from the sword channels."

Timur, whose intrepidity was never in question, sent a reply that he considered the Sufi's proposal not less just than reasonable, and that he had long cherished the idea among his own ardent wishes. To follow up on his answer he immediately armed himself and mounted his horse to prepare for the single combat. Timur's amirs hastily tried to dissuade him. Bayan, son of the defeated Mongol General Bikijuk, cried out: "Prince, it is our task to fight—your place is the throne and the canopy of command, and it is not fitting you should leave it." Several of the amirs vied for the honor to take his place but Timur pointed out that the Prince of Khwarazm had challenged him, not a noble or officer.

Under the troubled eyes of his amirs, Timur rode out from his camp in light mail, his sword bearer having held his shield high while girdling his belt and scimitar. He wore his familiar black and gold helmet with the horse plume topping. He seemed supremely happy on his bay charger, Brown Lad. The challenger then presented himself without attendants to the city wall. At the sight of his adversary sitting tall in the saddle, Yussuf Sufi had second thoughts and retired in confusion, pretending that his challenge had never been offered.

As the defendants crowded the city wall Timur called out to them: "Say to thy lord, Yussuf Sufi, that the amir awaits him." When a considerable amount of time elapsed with no sign of an adversary he again called out: "He who breaks his word shall lose his life." Timur then withdrew to his encampment amid applause and acclimation of his admiring soldiers. Kettle drums and cymbals greeted the amir, together with the sounding of trumpets and the neighing of horses.

Rather than risk an unnecessary loss of life Timur ordered that the siege continue without individual assaults on the walls, although his battering rams were in place. In a liberal gesture he sent a contingent all the way to Termed, on the north bank of the main branch of the Oxus, to gather loads of melons. These melons were of special quality and his intention was to give them to the inhabitants of the citadel of Urganj as a gesture of compassion. In actuality he hoped it would be a means of dividing the loyalty in the defensive ranks.

Arriving on trays of gold, the melons and the bearers were given safe passage within the walls to be presented to the citizens who were beginning to feel the pinch of hunger, particularly for fresh fruits and vegetables. Yussuf was livid at having to deal with this difficult situation and ordered them all thrown in the ditch. This caused considerable consternation in the eyes of the Musulman chiefs who could have used them to placate their people.

A renewal of hostilities was not precipitated by Timur, but one of the garrison captains opened up the confrontation. He and his warriors attacked the sector occupied by Omar Shaikh with considerable vigour, but were driven back with substantial losses to the safety of the city walls. For Omar Shaikh, Timur's second son at age twenty-one, it was his first decisive victory in full battle. For Timur this incident triggered a response—the siege was continued on a round-the-clock basis. The defenders were again subjected to an attrition by catapults and Greek fire.

Most of the catapults were brought to bear on the prince's palace and it was reduced to ruins in a few days. As the people were becoming both desperate and exhausted, there were signs of rebellion in evidence. At this time Yussuf Sufi was suffering a collapse of body functions, later described as apoplexy, and was taken to his bed. He died shortly thereafter and the Jalayrs were fighting among themselves to name a successor.

Yussuf's elder son, Khadjah Lauk, left the city to seek the protection of Timur as soon as he perceived that his life was threatened. Yussuf's brother Mounek, together with the other lords seeking power, elected to still defend the city, and it had to be stormed with superior forces to bring a final conclusion to the attack.

Following the usual resentment at futile resistance and considerable loss of life, the city was pillaged and fired. The most distinguished of the surviving inhabitants and the tradespeople were removed across the plains and placed in Kesh. The city of

Urganj never fully recovered and many of the Jalayr warriors were added to Timur's army.

Sometime during this period Timur added two more to the list of his wives (and concubines). Yaugur Agha was named by him as the "Queen of Hearts." The other, simply named Mekhribon, came to him in 1376 also. Little is known of them except that neither bore him a child.

In the Mongol hierarchy of valors a prince of the noble blood had challenged Urus Khan, ruler of the White Horde, and was killed in the process. The prince's son, Toktamish, vowed to take over where his father had failed (in 1376). He had sought out Timur for refuge, the latter giving him gifts and outfitting him for the campaign. Twice Toktamish had given battle to Urus, and twice he had been defeated. In the second engagement the son of Urus Khan was killed and his father swore to revenge him at all costs.

In the pursuit of Toktamish he was driven to the banks of the Jaxartes River where he stripped off his armor and swam the cold waters to safety. From there he was able to hide in the bush country where he was found by Timur in time to save his life.

When Khan Urus heard of Toktamish's escape, and that he was being protected by Timur, he flew into a rage and sent a message of reproach to Timur. It read: "Toktamish killed my son and has taken refuge in your territory! Give up to me my enemy! if not, prepare for battle!" Timur refused the khan's demand and prepared to lead his own troops to war if necessary. During the winter of 1376–77 the two armies reached a stalemate as the severe weather prevented mounting an attack. Neither army could gain an advantage as they were merely sustaining themselves in their felt tents for a period of three months.

Finally forced to withdraw without consequence, Timur once again decided that he should initiate the attack when the spring weather returned. Using Toktamish as his vanguard, they came to the Jaxartes River only to find that Urus Khan and his second son Tokhta Kaya, had both died. Toktamish was now confronted with the defeat of the new leader of the White Horde, Timur Malik, the departed khan's third son.

Surprising enough, the young khan was also successful in defeating Toktamish, even with fresh supplies and troops furnished by Timur. Only a swift horse, given as a special present by his friend, saved his life as he fled once again headlong into the bush country.

Toktamish was finally able to achieve victory in the neighborhood of Karatel in the present day country of Kazakhstan. It was a result of new equipment and military training given to him by his newly acquired mentor, Amir Timur. Toktamish proceeded to behead the young son of Urus Khan in the traditional Mongol fashion. With this renewal of life, Toktamish started to consolidate his forces, now as leader of the White Horde.

In a rebuke to his promise with Timur, he started a ruthless campaign of sacking and pillaging in the western Kiptchak in order to pursue his eventual goal of subduing the Golden Horde to the west, thereby assuming supreme command of former northern Tatary.

Timur spent the following winter in his palace near Karshi and issued orders in the spring of 1379 to fortify Kesh with new walls. Architects were enlisted from all parts of the country to erect public buildings, but the show place of this renewed building spree was to be a sumptuous villa outside of Kesh. This, when finished, was to be called the Ak Sarai, or the famous White Palace.

From his winter quarters Timur had sent an envoy to the young Malik of Herat to prepare for a koureltay, or top level council meeting, to be convened later in the spring. The Malik Ghiath-ad-din replied that he would welcome the Chaghatay chieftain Saif-ad-din to Herat and then accompany him at a later date to the council in Samarkand. Although assuming the throne of Herat in 1370, he was still young and uninitiated in the world of power politics.

In the process to follow, the court ambassador made his journey to Herat only to find that a series of protracted excuses prevented the malik from keeping his promise. Finally, in disgust, Saif-ad-din returned to the court of Timur to report his failure. Timur then sent another ambassador to Herat, but he also met with failure and was detained as well.

This was too much for Timur. Up went the standards and the army was again on the move, this time southward, building the usual boat bridge across the Oxus. On this occasion Timur's third son Miran Shah, just fourteen years old at the time, was sent with an advance party of five hundred men to set up quarters in Balkh and Shabreghoun*. The large army then prepared winter quarters in the area to ready for the coming invasion.

While in the winter encampment Timur sought out several holy men of the district. One of these, Baba Serkou, considered to be one of the most devout and enthusiastic, performed in a curious way. As Timur entered the holy man's quarters a breast of mutton was thrown at him. This act was interpreted to be a good omen as the "King of Kings" was destined to conquer the Khorassan which represented the breast or bosom of the habitable world.

As the first indication of Timur's good omen, the brother of Malik Ghiath-ad-din called upon him to tender his submission. Malik Muhammad was greatly flattered by the attention given him and set about to bring his followers into the Timurid camp, The two brothers, from a Persian family, had been left fatherless at an early age and were unaccustomed to certain measures of protocol.

The first move in the following spring thaw was to cut the lines of communication between Herat and Nisapur to the west. Next in line was the stronghold of Fushanj, a citadel whose windmills dated back to the time of Moses. This obstacle was surrounded by a moat but Timur was in no mood to delay longer than necessary. For three days they showered arrows and rocks to protect the engineers as they prepared planks over the water.

At sunrise on day four the Timurids rushed forward with ladders to storm the walls. Soon after they were breached in several places, but it was an aqueduct which was broken into which provided most of the access. Under a steady din of drums the warriors swarmed into the citadel with Shaikh Ali and Mubarak leading the way.

---

* a nearby stronghold

Timur himself went among his soldiers without his usual armor to encourage them in their efforts. As a result of being exposed he was wounded twice with arrows but managed to continue at the front of the attack. The resistance continued for one more day but then collapsed to a great extent during the night.

News of the fall of Fushanj cast a pall over Herat. The city sent out detachments to meet the first intrusion of Timurids to arrive outside the walls. They were repulsed with heavy losses and the survivors of the probes returned to the temporary safety behind city walls.

Timur then let it be known that all who forbore to lend assistance in the defense of the city and confined themselves to their houses would be protected. Many of the citizens did indeed, leave their posts on the ramparts, however, these moves were quickly countered by a threat from the defending nobles to put to death one person in every ward, an edict which terrified the population. Although this threat was never carried out, it somewhat mediated Timur's offer of clemency.

As a matter of establishing legitimacy in the operation, the malik received a message reminding him that the territory of Herat and environs had always been considered part of the dominions of the Mongol sovereigns and that the proper response would be to cease all hostilities. Ghiath-ad-din, seeing the inevitability of the outcome sued for peace through his son Pir Muhammed.

Strangely enough, Timur's second grandson who was born in 1376, was also named Pir Muhammed. Perhaps this tempered his judgement as to the disposition of the malik. The conference of surrender terms lasted three days after which time Ghiath-ad-din himself appeared at Timur's pavilion. He was permitted to return to the city wearing a diadem of precious stones and wearing a girdle of singular beauty that was presented to him by Timur.

Surrender terms included ransom for the city in gold, silver, uncut precious stones and artifacts of the malik dynasty. The northern iron gate of Herat was shipped back for display in Kesh, later installed in the new town of Sheri-sebz, Timur's birthplace. The malik was sent to Samarkand where he was kept in partial confinement. Before leaving the city Timur ordered the walls to be torn down so that it henceforth could not be defended in the same manner again. The nobles were all received in turn and given honor due to their station in the former court.

Adding Herat to a growing empire was an accomplishment of some account. It was a city of nearly one quarter million population, acting as the gateway to Hindustan and the center of commerce between Kabul, Bokhara, and Persia. A tally of the city's physical features numbered three thousand bath houses and ten thousand shops. It was said that after the victory Timur's dominion became so secure that luxury was its only enemy.

While in the area Timur visited Muhammed Sarbazal, a holy man who was purported to be the wisest in the city. Timur said: "Tell me how I shall gain the kingdom of Khorassan and occupy it, and how shall I win its near and distant territories; and what must be done that I may accomplish this business and climb this steep and rough path?" After some self deprecation the holy man answered, "If you desire for yourself a clear spring of water and occupation of kingdoms without wearying yourself, you need Kwaja Ali Muid Tusi, who is the hub of the wheel of these realms and the centre of the circle of these paths, and if he joins you outwardly, he will not inwardly be anything but your ally, but if he turns his face from you, no one else will help or profit you. Be, therefore, resolutely eager to conciliate him and attract him, for he is a staunch man, the same without as within, on whose allegiance hangs the allegiance of the rest, by whose counsel the acts of all are bound, who do what he does, stand if he stands, and go where he goes."

Timur sent a messenger to Kwaja Ali with many gifts. Later, as he was to invade all of the Khorassan, he would be joined by him, and with his influence the several governors of neighboring provinces would also be part of the alliance. The return to Samarkand was one of great expectations for the new ruler as his dreams of empire were forthcoming.

Having subdued the eastern Khorassan Timur returned to that portion south of the Caspian Sea known as the Mazanderan. The prince of this district was so intimidated by the show of force in the area of Nisapur that he readily agreed to the honorable terms offered him to become an infacto vassal of the great Chaghatay amir.

For Timur the book was not yet closed in the conquest of the Khorassan. He ferreted out the inhabitants of Kheraushah for the murder of his countryman Hadji Barlas. The punishment was not stated, however, it apparently was something short of a death sentence. He then returned to Samarkand for a short stay before wintering in Bokhara. It was a stay of satisfaction that his territorial expansion had been a success. Miran Shah, together with some of his ablest commanders, was sent to occupy the eastern Khorassan.

Ominous news was received soon after the fall of Herat. Toktamish had been successful in recruiting and using the tactics learned from his association with Timur to finally defeat the Golden Horde. He was able to form a combined army as formidable as that of Timur. With help from the Tatar khans who had fought with Amir Mamay* and nearly defeated him in battle at Kulikoud, the weakened Golden Horde was not able to hold off the Toktamish army when they met near the Sea of Azov.

From Europe the plague of Black Death had spread into the Muslim world and was starting to demoralize large sections of the central Asian population. The loss of Timur's favorite daughter was closely followed by the loss of his youngest wife, Touman Agha. These personal losses may have triggered a certain measure of savaging, indeed he did develop at this time a relentless desire to pursue a life of conquest.

It was the news of an uprising to the south that stirred Timur into action once more. The Prince of Mazanderan, Shah Wali, had abrogated his vow of allegiance and had teamed up with a fellow lord, Ali Beg Jowny Kerbauny, to attack Subzawar, lying northwest of Nisapur and well into the Khorassan. The call to assemble the Timurid armies went out immediately.

Shah Wali had sent a letter to Shah Shuja (Sultan of Irak) and Sultan Ahmed (Sultan of Arabian Irak and Azerbijan) saying: "I am

* leader of opposition group known as the Blue Horde

your defense; if my affairs are well contrived, yours will be also; if disaster befalls me from him (Timur), it will also reach your kingdom.... I shall suffice to you for averting this trouble; if not, it will happen to you according to the saying of the poet: 'When the beard of a man's neighbor is shaved, he should water his own beard.'"

Shah Shuja, he who had plucked out the eyes of his own father, rejected the plan because he had only recently made a treaty with Timur. Sultan Ahmed replied in an ambiguous manner saying that he felt strong enough to resist the "maimed and lame Chaghatay...." Shah Wali was left to his own devices and remarked to his nobles that "both of them were careless with his wishes."

As winter was closing in, Timur's armies crossed the Oxus River and arrived at the walls of Khelat, a hill fortress in the possession of Ali Beg and some 280 miles east of Astarabad. The inhabitants had not been forewarned and all their cattle fell into the hands of the Timurids. As a possible siege was being prepared Timur was joined by the army of his son Miran Shah, together with the forces of Ghiath-ad-din who was anxious to prove his loyalty.

Ali Beg had become confident that his citadel was impregnable, having abundant water supply, therefore, had lodged his entire family within the walls. Timur then offered safe conduct for the lord and his family to his encampment to discuss terms of non-hostility and a renewal of friendship. Ali Beg turned a deaf ear to this entreaty and declined to discuss any terms.

In an uncharacteristic move, Timur then withdrew to the west and announced to his troops that they were about to enter the dominions of the Prince of Mazanderan. Ali Beg reacting to the withdrawal move which seemed like the fruition of his bluff, relaxed his guard and allowed his remaining horses, camels, sheep and oxen to range in the surrounding pastures.

Timur, once again the master of intrigue, suddenly appeared outside the walls as his entire army encamped in a ring around the citadel. Now, with the loss of all their livestock, the defenders were faced with a distinct dilemma. Ali Beg became completely subdued by his situation and resolved to humble himself in the face of overwhelming odds. His message to Timur elicited a sense of shame and remorse for his actions and requested an assurance of safety in the process of surrender negotiations.

With a small number of attendants as specified by the prince, Timur entered the citadel through a narrow defile and was met by a lord and several of his nobles. Ali Beg did not appear and indeed, it was a trap designed to assassinate the great amir. By sheer providence, and perhaps some foresight, Timur was able to escape back to his camp as his five cavalry officers sacrificed themselves to make it possible.

The flames of rage penetrated deeply into Timur's thoughts as he ordered a general attack from all directions onto Khelat. An elite corps of climbers succeeded in scaling the rock walls during the first night of fighting and lodged themselves at the summit of the mountain. They were counter attacked in the morning but Timur managed enough pressure from all sides to protect them from being overrun.

When the attrition of his army became evident to Ali Beg he once again found himself driven to make a desperate move. He called a truce and ordered his generals to retire to their quarters. This time Timur proceeded as far as the gates on horseback and the lord of the citadel was required to appear at his feet. With a show of compassion Timur allowed Ali to withdraw and prepare for formal negotiations.

What followed was what could only be called reckless bravado on the part of Ali Beg. Back inside the walls he heavily barricaded the gates and set up blocks at all places where the walls and rock had been breached, thus trapping the small force on the mountain top. This repeated treachery was most infuriating, however, the citadel had never been conquered and even Timur found it a difficult task.

For two weeks the Timurid probes did not bring hopeful results and Timur was unwilling to make heroic sacrifices to bring the matter to a head. The army temporarily withdrew to a fortress partly in ruins and proceeded to renovate it to make it habitable. An army under the command of Timur's nephew Amir Muyed was dispatched to cut off all access to Khelat.

With Ali Beg bottled up and no longer an effective foe, Timur decided to move on Turshiz, a mountain fortress on the northern edge of the Great Salt Desert. This garrison had been provided at an earlier time by Ghiath-ad-din, therefore, Timur called upon his ally to apply pressure to capitulate without incident.

At this time the malik was Ali the Sedeidian and he refused to honor his former lord, deciding instead to defend his fortress. Upon hearing this Timur sent his engineers to work in cutting a diversion ditch to drain the moat surrounding the stronghold. When the battering rams were put into place it became obvious that the towers were being shaken to pieces. The malik did not hesitate unduly and sent a messenger to Timur for terms of surrender.

As a result of a timely withdrawal in the defense of the fortress, the warriors and their families were moved to Transoxania. Most of them were given important posts in the administration of the frontiers. The general population was allowed to remain as the government of Turshiz was given over to a noble under the authority of Miran Shah.

Soon after the fall of Turshiz a Persian ambassador arrived at the encampment to bring greetings from Shah Shuja, Prince of Shiraz. The message included overtures of peace and friendship, all accompanied by a large offering of costly gifts. Timur, in turn, dispatched the ambassador back to his prince with lavish gifts. He did include, however, a request for the princess from the race of Muzaffars to become the eventual bride of his grandson Pir Muhammed.

The Muzaffars were a race of Persians who started a dynasty of their own when their leader captured Shiraz and the province of Fars, later the important city of Ispahan, all in southwestern Persia. During Timur's time the monarch was Shah Shuja who had extended his small empire well eastward to Kerman, on the edge of the Great Desert. The renowned poet Hafiz resided at the court of Shah Shuja, now known as the Sultan of Irak.

Timur's attention was once again turned to the problem with Shah Wali, the Prince of Mazanderan, and his ally Ali Beg. When Timur moved his main army toward the Caspian Sea the shah became alarmed and promised to appear at the Timurid encampment for negotiations to affirm his formerly declared allegiance. Upon hearing this Timur halted the move to Mazanderan and changed directions to arrive near Raudegan, still in the Khorassan, where the pasture land was lush.

In the meantime the blockade of Khelat had been continuing but an aberrant attack by Shaikh Ali Bahaudur provided a new aspect to the situation. This formerly trusted commander of Timur's army had decided on his own to break the stalemate and attack the rock walls of the citadel. His expedition managed to scale the walls but became disoriented during the night, finding themselves in the morning on a summit of a neighboring hilltop and in a vulnerable position.

The garrison at Khelat was able to ultimately defeat the small Timurid force as they ran out of arrows and were forced to surrender. It was only because the garrison was suffering heavily from the blockade, now subjected to infighting, that Shaikh Ali Bahaudur was saved from beheading. Instead, he was sent to Timur's camp at Raudegan as a mediator. The commander reported at the encampment in disgrace, only partially forgiven by Timur. As a result of this incident Khelat was spared a direct attack but continued to endure a blockade.

Timur decided to return to Samarkand, and it was on this journey that he received word that his daughter, Princess Aukia Bekki, had fallen into decline and had died from a brief illness. She had married a noble of the Chaghatays and borne a son called Sultan Hussein. This son of Timur's daughter was destined to have a spotted career and not be a part of the inner family circle.

To honor his deceased offspring Timur built a memorial in Sheri-Sebz just a short distance away from where he was born. This family loss was said to have affected Timur for some time and left him irresolute and melancholy.

There was cheering news, however, to close out the year 1382. Alibek Kurbani, the Turkoman who had imprisoned Timur and his wife Aljai for sixty-two days back in 1362 had been detected and sent back for imprisonment. In a local council meeting the circumstances of the incident were reviewed and the Turkoman was executed for criminal behavior. The book was closed on Timur's greatest humiliation.

# 7

# The Expedition to Persia

*Will the searching soul transcend*
*The message so macabre you send?*
*What Mongol custom that one dreads*
*Lies in those pyramids of heads?*

Early in the year 1383 Timur returned to his beloved
Samarkand to pass the balance of the winter season there. Miran
Shah was then encamped on the banks of the Mourghab River just
south of Merv to consolidate the countryside. Disturbing news then
arrived in Samarkand from the province of Ghur, the home of fierce
mountain tribes.

The Malik Muhammed, liberally treated by Timur during the
previous year, had been raising an army of men from Ghur and was
threatening Herat. He had been joined by another chieftain who had
been rescued from prison by Timur. Upon arriving at Herat they
were able to intimidate the population into joining them as they
occupied the city and prepared to fortify it.

When two of Miran Shah's generals were sent to the vicinity
of Herat they were immediately opposed by the Ghurs outside the
city. After a fierce battle the Timurids were successful in defeating
their adversaries, driving them back to the confines of the rebuilt
city walls. Miran Shah himself arrived shortly thereafter at the head
of the main force.

In the battle that followed there were significant losses on both sides but the garrison held out until finally overrun by superior numbers commanded by Miran. To say that the rebuilt city was razed does not adequately describe the blood letting which followed. Only those city dwellers who did not resist were spared. In a fashion borrowed from the Mongols, the skulls were piled into macabre pyramids as a symbol of ultimate revenge.

Historians differ as to whether Timur ordered the beheading orgy but his distance at the time and the fury developing in the final hours, would likely belie this theory. Timur, on many occasions, had demonstrated that he removed himself from distasteful acts. It must be remembered that a measure of *laissez faire* had to be employed in the pursuit of a proper aura of power in the eyes of warriors of his day.

While in winter residence in Samarkand Timur's young Jete wife, Dilshad Agha, had developed a serious illness and died within a few days. Within two weeks after this loss Timur's elder sister, Kutluk Turkham Agha also expired. It was reported by his close followers that Timur was so absorbed with grief that he was unable to attend to the affairs of state for a period of time.

Only the news of uprisings to the north in the Jete tribes shook the mental lethargy that was holding the great amir in check. Two armies were dispatched to seek out the rebellious Jetes, and after receiving intelligence as to the extent of the incursion, a third division of horse warriors was also sent to bolster the Timurid forces.

In the first news to come back from the insurgent front it was evident that Qamar-al-din was being outmaneuvered north of the Ili River. The advance unit than pulled back to Ata-Qum before the main army caught up. Further probes to find traces of the elusive khan eventually failed and the army was ordered back to Samarkand. They brought back a great deal of booty and a considerable train of captured women and children.

After the Mongol uprising had been put down Timur's attention was directed once again to the south. It was the autumn of 1383 and his next move was to launch an expedition which was destined to be one of his greatest feats. Before the main thrust of his

*Pyramid of Heads*

protracted plans could unfold there was a problem developing in the Seistan which he needed to address. It was of particular interest because it was in this province that he had received the crippling wounds back in 1362.

Crossing the Herat River the Timurid armies came upon the desert country north of the large lake of Zarah. In the city of the same name Timur found that the local shaikh had suffered many of the locals to do penance by fastening iron rings to their ears, hands and other parts of the body. In his hurry to reach several famous shrines in the area, he chose to ignore these ignominious deeds and pressed on to do honor to the holy places of Islam.

In 1383, after marching down the Farah River and devastating the countryside on the way, Timur's army halted briefly while part of the cavalry was sent to the mountains on the frontier. The lord of the city of Farah called upon Timur in his encampment and was received with distinction. Before retiring, the shah pledged his allegiance to the Timurid empire and enlisted many of his followers into the imperial army.

Timur then arrived suddenly with his army before the city of Zaranj. He had already taken and destroyed the fortress of Hisar Zarah, near the lake of Zarah as the residents of Zaranj were feverishly preparing for an imminent attack. The city had a forbidding moat as they tapped water from a canal tributary to the Helmund River. Considerable area of the environs was covered by salt marshes and date plantations. The countryside was noted for heavy prevailing winds where drifting sands had to be contained with a great dike system.

As the story unfolds, Timur separated himself from the army and appeared on a hillside alone where he could be viewed by the city's inhabitants, having first placed two thousand warriors in full armor at a strategic ambush. The Prince of Seistan, Shah Kutbudin, sent out two scout parties to reconnoiter his enemy's positions; meanwhile the residents stormed out from behind the walls unexpectedly with the intent of destroying the invaders.

Timur used his favorite ruse of feigned retreat to draw out the undisciplined peasantry, then struck with force to drive them back to the walls with heavy losses. The people of Zaranj, now becoming desperate to preserve their homeland, attacked Timur at night in a surprise move. This caused some confusion but the discipline in the Timurid ranks quickly turned the tide of battle and, once again, inflicted heavy losses on the Seistanis.

Although the attack on Zaranj was prompted to some extent by a measure of revenge for his previous wounds, it was a further attack after surrender negotiations were made that brought about the carnage to follow. Everyone who had resisted was put to the sword and the city never fully recovered from the devastation.

Very likely it was the savaging of the people of Seistan which prompted Marlowe to include the following part in his writing of Tamberlaine the Great:

> *For he shall wear the crown of Persia*
> *Whose head hath deepest scars, whose breast most wounds,*
> *Which, being wroth, sends lightning from his eyes,*
> *And in the furrows of his frowning brows*
> *Harbours revenge, war, death and cruelty:*
> *For in a field whose superficies*
> *Is covered with a liquid purple veil*
> *And sprinkled with the brains of slaughtered men,*
> *My royal chair of state shall be advanced;*
> *And he that means to place himself therein*
> *Must armed wade up to the chin in blood.*
>
> from Act 2 I iii

With the reduction of Zaranj accomplished Timur next moved on Bust, a city near the junction of the Helmund and Kandahar Rivers. On the way he subdued a fortress in the town of Tak which was located just one day's journey north of Zaranj. The "Fortress of the Arch" which was located on a hill where the Helmund made a large bend surrendered quickly through intimidation. Strangely enough the community outside the fortified area destroyed their own dike as a sort of subservient gesture to show lack of hostility. In any event they avoided any looting as the large army bypassed it.

The Nikoudrian tribes near Bust* were an unknown factor at the time of Timur. Taking no chances, Miran Shah's army was sent into the area as a precaution to detect any hostility. On the plains of Keren they came upon the old chief Hadji Saif-ud-din with the intent to persuade him to attend Timur in his encampment.

Unfortunately the advance guard, unaware of a previous friendship with the old chief, cut off his head in a brief battle to be presented to Timur as a symbol of conquest. Soon after this incident the prince of Memkatu** showed up near Timur's pavilion in a surprise visit, bringing with him several costly gifts. Although he had counted on time healing old grudges, he was recognized as the lord who wounded Timur severely in the hand back in 1362. Before any overtures could be made the prince fled from the area but he was cut down by a flurry of arrows from an avenging guard contingent.

In late December of 1383 word came to the Timurid camp that the followers of the old Nikoudrian chieftain had assembled an army of three thousand and were preparing for a siege in a fortress south of Kandahar. These warriors were considered infidels and, therefore, prime targets in a holy war. Apparently they had, in any event, been terrorizing the Musulman inhabitants with all manner of outrage and violence.

Very little is known about the actual attack on the fortress except that it held out for only a few days. Retribution, once again, manifested itself in several pyramids of severed heads to remind the countryside of the high price in continuing hostilities. Those that remained passive were allowed to stay or were repatriated in neighboring villages. The large dam on the Helmund which irrigated the western part of Seistan was destroyed before leaving the area.

One more pocket of resistance remained in the mountainous area south of Kahdahar. They had originally signified their willingness to submit to Timur's authority but the fierce Afghan tribes would not hear of it and assembled to do battle. During the fighting

---

* on the Helmund River
** from Afghan lineage

which followed several of the Timurid generals were wounded and the son of Mubarek Shah was killed. Timur was forced to temporarily withdraw to seek a new avenue of attack.

One branch of the Timurid army had been severely put upon and was in danger of being surrounded. It was then that Timur renewed his flanking maneuver with all the reserves and succeeded in finally putting the Afghans to rout. During this last stage of the battle an adolescent of Timur's army ambushed one of the enemy, "dehorsing" him and severing his head. After presenting this trophy to Timur the young boy was lionized by the court of nobles.

Following the defeat of the mountain men the operation near Kandahar became a series of mop up excursions. Miran Shah's army had ranged eastward for a short distance and then returned to Samarkand in the fall of 1384, a distance of some 500 miles. With the high plain country now neutralized Timur needed to assure himself that the second city of Kabul, over 300 miles northeast on the road to the Hindu Kush, was still friendly territory.

Leaving Kandahar, the capital of Afghanistan, Timur was anxious to set up his winter quarters near Kesh. Crossing the Helmund he headed north through the city of Balkh, then to his favorite Ak-Sarai, or White Palace. There, he spent the time in visiting with his family and planning for the next westward foray. There was still the Shah Wali challenging the sovereignty of Timur in the Mazanderan. From his memoirs it was evident that the ultimate prize had been for several years the subjugation of all of Persia. Sequentially he first moved the main army across the Oxus near Termed as soon as the winter weather abated. Next, he consolidated this and his special divisions at Balkh. He was now poised to start his grand campaign.

Timur paused long enough to receive the proffered princess of Shiraz, a tribute from Shah Shuja, her father. The princess was betrothed to Pir Muhammed, the second son of deceased Jahanghir. Also present before the departure of the army was Khalil Sultan, the two year old son of Miran Shah. Mulkh Khanum, Timur's fourth and favorite wife, accompanied the princess from Shiraz and the grandchildren back to Samarkand.

The combined army was now on the move, crossing the Moorghab River, then stopping for a time at Abiwerd, northeast of Khelat. Here, scouts reported that Shah Wali was fortifying himself at a stronghold called Dezenkellah, south of the Caspian Sea. An advance unit was sent ahead to probe the shah's defenses.

In an initial skirmish the Timurid commander Mubasher received an arrow directly in the mouth which passed through his throat. In an intrepid move this brave warrior carried on with his charge and was able to behead the archer who had wounded him. Later on, upon presenting the head as a trophy, Mubasher was given the district where the battle was fought as a commemorative.

As the army moved on they crossed the River Jurjan near Astarabad, a major city at the southeast corner of the Caspian Sea, where they entered into Mazanderan proper. They were obliged to literally hack their way through dense forests while moving westward. It was while this slow progress was hampering them that the Timurids were harassed by units of the shah's army in frequent raids. For nineteen days these quick probes continued, but on the twentieth day the invaders ran into Shah Wali's main force.

What transpired at this juncture is an interesting story of the tactical expertise employed by Timur. When his intelligence reported that the shah had ringed his perimeter with a ditch studded with sharp stakes, he countered with the same tactic. It was then up to the Mazanderan army to entice an attack, a ploy which required a feinted charge toward the Timurid army.

When Timur's warriors retreated in the face of this feint, the enemy became emboldened and called up the main force to continue the charge. Shah Wali's army was then ambushed on the flanks and many of them ran headlong into the ditch and impaled themselves on the sharp stakes. Those that retreated were closely pursued and fell into their own ditch with its trap of stakes.

Completely discouraged by this turn of events, Shah Wali was obliged to flee with his wives and children to the relative security of a fortress near the Elburz mountain range to the south. In the succeeding days he was dislodged from this redoubt and fled to the ruins of the ancient city of Rei. Although a far cry from its glory days as a crossroads of caravans, this place, on the northern edge of the Great Desert (also called Great Salt Desert), was still habitable.

Timur first returned eastward to take possession of Astarabad which had been bypassed earlier, then sent a portion of his army to Sultanieh, a relatively new city which had been established by the Mongols. This route led westward along the southern foothills of the Elburz range which, in its east to west extension, ran for 650 miles and divided Persia's high plateau from the relatively lower lands to the north along the Caspian Sea.

At this time the Sultan Ahmed Jalayr, titular ruler of part of Persia, was residing in Sultanieh and was presented with a dilemma of how to handle the advancing army of Timur. Before reaching Rei which lay on the route to Sultanieh, Timur was diverted for awhile to contend with a band of renegade monks, called the Sebgevars. They had been raiding the countryside but were scattered over a large territory. Timur was obliged to divide his army into small units in order to seek out and destroy this menace to the country-side. He then felt free to confront Sultan Ahmed.

During the winter of 1384–85 Timur set up headquarters at Rei in order to monitor any traffic between Mazanderan and Irak. Once one of the great cities in this area, it had never risen to promi-nence after being razed by the Mongols. The main castle was one called Kalah, situated to the north of the city; the remainder in a ruined state at the time of Timur. The city walls had been nearly restored, but the main gate to the south leading to Baghdad had been entirely rebuilt.

After keeping Persia off balance with threatening moves toward Sultanieh, Timur received news that the sultan had fled northward, leaving his son Aukbouga to organize an army to resist the threat of a Timurid invasion. When the advance units arrived at Sultanieh it was interpreted as the main army. After a hurried conference Aukbouga and his generals left the city to follow his father in a refuge encampment, the city of Sultanieh thus literally abandoned, was entered without incident.

This was a new city built by the Mongols in the first part of the 14th century and boasted beautiful buildings only rivaled by Tabriz. Its extensive fortifications had a perimeter that was said to be 30,000 paces in extent. The Mongols had selected this site as the hub of a road system which continued to reach all parts of western Asia. Realizing its importance as a headquarters, Timur selected Sultanieh as his command center for the winter of 1385 and on into the following spring. It was there that he received Audel Agha who had been previously deposed by Sultan Ahmed from his home in Irak. Timur perceived a ceremonial coup here and announced the restoration of his government and placed an army under Audel Agha's command.

During the spring of 1385 Timur's legions fanned out from Sultanieh to pillage the countryside and to bring into submission the minor village areas. Meanwhile he had accumulated a great deal of booty from northern Persia and the Mazanderan which was sent back to Samarkand. Timur himself followed soon thereafter to follow the placement of new governments in Amul, Sari and Astarabad.

It was incumbent upon those who tarried at Sultanieh to visit the ancient city of Shiz, lying almost due west of the city. It was the birthplace of Zoroaster, the Persian prophet, whose followers enjoyed a temporary revival of their religious beliefs during the early days of Christianity. The main feature of the area was a deep pool only one third of an acre in extent which was kept at a constant level by a siphon from surrounding springs. The ruins that persisted for many centuries was given the name of "Solomon's Throne."

Amul, near the Caspian Sea was in the middle of a rice producing country with a hot and damp climate. It served as a source for many products which were needed to sustain Timur's large army. He had previously ravaged Amul and destroyed the three castles which served as a protective cordon around it. Sari, lying to the east of Amul, was important for its production of corn, grapes and silk.

Timur was now poised to move into the non Arabian portion of Irak. His target was Feyrouzkoh, a fortress in the northeast corner of the country. Timur, always searching for legitimacy in his conquests, now found one. The ancient caravan routes to Hijaz and the sacred cities were being exposed to the Prince of Lauristan, ruler of the province in southwestern Irak. With his diversion army on the move, Timur led a series of forced marches to the troubled area, hoping not to alert his adversary.

Passing by the ancient city of Kum, Timur stopped long enough to find the tomb of Fatimah. Legend had it that the daughter of Muhammed was poisoned while visiting there. Timur found both the shrine and the city to be in an advanced state of ruin but did not deem it a propitious time to institute repairs.

The Timurid army arrived at the gates of Khorumabad, home of the plunderers, in complete surprise to the garrison. They were easily overwhelmed and the resulting carnage was applauded by all the caravan chiefs who had tipped off Timur of their whereabouts. In the fury of the engagement the robber bands were literally hacked to pieces.

Word came to Timur on his return to his encampment that his primary nemesis, Sultan Ahmed, had attacked and conquered the northern city of Tabriz, capital of Azerbijan. Miran Shah was immediately dispatched to secure the area south of Tabriz and await his father's arrival. Tabriz had been captured some months before by Toktamish and his Golden Horde, who then left it in nearly hapless shape as he returned northward.

This incursion by Toktamish, allowing the sultan to easily conquer Tabriz, was more worrisome to Timur than the disposition of Sultan Ahmed. He had been known as the protege of Timur but now his powerful Golden Horde matched that of the Timurids in size and threat. It was obvious that both great lords were heading for a collision course.

Leaving several divisions to administer that part of Irak then overrun, Timur proceeded northward toward Tabriz. Hearing of this still massive army coming his way, Sultan Ahmed decided to retreat to Mesopotamia by way of passing through Armenia. Amir Saif-ud-din, Timur's old friend, was assigned the duty of pursuing the sultan. Ahmed had abandoned much of his baggage in his hasty departure which served to augment the wealth already accumulated from western Persia.

In the city of Maraghab, some seventy miles south of Tabriz, Timur tarried only long enough to inspect the early capital of Azerbijan. It was in partial ruins but the observatory just outside the city built by Nasir-ad-din was still worth visiting. Close by was a famous garden in isolation between two clear streams that Timur also visited. Seeing no hostilities being offered, he pushed on.

During Timur's time the throne of Persia was subjected to a great deal of treachery and intrigue. Sultan Aweis, who reigned until 1356, passed on the government to his second son, Hussein. The older brother had been murdered when his father expired, but Hussein was able to gather enough followers to consolidate his rule. He proved to be an excellent prince who was noted for his love of justice. Through bribery his younger brother Ahmed was able to have him assassinated and brought about a cruel and unjust regime. The nobles of his court secretly asked Timur for help. This, in large part, is what brought the great amir to the gates of Tabriz.

In the process of expelling the sultan's remaining forces, much of the region known as the Karabagh (black garden) was laid waste. At one point five hundred individuals suffocated in the smoke of the burning palace of the reigning prince. While in the area, the greater part of Azerbijan was conquered and pledged to Timur's growing empire. The main army then withdrew to Tabriz where they continued to be active during the summer of 1386.

At the time of its occupation Tabriz was considered one of the most beautiful cities in Azerbijan and the Karabagh. Its centerpiece was an expansive mosque with high pillars of multi colored stone. Before the mosque's main entrance a stream ran under stone arches as it fed a natural fountain in a court with six marble pilasters.

The lofty Gur Kalah (castle of the tomb), recently abandoned, still boasted a magnificent palace, built partly into a hill. The decor of the walls and ceilings was of ultramarine and gold. Nestled at the base of the mountainous area just to the east of the large Lake of Urmigah, it overlooked the countryside rich in fruits, olives, grains and spices. Made up of Persians, Turkomans, and some gypsies, the population often wore a traditional red Caftan (long sleeved garment) and played host to the travelers and merchants from all over Asia Minor.

While holding court in Tabriz Timur learned of the excesses of the reinstated ruler of Irak, Audel Agha. His arrogant demeanor, coupled with a penchant for unrestricted expenditures, was causing a great deal of consternation within his government at Sultanieh. Timur was obliged to order his arrest but news of this preceded the appearance of the appointed administrator. He offered resistance for a few days but was subdued when the officers were able to collapse a wall on him.

As winter approached Timur once again turned northward to cross the Araxes on his way to invade Georgia. After putting down all resistance between the Rivers Kur and Araxes, he appeared at the gates of Tiflis, on the upper reaches of the Kur. The defenders of this city decided that they had resisted all other invasions and with their double walls and three fortified gates, could withstand one more.

After several days of siege from the main Timurid army the garrison became suddenly infiltrated with Timur's warriors, swords in hand, who proceeded to put down all resistance. Malik Bokraut, the Prince of Tiflis, was brought before Timur loaded in irons to plead for his life. He had fallen into disfavor, particularly because one of his generals had plundered a caravan on the way to Mecca. After swearing to embrace the religion of Muhammed he was spared but relieved of any command.

When Timur occupied Tiflis previously he had taken among his prisoners King Bagrat and his queen. To retain his regency the king had embraced Islam (actually feigning conversion) and presented his conqueror with a coat of mail said to have been forged by the Prophet David. The frailty of this conversion to Islam was to cause repeated violations of allegiance by the king which had to be reconfirmed from time to time.

Through an emissary Sultan Ahmed sent a message to Timur wishing to renew their bond of friendship and reminding him of their previous treaty. The answer he received was conciliatory as Timur expressed his wish to link the two great dynasties for an indefinite time. Shortly thereafter the exchange of letters brought news to Timur which fulfilled a prophecy made by the sultan some time before.

Shah Shuja of Persia who had previously put his own father's eyes out, curiously made considerable preparations for his own funeral, overseeing the making of his shroud and coffin. Having sworn allegiance to Timur he dictated a letter to the great amir. It went in part like this: "As to the treaty between us, deigning never to break it, I look upon the gaining of the imperial friendship as a great conquest, and my chief wish, dare I say it?, is to have in my hand this treaty with you at the day of judgement, so that you should not reproach me with breaking my word...."

Anticipating his demise, the shah further praised Timur as being as wise as Solomon and as great as Alexander. Then, as a further ploy to insure the future sovereignty of Persian rulers, he added: "...to commend my son Zain-al-Abaidin, God grant him a long life under the shadow of your protection, I leave him to the care of God and your majesty. How could I doubt that you will keep the treaty?"

As many as ten princes vied for parts of the Persian empire when the shah died in 1386. Each established a monarchy; some produced their own money system, but all were hard pressed to maintain their boundaries. Shah Yahya established himself at Tazd, Sultan Ahmed at Kerman, and Shah Mansur at Ispahan. Timur felt only compassion for Zain-al-Abaidin because of deference to his late father, the shah. Nevertheless the army, now numbering seventy divisions, moved against the Muzaffars in the winter of 1386.

Following the occupation of Tiflis, Timur indulged in one of his favorite pastimes, that of hunting and the chase. It was customary to form a grand circle or nerkah, driving the game within where they could be ridden down in the pursuit by singling out a particular quarry. This was combined with what we now call "war games" where tactics were refined and practiced. Tiring of this after several weeks, Timur was again on the move. This time he chose to march eastward toward the Caspian Sea.

He was accompanied by Malik Bokraut who was busy engaging in currying favor with the great conqueror. In degrees, the former prince was making it known of his submission to both Timur and to the tenets of Muhammedism. Through some very artful flattery the prince was able to restore himself in the eyes of his lord. Among the presents he gave to the great amir were eight slaves, however, custom dictated that there should be nine. When Timur asked "Where is the other?" the prince quickly stepped into the ranks and declared: "I myself am the ninth!" This act of subjugation so pleased Timur that he restored the rule of Shirvan to the prince. As a following act the former prince of the province of Shirvan was restored to his dominions. Amir Shaikh Ibrzuhim was also given the exalted title of Shirvanshah.

Timur decided to winter over in the Karabagh at Gukchah Tangiz (Blue Lake) where he received the overtures of the prince of Guilan who had never previously paid homage to the Persian sultans. They had always before felt comfortable in their mountains and forests from hostile incursions. It was the spring of 1387 when Timur became restless once more and started on his way toward Berda, some fifteen days journey from Samarkand, where stories of local beauties abounded and the famed home of Keydefah, queen of the Amazons intrigued him.

These women were said to be from the lineage who were at Troy when it was destroyed by the Greeks. Their custom was to disdain all men except at one time of the year when, accompanied by their daughters, they chose their mates. For a week or two they lived with, ate, drank and slept with their choice before returning to their homeland. If they brought forth daughters from these unions they kept them, but all sons were sent back to their fathers.

Word came to Timur's encampment that Toktamish Khan, now with a sizeable army, had been sighted across the Kur River. Two of the Timurid generals were sent to the vicinity to determine the extent of this expedition but were warned that to engage in any hostilities was forbidden. Timur expressed the hope that his previous offer of friendship would still hold and not deter him from his longer range plans for Persia. The warring princes in the west, by contesting each other for territory, were playing directly into his hands. He was poised and ready to move at an opportune time, and the news of his potential nemesis to the north was disturbing.

Timur was obliged to counter the threat of Toktamish by sending Miran Shah with an army to confront him along the Kur River. The Mongols were driven back with only a few tactical skirmishes and Timur treated the incident lightly and agreed to a truce. His message to Toktamish read in part: "Disputes are slumbering; the curse of God rests on those who awaken them."

# 8

# The Extended Empire

*To tarry at the Lake of Van*
*Delays the march to Ispahan.*
*Shiraz is next but not toward*
*The problem with the Golden Horde.*

Timur was chafing at being delayed in Tabriz while waiting for intelligence on the intentions of Toktamish, then threatening Georgia. With his timetable at stake, he was obliged to hold all plans in abeyance. When his two generals arrived back from their probe they brought the news that the Mongol khan's presence to the north was designed to deter any expedition by Timur into the territory of the Caucasus.

Having followed instructions on not engaging the Mongols, the withdrawal by Timur's patrols was interpreted as one of fear. The khan's army attacked and killed forty of their number. It was only the timely arrival of the army of Miran Shah, sent earlier for possible support, that prevented a headlong retreat by the Timurids.

Timur invoked his best manner of conciliation and sent a reminder to Toktamish of their pledge of mutual friendship, warning him, however, of consequences if the pact were broken. He then moved the imperial army to the large lake of Erivan just east of the city bearing the same name where he prepared to meet his fourth wife and the young princes Shah Rukh and Khalil Sultan, recently arrived from Samarkand.

This brief conjugal and family visit was interrupted by the news that the generals of Sultan Ahmed were entrenching themselves near the source of the Euphrates at Alanjik to challenge him. Timur immediately accepted the calling, and three days after his arrival at Alanjik the famed fortress was overrun and the defenders cornered in the citadel of the upper fort.

A plan of attrition was decided upon as the attackers were able to cut off all food and water supplies. It was ultimately the need for water which drove the garrison to sue for surrender and clemency. Timur had just decided favorably upon this request when providence played into the hands of the defenders. A heavy rain fell which was captured in the reservoirs and cisterns. Having tired of this siege and its effects on his time table, Timur moved on and left a detachment under Shaikh Ali Bahaudur to eventually starve them out.

Envoys appeared at the Timurid camp to ask for an engagement against the Turkoman tribes who were at that time plundering caravans going into Arabia. Timur, always reveling in the prospect of perceived righteousness, proceeded to Van, a city on the east shore of a large lake, also by the same name. His immediate foe was Kara Muhammed, chief of what was called the Black Wether tribe*.

In the process of driving out this menace Timur passed close to the fortress controlled by Bayazid, the most formidable of his later enemies, and one which would afford him the many titles of world conqueror still latent at that time. In the end four units of the main army were sent out to seek and destroy the scattered remnants of Kara Muhammed.

Only Miran Shah was completely successful in the pursuit of the Turkoman tribes as he returned loaded with booty and a number of captives to rejoin the imperial army. Two other units were mildly successful, coming back with horses and arms, however, the fourth lost its leader in a tragic death, still managing to disperse their adversaries.

---

* so called because of the black sheep they tended

Following this diversion of primary purpose Timur assembled the combined armies once more and plundered his way through the plains of Moush in western Azerbijan to the capital of lower Armenia next to Lake Van. This brackish lake, some 80 miles in length, was said to be the cradle of the civilization in Armenia. The city of Van is on the eastern shore near the two major inlets. Since there is no outlet to this expansive lake, centuries of leaching minerals have made it quite salty and barren of most life.

When Timur appeared at this principal city, the magistrates did not resist occupation, therefore, were treated with courtesy and kindness. Favorable treatment was also given to the smaller city of Adeljouz, in the far south of Armenia, where the governor was given lavish gifts for his compliance.

Once again entering Irak on his southward incursion, Timur reminded Zain-al-Abaidin, the son of departed Sultan Shuja, of the terms connected with his ascendancy to the throne. He also added that the prince was in need of support at a time when a play for power was rampant throughout the land. Zain-al-Abaidin proceeded to dither as he weighed his chances of displeasing Timur against favor with the other princes of western Persia. In the end he displayed hostility toward the amir by detaining his envoy.

Apparently the master plan was to conquer all of Persia in an orderly fashion. The large province of Fars in the southwest became a prime target because of the number of fortresses held by the Muzaffars. It was a rich province that extended all the way to the coast of the Persian Gulf (called Bahr Fars in Timur's time). In the autumn of 1387 Timur started his long march southward, first to the city of Ispahan, just north of the border with Fars.

There he found a friendly greeting where Zain-al-Abaidin's uncle was the chief magistrate. The Timurids were welcomed into the city where they proceeded to occupy the citadel of Tabarek. Actually there were twin cities lying on the north bank of the Ispahan River, where the eastern suburb was called the "Town of 100 Towers." The river flows in a southeasterly direction where it sinks at the edge of the Great Desert, only to reappear near the city of Kerman.

Timur set the tone quickly for the inhabitants of Ispahan. They were to be granted immunity from sacking by providing a moderate ransom. With such a formidable army in their midst, it was agreed that a settlement could be reached with Timurid nobles dividing up the city into temporary responsibility zones.

Tribute was agreed upon and the conscription was in the process of being collected when an incident occurred which triggered a chaotic condition. As the story goes, a young blacksmith happened one night to beat on a drum, presumably for his own amusement. A number of citizens, mistaking it for a call to arms, suddenly exploded into the streets with whatever arms they could muster.

At first the presumptive revolt succeeded and the nearly three thousand occupying warriors were largely slaughtered. Following this the gates were shut but the makeshift defenders had no chance against the massive army arrayed against them outside the walls.

On the morning of November 16, Timur stormed the walls and gates with orders for each soldier to bring back a Persian head. Those quarters of the city which had not joined in with the mob were spared, the Timurid forces forming a protective cordon around them to insure the safety of the innocents.

It was estimated that up to twenty thousand Persians died in the fighting before the city was secured. Timur later regretted that his plan of non violence couldn't have been carried out, but he had to react to the circumstances at the time. News of the vengeance heaped upon Ispahan reached the other cities and the Muzaffars, each in turn, decided on ransom as the wisest course of action.

Very likely it was the proliferation of horror stories which affected the decisions to capitulate, as it was alleged that the children of Ispahan were taken outside on the plain country and trampled under the horses' hooves. There is no evidence that this was true as it was quite apparent that Timur was satiated by the turn of events which had gone well beyond his fondest hopes. The only possible explanation of the trampling incident could have been a later time after the fall of Ephesus when it was said that some of the errant warriors did just that in a fit of rage.

*Soldier with Persian Head*

Shiraz, capital of Fars, was next to feel the threat of the Timurids. Founded in the early years of Islam, its protective walls were not in place until late in the 10th century. Its name came from an old Persian manuscript which in translation meant "lion's pouch." It was said that the wealth of the countryside was taken there, never to return.

By the year 1387 the city had fallen upon more desperate times. Although well known for its attar of roses, palm flower water, perfumes distilled from jasmine and other exotic scents, it could not mask the stench of human wastes. Its lack of privies and careless approach to minimal sanitation had to be particularly overcome by the profuse use of herbs and other pungent odor producing plants.

Most of the people of Shiraz were then devoted to the poverty of holiness and had accumulated very little wealth of their own. When the main army of Timur arrived at the gates on December 11 it was decided to throw all nine of them open in order to save the city from perceived desolation. The tribute exacted for its preservation was meager, at best. The city did boast one famous person, the poet Hafiz. While in Shiraz Timur summoned him and asked for a composition in verse to commemorate the occasion. When the verse was delivered it was a mere couplet which read:

*"If that fair maiden of Shiraz would accept my love,*
*I would give for the dark mole which adorns her cheek,*
*Samarkand and Bokhara."*

Timur, then sensing that his invasion had been trivialized, responded: "With my sword and after years of conflict have I taken Samarkand; now I am taking from other cities great ornaments for Samarkand. How is it that thou wouldst bestow it upon a wench of Shiraz?"

When Hafiz bowed to the ground and answered: "Alas O Prince, it is this prodigality which is the cause of the misery in which you see me." Timur was pleased with this reply and treated the poet kindly as the anger within him subsided.

Turning his attention toward his logical military heir, Timur pondered over the growing instability of his third son, Miran Shah. He was quite satisfied with his oldest living son, Omar Shaikh, but his youngest son Shah Rukh had little stomach for the military service in his youth. Like his grandfather Teraghay, he favored quiet consort with learned men and was usually found with his books. Timur was left in a sort of dilemma as to the disposition of his favors.

When he reached manhood Shah Rukh developed a feeling for that branch of the military which dealt with tactical and logistical problems and, like his father, developed into an excellent chess player. By this time, he had become a distinct favorite of the council and was destined to inherit a portion of the dynasty when his time came. He never lost his feeling for the arts and always chose peace over war when confronted with that decision.

At the age of fifty-one Timur had filled the vacuum which characterized the unrest in Persia and other parts of central Asia. He was given the title of Amir Timur Gurgan, or Lord Timur the Splendid, but certainly an emperor in everything but name. As before, he firmly retained the title of Amir of Tatary and refused to name his expanded empire. The term "gurgan" is literally translated into son-in-law, however, its significance is that of being in the Chingisid family.

One of Timur's titles was Sahib Keraun, which translates to "lord of the grand conjunctions." The Asians believed that in all of the great conjunctions of the planets there was an attendant evolution. Abraham, Moses, Zoroaster, Christ and Muhammed came into the world at a time of grand conjunction. Solomon, Alexander, Chinghis Khan and Timur were, each in their turn, "Sahib Keraun."

Ahmed Ibn Arabshah, Timur's primary detractor, describes his return across the Khorassan in the following way: "...and his cavalry advanced in corslets, and squadrons of horsemen, like hills of sand riding through tracks of roses and fragrant herbs circled in that distant country. Camels strode and mountains passed like clouds; with mind free from care, he returned to Samarkand and on the march had joy for his familiar, gladness for servants, mirth for boon companions, hilarity for nightly gossip and went with negligence and haste, until having crossed the provinces of Azerbijan, he halted in the kingdom of Khorassan, the kings of regions and wearing of the diadem doing him homage."

Following the inclusion of all of Persia into the empire, a koureltay was announced in Akiar, near Kesh. It was basically a gathering and feasting to celebrate the latest campaign, but it was also a forum to announce the appointment of Miran Shah and Omar Shaikh as new governors of Khorassan and Andijan respectively, the latter a big city just south of the Jaxartes River

Timur's form of government was a mixture of Turki–Mongol and Arab–Persian, but more of the former. He governed by individuals mainly, thus a title did not necessarily define the scope of the office. Some specific tasks were outlined for the administration, but to keep the far flung empire intact, he had to resort to certain rewards for most of his province governors.

Timur deplored weakness and he considered beggars a prime example. Giving them meat and bread as doles was only a modest success. Many of them continued to complain and resumed begging openly. This practice was then handled by the mysterious disappearance of the worst offenders during the night.

A simple law to deal with thieves was decreed throughout the land. Magistrates and guards were responsible for their districts and all stolen properties had to be replaced or accounted for in kind. If the thieves were not caught after an allotted time it was up to the department heads to make restitution.

Since Timur was nearly always on the move, he made many personal judgements while inspecting the improvements he decreed for the countryside. His pavilions would leapfrog on the route taken so that there would always be one ready and provisioned at the end of the day's ride. Historians confirm that he was accompanied by twelve thousand warriors which made up the royal guard.

The imperial army commanders all took part in what was to be the greatest expedition of that century, the invasion of all of Kiptchak. Toktamish, having made several hostile incursions across the Jaxartes, as well as into Armenia, was again challenging the reign of Timur. The council decided that a postponement of the engagement to the north would only provide a bigger problem in the future.

News arrived in late 1387 which precipitated the resolution to oppose the Mongol forces. One Mongol leader, having accumulated a substantial army from the province of Moghulstan, suddenly appeared near Taushkend and was pillaging the countryside. Early in 1388 preparations had to be hurriedly made on a grand scale. The officers were ordered to collect a year's provisions for their troops, each soldier to be supplied with a horse, a bow and quiver of arrows and a leather water bottle. For each ten soldiers there was to be a number of hand tools, repair kits, fourteen pounds of rope, leather knapsacks, a copper pot and a baggage horse. Meanwhile Omar Shaikh's army, being the nearest to the attack on Taushkend, was dispatched to meet the immediate challenge, now near the River Jaxartes,where a few days of sparring to seek advantage took place.

As the Mongol forces moved up river Omar Shaikh matched their progress on the west bank. After three days of this Omar Shaikh decided upon a plan of action. He ordered all the women to assemble and outfitted them with helmets and some armor. All prisoners and servants were likewise decked out in whatever gear was available.

Leaving a bogus force in a conspicuous encampment the Timurids took their regulars in the dark of night down river and crossed without opposition. Soon after midnight Omar Shaikh attacked the Mongol camp and routed them easily. The surprised Mongol warriors fled northward where they were able to regroup. In their hasty retreat they were obliged to leave behind many of their comrades and were never again able to mount a formidable force.

Meanwhile Toktamish, now in full command of the several hordes, had entered Transoxania by another route. A second arm of the Mongol army was threatening Bokhara which was defended, at the time, by the chieftain Bougha Barlas. The garrison of the city was able to hold off the attackers and force them to divert their attention to the countryside.

At that time Bokhara, located on the Sughd River, held both the principal prison and the treasury for the province. It was a sprawling urban community with five distinct towns within the perimeter walls. The seven iron gates were heavily fortified and manned by a considerable force of defenders.

Mongol attacks were next centered around Kesh and the banks of the Oxus as they poured southward to threaten Samarkand itself. Amir Abbas, in the defense of the Samarkand perimeter, was mortally wounded as he met the enemy in an attempt to cut them off at the river. News of this new threat reached Timur after seventeen days as he was deploying a series of new magistrates. He sent thirty horsemen to Samarkand to announce that he was on the way to relieve the threat.

It was late February of 1388 before the main army was moving by forced marches, the divisions under Miran Shah and Hadji Saif-ud-din were already in place with only a minimum supply train. Hurried arrangements were made for the various governments in and around the Khorassan to function as the slower baggage train was still on its way back from Persia.

Timur arrived in Samarkand to find that news of his relief army had precipitated a flight by the Mongol attackers. He was gratified to find that two of his generals had been able to decimate the ranks of the departing Toktamish divisions in hot pursuit. One of his commanders was rewarded for singular valour in the liberation of prisoners in the vicinity of Khojend on the Jaxartes River.

Revolts in the Khwarazm were starting to form under Shah Sulyman Sufi at the instigation of Toktamish who felt the need of a diversion in order to regroup. Timur immediately assembled his army and with forced marches, approached the city of Urganj. With his formidable numbers Timur overran the city once more, this time he levelled the city with a pent up vengeance. Only one mosque and several minarets were left standing as the exposed ground was sown to barley. All artisans and craftsmen were sent back to Samarkand to bolster the ambitious building program which was under way.

It was autumn before the final remnants of Toktamish's army was finally driven from the Khwarazm. This effort was abetted by the defection of two detachments of Mongols who placed themselves under the standard of Timur. Miran Shah had penetrated into the frontiers of Kiptchak and returned with a number of prisoners, all of whom were brought back to Samarkand.

Toktamish was still pursuing his notion to dominate all of Transoxania as intelligence coming to Timur revealed that an army under Eyghelmesh Oghlan was threatening to cross the Jaxartes. He had been able to augment his forces through conscription from the nations of Bulghar, Circassia and Azauk—those areas to the west, north and northeast of the Black Sea.

One distinguished prisoner taken by Miran Shah was spared only after he was able to identify himself and rank. He was taken to Timur for questioning, and after pledging to serve the amir's standard, was able to give a great deal of information about the state of the Mongol enemy. As a result of this intelligence Timur felt he could draw back to winter quarters at his station in Akaur (between Samarkand and Kesh).

One of the primary duties of Timur upon his return to his capital was to formalize the ascension to the puppet throne of Sultan Mahmud, son of the deceased former khan Suyurghatmish. In the old Mongol custom he also took as a wife the surviving spouse of the khan, Kichik Khanum, also known as "lesser lady" in contrast to Queen Mulkh Khanum. The newly installed puppet khan was to accompany Timur on several of his expeditions, notably in the engagement with Bayazid later, in 1402.

It was a time to complete the outfitting of the imperial army for the long campaign to follow. Once again Timur consulted his astrologers for signs of favorable omens and indications of favorable timing. It was a dream, however, which gave the great amir his most encouragement, one in which the sun was eclipsed, then went into retrograde and set again in the east. From Timur's memoirs: "…that he should advance against me, that he should be defeated, and compelled to retreat by the same road he came; thus it was that Toktamish Khan came against me with the fierceness of lions, and destroyed them, by which means the tribe of Jujy* were plundered and put to shameful flight, and I returned successful and victorious."

* named for the eldest son of Chinghis Khan who died six months after his father

# 9

# The Golden Horde

*Toktamish was your choice of lord,*
*But treachery lies in his accord;*
*He lives to threaten all Kiptchak*
*While you were still in old Irak.*

When Timur returned to Samarkand in the autumn of 1388 he arranged marriages for his sons and grandsons. Pavilions were erected in the Paradise Garden with pearls and precious stones very much in evidence. Princes Omar Shaikh and Shah Rukh (then only eleven years old), along with the two sons of Jahanghir, took brides from the four selected princesses. These young ladies were said to be as beautiful as the Houris, the nymphs of Muslim folklore whose beauty and innocence never faded.

It was well into 1388 before the massive combined armies of Timur ventured toward the Kiptchak in the effort to search out and defeat Toktamish and his army of Mongols. Timur sent his engineers ahead to build bridges across the Jaxartes at places where they would hope to find the least resistance. After crossing with the main army, scouting parties were sent afield to seek the presence of their foe. A trap was laid out for part of the southern division of Jetes and a crushing defeat for them followed. Only a small number were able to escape across the Aritch, a tributary of the Jaxartes.

Toktamish, now seeing that he was facing increasing odds, decided to withdraw farther away by moving his army back across the steppes. It was merely a question of time before the Golden Horde would strike again. Timur countered by marching northwest and encamping on the banks of the River Tik. It was while in this area that he received information about an uprising building up in the Khorassan.

Not wishing to deter his main thrust, Timur by necessity, had to answer the incursion by the revolting Hadji Beg. Once again Miran Shah vacated the imperial forces and hurried south with forced marches to arrive on the scene by June near the city of Tus, where the Persian army was holding forth.

Tus was made up of two parts and when the Mongols razed both urban areas, the part known as Mashad emerged as the most flourishing, while the old Tus never fully recovered. The importance of this part of the Khorassan was centered around gold, silver, copper and iron mines. Of nearly equal importance were the deposits of turquoise and malachite. This urban center was important as the main access to Nisapur which extended on eastward through Merv.

Hadji Beg's brother Yussuf, evidently thinking that Timur himself had arrived, decided to leave suddenly with his followers at a propitious time. In a hurried consultation with his nobles Hadji Beg decided to leave in turn, taking with him as large a detachment as he could through a place in the wall which could be easily broken. This escape was planned to emulate a sneak attack on the Timurids whereby the residents were left behind to fend for themselves. Miran Shah then easily entered the city and spared those citizens who offered no resistance. Some historians have said that each conquering soldier was to produce a head of an adversary. This notion was a holdover from a previous encounter and did not prove to be true.

After a futile attempt to pursue Hadji Beg and his brother, Miran Shah liberated those prisoners who had been confined, and treasures that had been captured were given to the several magistrates in the area. As far west as Nisapur the chiefs all pledged loyalty to Timur. Miran Shah then headed northward to join the main Timurid army. On the way he eliminated the last Kart prince, thus ending the dynasty which had survived since 1245. Timur had become impatient to continue the march against Toktamish, but demurred to the wishes of the council who wanted to wait for the return of his son's army.

In the area of Moghulstan a budding khan was starting to develop a threat to the stability of the countryside. Another son of Tugluk Timur, Khizr Khoja, was just a child when his father died. He had been nurtured by his family and secreted away in the mountains between Kashgar and Badakshan. In his youth he was presented to the Chaghatays when it was considered a propitious time. His acceptance was hailed as a good omen, and as a proper scion of the dynasty, he was installed as khan in 1389.

Timur's expedition into Moghulstan during that year encountered the new khan who was gathering his soldiers in the high country. Even though it was summer he encountered snow and ice in the high elevations near Atir. The Mongol cavalry was easily defeated in a short battle but the main force under Khizr Khoja had managed to elude Timur. It was three days before the Timurids were able to relocate the enemy.

What followed was a series of skirmishes as Timur had divided up several times to pursue the Mongols. Omar Shaikh joined up later with his father who started his march across the plains country nearby, a place commonly given a name which in translation means "the dog does not drink." Prisoners taken in this foray were sent back to Samarkand as Timur moved onward to arrive at the Irtish River near the south boundary of Siberia. The army of Khizr Khoja was encountered soon thereafter but they scattered so widely that the pursuit was impossible

The Timurid army wintered in Taushkend as Timur was receiving sporadic intelligence about the khan's army which had remained beyond the Irtish. Early in 1390 the imperial army was once again on the march toward the vicinity of Alma Alta, crossing both the Ili and the Karatal. The Mongols had retreated farther into their northland and Timur did not wish to weaken his ability to encounter the primary enemy at a later date, therefore, decided to withdraw and prepare for the campaign against Toktamish.

While in winter quarters Timur visited shrines and donated heavily to the charities. He fell ill and caused a great deal of consternation within the army. It was forty days before he recovered enough to again mount his horse and gather up his troops for inspection.

When he began his campaign to oust the Jettah population he found the Christian missions flourishing, and not knowing how to deal with it, allowed them to continue undisturbed. When the Jete army fell back to the mountains for support they had softened considerably, no longer with the instinctive will to fight in the traditional Mongol manner.

Although unaware of it at the time, Timur was about to cross and cut off the great highways of Asia. This would effectively mark the end of the roving bands of Scythian, Turk and Mongol tribes as a factor in the vast expanse of the steppe country. Timur's crossing of the Desht Kiptchak (Kiptchak desert) followed in the footsteps of Chinghis Khan who founded the dynasties of the Blue Horde in the west and White Horde in the east, now consolidated under the the horn standard of the Golden Horde.

Later in the year 1390 Timur contemplated taking the initiative as his foe was ever retreating westward. All provisioning had been completed and he felt satisfied with the makeup of his enlarged army as a division of Sufis joined with him and the Jettahs had been neutralized.

Crossing the great plains country was a hazardous venture as they nearly ran out of water. The spring snow melt from the mountains to the south watered enough pasture land for them to sustain the massive army. As a last gesture Omar Shaikh's army was sent into Siberia where they were able to decimate a group of 700 Jetes. Timur now felt secure from any attack at his rear.

On the continued march into Kiptchak Timur was detained for a few days to entertain certain ambassadors who were given gifts and sent on their way. Part of the ceremonial procedure was to mask the intent of the actual invasion. Even in the harshest of times

Timur retained the decorum of a great leader. After a hunt he would appear with his white ermine headgear adorned with rubies, an ivory baton tipped with a gold knob, and his lords in attendance. For some time Timur had trained himself to stand erect and to minimize his limp with a flowing style of weight change.

Proceeding westward, the army crossed the River Karasou (probably the modern day Isim), from there into a vast wasteland. At this time, in a rare occurrence for the great amir, two of his chieftains deserted him to seek protection under Toktamish. Timur, in council, addressed his generals and nobles about the coming campaign and reminded them of the importance of close adherence to duty and homeland.

The gamble being taken had to have a successful ending, the army had reached the point of no return. By the time they had crossed the River Yelanjouk (now Tobol) in April of 1391, supplies were running dangerously low. Except for the foray across the Irtish, there had been no sign of the enemy.

Daily hunts were made where the game was surrounded by the horsemen and driven into a central pocket. The warriors subsisted on the protein from wild boars, antelope, partridges, even wolves. The meat was always prepared in a stew with some flour and herbs added. To keep up the army's spirit, Timur and all his lords ate from the same stew pot as their lowest echelon warriors.

With the business of the chase at an end several days were employed in a review of the army divisions. While contemplating who should lead the vanguard, Timur's grandson Muhammed Sultan came to him and begged on his knees for the privilege of being at the point of the army. By the 10th of May, on a day that appeared favorable to the chief astrologer, the Timurid army was again on the move with the young prince leading the way.

After two days the track of the enemy was discovered as camp remnants were found near a tributary of the Ural River. Later, signs of seventy camp fires were discovered but no signs of any patrols or rear guard personnel. Timur selected the hardiest of his scouts to probe more deeply into the countryside. They were able to observe a few Mongol warriors but returned without causing an alarm.

When they finally came to the Ural River at the end of May the patrols found the first positive signs of the enemy army. History would record that if Toktamish had been encamped farther west it would have been impossible to engage him. Timur had violated military strategy but he depended on his knowledge of Mongol temperament to see his plan through.

With the capture of a prisoner it was determined that Toktamish did indeed, wish to lead his pursuers as far west as possible. His camp appeared to be somewhere between the Ural and the Volga. Murbasher, because of his fast moving cavalry, was chosen to make the initial engagement. They came upon a detachment of the main army and immediately pressed the attack.

After a fierce battle the Mongols were defeated and forty prisoners were brought back to Timur's pavilion. Unsatisfied with what intelligence he could get, another scout party was sent out to discover where the main body of Toktamish's army was encamped. They returned with news of finding an enemy scouting party together with a sighting of a large cloud of dust, indicating the probable location of a large force.

An initial probe was made by one of Timur's favorite generals, Eyku Timur. Unfortunately he arrived at a hilltop only to find a considerable force arrayed in battle formation ready to charge. Although he called for an immediate retreat, the Mongols were on him at first sight. In the furious battle that ensued Eyku Timur was mortally wounded as well as several of his nobles. The retreating army had to make their way back to the encampment through treacherous swamps and woodlands.

In the council of war that followed there was a distinct pall over the general staff as they mourned the loss of their close comrades. A counter attack was set in motion with a corps of twenty thousand horsemen under Omar Shaikh. Before any serious engagement could be made a sudden storm broke out accompanied by cold rain and sleet, demobilizing all units for a period of six days.

*Toktamish Charges Timurid Warriors*

As the weather cleared the attack was renewed with ten divisions moving forward in a gigantic crescent to confront Toktamish. It was the 16th of June, 1391 when Timur, near the center of his army, ordered the initial forward movement as he hoped to provoke the Mongols into headlong attack. As a further measure designed to confound his foe, the order was given to dismount and to pitch tents, getting ready to prepare the customary meal. Only after this show of confidence did they actually proceed forward once more.

What transpired next has been described as a brilliant series of cavalry engagements. By using his tactic of fluidity the great amir managed to divide and outflank his enemy, always cognizant of the superior numbers arrayed against him. Later he would list his three fixed rules of engagement which characterized his campaigns:

1. Never allow his own country in the maneuvering of a campaign,

2. Never to allow himself to be put on the defensive,

3. Always to attack as swiftly as hard driven horses can travel.

Even in June the damp tundras were pelted by showers and direct engagements were sometimes postponed. The march of nearly eighteen hundred miles had actually hardened the Timurids as the Mongols wondered at the resilience of their foe. The right wing of Timur's army under the command of his son Miran Shah contained the heavy cavalry and a group of the so called "madly valiant," sometimes called also the "death seekers." This was in variance to the normal disposition where the left flank contained the elite corps.

Nobody doubted that the final confrontation was at hand. Timur personally visited all of the commanders and showed supreme confidence in achieving total victory. Many of the warriors were thinking fondly of their homeland, fingering personal icons and offering up prayers for survival.

On the morning of the big battle (June 18) Timur dismounted and prostrated himself on the ground imploring God for help in the coming confrontation with those accused of treachery. Upon remounting he led all his troops with hands raised to the skies in the cry "Allah Akbar!" His faithful old friend Imam Baraka turned to his leader and said: "Go where you will, you will be victorious!" The signal to advance was given and the battle of the Kiptchak had started.

It was the right flank which led the first charge into the ranks of the Golden Horde. While they were thus engaged, Toktamish broke through the center of Timur's lines, and sensing victory in his grasp, proceeded to penetrate as far as resistance was offered. Omar Shaikh, on the left flank, countered with his army and headed by swift horsemen, swept in an arc which carried for some distance. Toktamish then veered to his right to try a flanking movement of his own, thus causing a considerable attenuation of his lines.

Timur, from his central position, then reacted to the trap he had set. With all his reserves the Timurids attacked both flanks and drove a wedge between the two strung-out portions of the army of Toktamish. A portion of the divisions under Miran Shah then wheeled around to attack the Mongols in the rear. Toktamish was obliged to attempt a breakout by attacking a unit to his right but was met with determined resistance.

One of the significant aspects of the fierce battle was the defection of an elite squadron which was displaying the horned standard of the Mongols. Timur rightly surmised that the fall of it usually denoted the loss of the leader. The Golden Horde scattered to the protection of the forests and Toktamish, very much alive, was unable to rally his forces. Later it was discovered that Timur had bribed the standard bearer with rich gifts to lower the horned scepter upon his signal.

This defeat of Toktamish was known as the Battle of Kunduzche* and the chronicler of the event described the melee in the light of a dry land encounter. His questionable transcription runs as follows: "The earth became a cloud of dust, and was transferred into a raging sea whose threatening waves washed hither and

---

* near the east bank of the Volga close to the present day city of Dimitrovgrad

thither. The sun, the source of light, was darkened by the dust thrown up by the furious riders, and the countenance of the moon was soiled by the dust. The heavenly sphere emitted a longdrawn groan, and the world plaintively petitioned for grace."

As the remnants of the khan's large army fled westward they were pursued by nearly three fourths of the Timurids. Some were trapped and slaughtered on the banks of the Volga, while others who had escaped to some of the river islands were taken as captives and brought back in chains. The booty captured was like manna from heaven to the warriors who had subsisted on meager rations and limited supplies, all of which had caused considerable weight loss throughout the ranks, including the horses and camels.

One noticeable feature found in the prisoners was their method of transporting their tents. They did not dismantle them and then go through the time consuming job of reerection—they had a special mount on the camels to transport them intact. These typical round felt tents were called a kibitki by the Chaghatays and nearly always taken apart for transport. A few of the more special ones could be mounted on wide wheeled vehicles. Later, almost to a man, they copied the Mongol type of shelter.

There was an unsavory side of the victory which centered around the captives, largely with the women and boys. The more desirable women were made to dance and sing songs, then taken to the tents for love making. The boys were forced to become servants and pressed into the most menial of duties.

It was well into July when the Timurid army, now with a great deal of loot and captives, started the long trek back to their homeland. The army under Saif-ud-din became particularly anxious to return and responded with protracted marches which outstripped the others. Timur was content to celebrate in a more leisurely manner as he virtually dawdled for twenty six days, while sending his armies back in sequence.

Those sections of the Mongol jurisdiction which had separated themselves some time before from Toktamish were entertained at Timur's pavilion. They were given certain grants, but still fearing a future uprising from the fleeing Mongol khan, exacted written commitments of support should they experience danger from this quarter. One chieftain, Kounjah Oghlan, was singled out for a large share of the spoils because of the scope of his adherence to Timur in the past.

Having been away for eight months, the victors were warmly received upon arriving back in their homeland near the end of 1391. After choosing a Mongol officer as khan for the northern territories, Timur then looked forward to other pursuits. Unfortunately the conquest of Kiptchak was not to be of long duration as his nemesis, Toktamish, was destined to rise again to challenge the great amir.

# 10

## The Return to the West

*Beyond the plains of Khorassan*
*Lie desert sand and Turkoman.*
*To the Tigris and Euphrates go,*
*To seek the sultan as your foe.*

Back in Samarkand Timur's first act was to inspect the tomb he was having built for Jahanghir. It was also time to assemble another koureltay in order to set the stage for his desire for further conquest. One of his primary purposes was to insure a continual supply of men and officers for his growing army. This was accomplished with written agreements which reached down into the ranks of imams* and chieftains.

Apparently there had been no extended reoccurrence of the illness which had overtaken him in the winter of 1390–91. Timur does not refer to the more frequent bouts with his illness, nor do his scribes, except to duration. From later evidence it seems that he suffered much in later life with pulmonary problems. This he resisted with the same pride and resolution as his pronounced lameness.

Timur was obliged to turn his attention to his perennial antagonists, the Jetes, whose homeland of Jettah was also

---

* order of Islamic holy men

---

somewhat threatened by the Golden Horde. Omar Shaikh, now as governor of the province of Farghana (northeastern Transoxania), was sent out to determine the extent of their hostile activity. One patrol ran across a killing field where two of the pretenders to the Jettah throne had vied for dominance, leaving behind a bloody battlefield.

The amirs under Omar Shaikh took advantage of the attrition which attended this struggle between two rivals to pursue the victor. This expedition brought them all the way to the Irtish River which runs northward through Siberia. After six months of following their quarry with very little positive results, they had to retire for lack of supplies.

Back in Samarkand, Timur once again felt the pangs of his illness for a few weeks as the doctors fought his congestion and fever. His nobles became quite concerned, but the great amir was more concerned about his coming campaigns and declared himself fit within the month. During this time he decided to confer the government of eastern Afghanistan upon his grandson Pir Muhammed, a territory which extended all the way to the upper Indus River.

As Timur reconvened his court, foremost among his official duties was to prepare for a double wedding to unite his two grandsons with families of the Karts (from Herat). Both Pir Muhammed and Muhammed Sultan had been betrothed to the daughters of Ghiath-ad-din, the malik and now a close friend of Timur. After the elaborate ceremony was concluded it became the chosen time to set the stage for the grand plan to subjugate all of Persia.

Since the demise of Shah Shuja at least five princes of southwest Persia had been feuding and creating the vacuum which Timur found most inviting. Aside from these Muzaffars, Sultan Ahmed was the only ruler who commanded a large enough force to meet an invasion threat. Timur, once again, found a passage in the Koran which could be interpreted as a license to set matters straight, where peril to the holy faith could be perceived.

On May 27, 1392, Timur took his army across the Oxus which formed the traditional boundary between Persia and Tatary. In the neighborhood of Balkh the Oxus winds its way through limestone hills where fields of rice, barley and melons grow. On the lower plains, before emptying into the Aral Sea, it is dotted with mulberry trees, alders and vineyards. Further up the slopes is the grazing land for sheep, cattle and horses where the tamaracks grow in abundance. This is the land that the army traversed before entering the plains and deserts of the Khorassan

After a few day's march Timur dismissed the princesses who were in his retinue, to be conducted back to Samarkand by Shah Rukh. Following several forced marches he was able to catch up with his advance division under Muhammed Sultan and Pir Muhammed at Kaboushan, on the road to Astarabad. He was then met also by Khan Zada, his daughter-in-law who was on her way through the Mazanderan, an episode which would end with the discovery of a covert liason with Miran Shah.

From Astarabad the progress westward was impeded by thick forests which necessitated some delay while passage for the army was cut through its entanglements. They came upon an abatis* made from large trees where the people of Sari had stashed their treasures of gold, silver and jewels. After confiscating this find, the army continued over swampy land to the city of Amul, just south of the Caspian Sea.

Near Amul, in the Elburz mountains, was the headquarters for a wild fanatic group called the Assassins or Fedagis—Fedaj is Arabic for one who sacrifices himself. After fierce fighting a massacre of this religious sect followed which chroniclers label as one of the bloodiest in all of history. The way was then open to proceed westward.

As Ghiath-ad-din was sent ahead to dissuade his former family members from offering resistance, the army found itself passing through marshy lands where some man made impediments were placed in the way. It was October 11, 1392, when the advanced scouts ran into their first evidence of resistance. In a skirmish which followed Shaikh Ali Bahaudur, long a companion of Timur, was killed.

---

* a blockade to deter passage

Although a few leaders of the resistance forces sought out the great amir in compliance with the old agreement, most of the garrison at Mushedsur were being militantly defensive. For the first time in his career Timur found it necessary to attack by water. He sent for his Greek fire slingers and boatmen from the Oxus to confiscate all vessels on the south of the Caspian Sea.

In combination with a small force crossing the marshes to the southwest of Mushedsur, the Timurids main attack by sea proved to be demoralizing to the inhabitants, many shortly thereafter fleeing to the west. A large part of this hurried exodus was prompted by the cacophony accompanying the initial charge provided by trumpets, cymbals and kettle drums emanating from the sea. Those that stubbornly resisted were forced to surrender after a few days.

Here was another occasion where Timur treated the city survivors with kindness and liberality. After a lecture on the tenets of the Koran he sent them to the safety of the castle at Sari with orders to guard them at all costs. The fortifications at Mushedsur were then levelled to the ground before the army proceeded onward, having been satisfied that the conquest of Mazanderan was complete.

Although treating the Shiite Muslims as brothers-under-the-skin, Timur had always put theological pressure on captives to embrace the Sunni doctrine. While in the Mazanderan, he sent back to Samarkand and Taushkend many captured nobles whom he felt could be converted and thus eventually carry the ethic to their followers at a later date.

Much booty was returned to Samarkand as Timur welcomed his favorite wife, Mulkh Khanum, together with Shah Rukh and grandson Khalil. He then ordered the construction of a winter palace in the territory of Jirjan, located southeast of Astarabad. He arrived at the building site on December 5 where he met with his architects and builders who, at the time, were well into the foundation construction.

Again, restlessness overcame Timur, and not waiting for the winter thaw he headed westward once more. Two branches of the army under Muhammed Sultan and Pir Muhammed had already left earlier. The voluminous baggage train was ordered to follow at a more measured pace. Word had come that his two grandsons had penetrated to the frontier of Irak and were ready to enter Sultanieh in Azerbijan.

Seven days after arriving at Sultanieh the Timurids were again on the move, this time on the road toward Baghdad through the province of Kurdistan. The two armies interrupted their southwestward progress when a messenger arrived to inform them that they were to proceed to the frontier between Kurdistan and Azerbijan where Timur feared they would find pockets of resistance which might threaten their rear. Within a few days he reversed this order because of new intelligence, sending word to his grandsons to resume their primary course.

Ibrahim Shah, then the reigning prince of Kurdistan, dispatched his son with presents and Arabian horses to the Timurid camp. Timur, in the meantime, was in the process of catching up with advance armies. He left behind the army of Miran Shah to await the baggage train, then pushed on in a southwest direction to the fortress of Keyou*.

He immediately attacked the fortress which yielded within a few days. The governor of Keyou then quickly surrendered and Timur rested for several days in the governor's residence. Meanwhile Omar Shaikh turned southward and entered Kerrahroud where he sent the governor to Timur's pavilion to pay homage.

Saif-ud-din was given the government of Keldaush and Nehawend, the latter having been named after Noah who was said to have resided there. The fortress at Khoromabad on the border with Lauristan was attacked and laid waste by Timur's personal army before he started to clean out several bands of marauders who were plundering and terrorizing people in their area.

Omar Shaikh, having penetrated to the banks of the Tigris, now joined his father. He had to report that he had been unable to overtake the Prince of Lur who was his assigned quarry. It was early in 1393 when word arrived that Miran Shah was camped just

---

* at the foot of the Kurdish Mountains

north of Ispahan with the baggage and heavy equipment. With the appearance of this formidable unit the Muzzafar Melouk* of Ispahan readily surrendered without even a token resistance.

Timur's next move while skirting the mountain chain running all the way to the Persian Gulf, was to the ancient city of Tustar (Arabic name) which was called Shustar by the Persians. The city was surrounded by a garden area where grapes, oranges and dates grew abundantly. It had a pleasant climate much of the year but was exceedingly hot during the summer season. The city was historically important for having been the place of captivity for the Roman Emperor Valerian from 260 to 253 B.C.

Timur was joined there by the armies of his grandsons, at which point the two chiefs who commanded at Tustar abandoned their city and fled to Shiraz. In this latter city the titular head of the Muzzafars, Shah Mansur, was feverishly preparing his defenses for the coming invasion. Before moving on Timur and his nobles inspected the great weir that was then over sixteen centuries old, still holding back a large portion of the waters from the Dujayl River.

It was early March in the year 1393 when Timur, at the head of the combined armies, marched toward Shiraz. With orders to Omar Shaikh to continue with the progress of the baggage train, the main army waited in encampment where the Prince of Lauristan presented himself at Timur's pavilion. Having previously fled, his presence at the feet of the great amir indicated that some of the feuding Muzzafars were having second thoughts about their troubled dynasty.

The great army was still some distance from Shiraz as they proceeded across the many tributaries that emptied into the Persian Gulf to one of the strongest fortresses in Asia. Lying on a mountain top southwest of Kazeroom, the stronghold was known as the "White Castle," and its governor, Saudet, had been named to signify good fortune. From the description of his countrymen it would belie this—he was said to be "an unfortunately wicked fellow."

---

* from the same derivation as malik (king)

The strength of this fortress was centered upon the one and only possible road, a tortuous way through rugged rock formations. The mesa on the top had been described as a veritable Eden with clear streams, fountains, fruit trees, myriads of birds, and teeming with all manner of animals. Timur set up his encampment on a neighboring mountain top which commanded a view of this beautiful but forbidding place.

Notwithstanding the problem that the fortifications presented, Timur divided up his army to attack it from all possible sites. After a full day's assault several units were able to scale the rocky slopes and attain a position of strength which they were able to hold through the night.

At dawn on the following day the entire might of Timur's army renewed the attack to the sound of trumpets and kettle drums. They were met by a shower of stones and arrows. It was only after much loss of life that Ak Beg, one of the strongest of warriors, was able to move his way to the top of the mountain through a narrow crevice, surprise the defenders, and manage to hold out until his companions could join him. As his fellow warriors made it to the top, Ak Beg led the growing force to higher ground where they diverted much of the attention of the defenders.

This access to the mesa so demoralized the inhabitants that they scattered to try and defend all possible entrances, and in doing so, fell prey to the growing numbers pouring in from the one entrance point at the top. Within a few hours the rout was complete and the one road to the top was teeming with Timurids. Saudet, the governor, was captured without injury and brought to Timur where sentence was placed on his head to expiate for the considerable blood letting.

When all of the remnants of resistance had been rounded up it was discovered that Shah Mansur had escaped during the previous night with a small band of followers. News reached Timur in the following days that the prince of the Muzzafars had rounded up all of his remaining faithfuls and had retreated to Shiraz. News of the sacking at the castle had reached the other lords and most of them opted to ransom their cities to spare the devastation which would have awaited the resistance to Timur.

Shah Mansur sought the help of his other rulers in Irak but they were busy fighting among themselves. Word had long since leaked out that Mansur had put out the eyes of his cousin, Zain-al-Abaidin, ostensibly because of a possible threat to his monarchy, but perhaps abetted by the cousin's close friendship with Timur. Shah Mansur had assembled 2,000 mail clad cavalry and back in his fortress, was asking the inhabitants to support him.

The city dwellers, mainly Sunnis, had long studied the frailties of their monarch and decided on an appropriate response which they delivered in the following form: "When your necklace is broken and your army overthrown you will think in the struggle that no counsel is so wise for you as to seek escape and flight, and you will leave us, like meat on a butcher pole, after our foot is entangled in battle with them, and belated repentance will not help us after establishing our enmity, nor will this fracture then be repaired by us unless by slaughter, rapine and chains."

Shah Mansur did indeed leave Shiraz to give battle to Timur in the field, enraged by the characterization of his cowardice. The night before his decision of confrontation he turned an unbroken horse loose with a heavy kettle tied to its tail in order to disrupt the encampment of his foe. By morning he had not lost his resolve to engage Timur in a show of bravado to regain lost favor with his own people.

In the battle that raged outside the walls of Shiraz an account by Timur's faithful comrade-in-arms, Saif-ud-din seems to be the most authentic, having been in the thick of it. He writes: "Shah Mansur advanced at their head like a furious lion, and in opposition to his reason, which should have preserved in his mind a suitable idea of the person he had to do with. On a Friday, at the hour of prayer, he attacked our main body, composed of 30,000 Turks, the most dexterous men of their time, in a place called Patilla: he, however, overthrew their squadrons, broke their ranks, made his way into the midst of them and gained posts of the utmost consequence behind our army. Then he returned, furious as a dragon to the fight, seeming resolved to lose his life. Timur stopped short with some of his favorites to consider the extreme vigour, or rather rashness, of the prince who dared to attack him in person. Timur, seeing him come directly against him would have armed himself with his lance to oppose him, but he could not find it because Poulad Chourz, the keeper of it, had been so vigorously attacked that he had fled and carried away the lance. Timur, who had only fourteen or fifteen persons with him, did not stir out of his place till Shah Mansur came up to him. This rash person struck the emperor's helmet twice with his scimitar, but the blows did no harm, for they glanced along his arms; he kept firm as a rock and did not change his posture." (In point of fact Timur did receive some minor wounds on his neck and shoulder).

Prince Mansur found that his followers had scattered during the charge and he was left with only a handful of faithful Some of Timur's warriors ran across the wounded prince after he was forced to dismount from his horse. One of the scribes favorable to Shah Rukh described Timur's youngest son as defeating Prince Mansur in a fierce battle, after which he cut off his head. The likely scenario is that the seventeen year old favorite had a relatively easy time of it and arrived at his father's encampment to throw the head at his feet exclaiming: "May the heads of all thy enemies be laid at thy feet as the head of the proud Mansur!"

The remainder of the Muzaffar army was routed and the city of Shiraz was secured. It was the end of any organized resistance by this group which had ruled from the time of Hulagou Khan (grandson of Chinghis) until defeated by Timur in 1393. Their name had been derived from the founder Mubariz-u-din Muhammed whose title was Ui-Muzaffar or, "the victorious." Shah Mansur was the fifth of this dynasty—the sixth and seventh were unable to unite the clans.

Much of the fury behind the attack on Shah Mansur was prompted by the news that had reached Timur months before, that his claimed follower, Zain-al-Abaidin had been blinded in a fit of rage by the prince. Thus it was that the son of Shah Shuja was avenged. He and his companion Chelabi, also blinded by Shah Mansur, were taken back to Samarkand to live out their lives in relative comfort. The wounds sustained by Timur healed quickly and did not prove a deterrent to his plans of consolidation for all of Persia.

Muhammed Sultan was sent to Ispahan with instructions to see that the city was properly garrisoned, albeit with contributions from the citizenry to insure their safety. Omar Shaikh, still with the baggage train, was able to eliminate some remnants of the rebel parties who were out pillaging the inhabitants of Lauristan. A great deal of booty was recovered from the flight of the Muzaffars, including a number of precious stones, horses, mules, pavilions and other goods which were proffered by the conquered tribes.

Timur conferred the province of Fars, actually the heart of much of the empire, on his son Omar Shaikh. Each of the remaining Muzaffars agreed to submit to the Timurid rule, even Sultan Ahmed's ambassador presented himself at court. Timur and his nobles spent the month of April largely in Shiraz as they offered continuous entertainment with cups of gold being used, as the most beautiful maids in the city became servants of the court. The famous amir ingratiated himself with the inhabitants by removing many taxes and promising protection through his standardized laws.

On May 8, 1393, Timur left Shiraz on his way to Ispahan. After refreshing himself there for some time he saw to the further elimination of the plundering Ismaelite* bands which were still causing problems in the area westward from Kashan. On the desert border between Ardistan and Kashan were the "Vulture Hills," the highest of the great desert. It was in the neighboring "Black Hills" that the robber bands were known to be hiding.

When Timur was satisfied that he had reduced the numbers of Ismaelites to a tolerable residual he once again was on the march— this time into northern Irak. Several ladies of the court, including two of Timur's wives, joined the army at their encampment near the fortress of Hasby.

When the agent of Sultan Ahmed presented himself he was given the usual dress of honor, horse and sum of money, but sent

---

* early breakaway Islamic sect

back without any assurances of particular friendship. Timur had in mind to move on Baghdad and did not want to give out any false impressions. On August 20 he started the journey to the capital of Mesopotamia.

While in the area of Dizful in southern Irak Timur repaired the famous dike across the Dujayl River. It had been constructed centuries before by the then Sassanian* King Nourshirvan. It was made of hewn stone with lime cement and fastened together by clamps of iron, twenty feet wide and one thousand two hundred feet long. Two arches near the center allowed a portion of the water to flow through while the excess was used to irrigate the surrounding farm lands. Finding low water, it was expedient to put the engineers to work, as the rest of the army continued on toward the west.

Dizful took its name from the famous bridge on the river of the same name, called the "Castle Bridge." It had 42 arches and was 320 paces in length. The city occupied both banks and a canal was cut through solid rock to irrigate the surrounding fields, being lifted to the higher level by means of a gigantic water wheel. The Dizful River continued due south to join the Dujayl before emptying into the Persian Gulf.

Timur paused long enough on his incursion toward Baghdad to visit the mausoleum of Kubbeh Ibrahamlik which was described as being twenty-seven leagues northeast of the metropolis. After recounting his vows to Islam he sent a message by carrier pigeon which had to be repeated, as a passing of Turkoman tribes was mistaken for Timur's legions.

When word came that the Timurid army was approaching, Sultan Ahmed sent what gifts he could muster, at the same time sending gifts to Kara Yussuf in the hopes of help from this quarter. Timur returned all of the offerings with a note that he was seeking peaceful submission only.

Ahmed, sensing that disaster could be at hand, hastily assembled a body of horsemen and prepared to flee to the border, some eighty miles away. He gathered up his personal treasure and

---

* former Persian dynasty which ruled from third to seventh century A.D.

posted scouts with carrier pigeons to prepare for as much advance warning as possible.

It was certainly Timur's intention to take Baghdad, but he had in mind a clever plan to accomplish his ends in a circumventive way. First, he sent a cavalry division to occupy the Turkomans in a static confrontation, then assembled the main army for a move toward Baghdad at a propitious time.

Under cover of night he took most of the army away from the main road and into the mountain foothills to the north. The sultan's scouts, sighting a large cloud of dust caused by a fast moving body of horses, loosed their pigeons to warn the sultan of impending danger.

Timur's own advance scouts detected the warning flight of pigeons and traced them to their source. The imprisoned scouts of Sultan Ahmed were then made to send a second message stating that the first warning was in error, that it was a large body of Turkomans coming to his rescue. The sultan, always suspicious, did not entirely believe the second message and decided to prepare a boat bridge across the Tigris. In any event Timur was able to enter the metropolis without a great deal of resistance and was able to send a tardy contingent to follow Ahmed in his retreat.

Timur, not cognizant of the sultan's flight in time, neglected to cross the river in force, instead electing to enter the city. When he discovered his mistake, a pursuit which ranged ten leagues to the northwest, was doomed to failure. He then, bending to the entreaties of his nobles, returned to Baghdad.

On the other hand, the amirs in his command did actually pursue the sultan for several days until they found he had crossed the Euphrates ahead of them and was well on his way across the trackless desert. The chase was further complicated by the discovery that all available boats had been destroyed. After eschewing the idea to swim the river it was found that four boats had been miraculously saved and were cleverly hidden by their owners.

Spurred on by the amount of booty involved, the pursuit continued. It finally developed that the exhausted horses were the defining factor and it called a halt to any meaningful pursuit by the main body. A small group that was able to continue ran into a superior force which repelled them with severe losses. No chance to regroup was possible and the last of the pursuers had to withdraw. It was a disconsolate band of warriors who had to report their failure to Timur.

Sultan Ahmed, finding himself in a relative safe mode, sent his possessions to the fort Al Naja which was situated high on a mountain top and considered almost unassailable. The fort was located in the province controlled by Sultan Zahir, he who had previously put his own mother to death along with her alleged adulterer. He eventually averted a confrontation with Timur and threw open the gates of the fort to withdraw and become an obedient adherent to Timur, thus allowing himself the retention of his title. In the meantime Sultan Ahmed sought refuge in Karbala (in Syria) where the Sultan of Egypt was in residence.

With the place of refuge discovered, a considerable force was sent to apprehend him. After only a token resistance, the sultan was taken in bondage to Miran Shah at Hillah, just down river from Baghdad. There, he was treated kindly and given considerable freedom, indeed too much freedom. As the army was on the way north to Mardin, in Mesopotamia, he was able to escape during the night. Eventually he fled to the protection of his benefactor in Egypt.

The occupation of Baghdad was described as benign as the sons of Sultan Ahmed were received with approbation on their return to the city. They were given the stewardship of various quarters of the city as pledges of continuous friendship were made to seal the bargain. The only conspicuous looting was the emptying of the contents of the sultan's wine cellars into the Tigris. Certain families, however, were required to pay ransom for the ones who were captured in the process of waging war.

Before leaving Baghdad Timur sent envoys to Egypt and Syria, in particular a reminder to the former concerning certain indignities suffered at the hands of the Mamluks. As a claimant to all the territory from Cathay to the Persian Gulf, he warned of any hostile acts as subject to retribution. Meanwhile commerce in and out of Baghdad returned to its normal state.

In the month of October, 1393, Shah Rukh was sent in advance of the main army whose next move was to be Takrit. On his march through Mesopotamia Timur encountered a lion pride which he set out to hunt as a welcome diversion. By early November his main army was in sight of Takrit.

Located on the west bank of the Tigris, Takrit was famous for its strong castle which was said to be 6,000 paces in circumference. Many of its population were Christians who had been allowed to practice their religion in peace. In the surrounding fields were large flocks of sheep and gardens yielding tasty melons and sesame seeds.

Amir Hasan, the prince of the city, was overwhelmed by the sight of the powerful army. With the knowledge that his previous acts of plunder and outrage would need to be accounted for, he dispatched his brother to offer terms of submission to Timur. Returning with only a horse and dress of honor, the minimum for an envoy, the message from the great ruler was to appear at his court.

After only a short contemplation, Amir Hasan was overcome by sheer terror. He decided to chance it with the total means under his control to defend the city. When his hostility became evident the battering rams moved in and proceeded to demolish the walls of Takrit into rubble. On the third day of the assault the prince sent out his own mother with many lavish presents to beg for clemency. Again, the demand for Amir Hasan to appear in person was the final answer from Timur.

When the last stronghold of the city was undermined and it became evident that resistance could not succeed, the prince tried once more with his brother to mediate his chances, again with the same results. In their last stand the brothers, together with the remainder of the garrison, were stranded on the only remaining rock promontory left to them.

The amir was brought to Timur shackled in irons. At this time it was decreed that all who bore arms were to be put to the sword, but that the defenseless inhabitants were to be spared. Once again the pyramids of heads were erected with clay from the river used in the cementing process. This was the first time that Takrit, hitherto deemed impregnable, ever succumbed to enemy capture.

On December 6 Timur left the ruined city, this time moving northwestward where he first amused himself with hunting trips, then returned to the consolidation of power in the countryside. The eventual target city was Diarbekir on the upper Tigris, not far from the border with Armenia. Following a series of feints, the armies of Timur infiltrated both sides of the Tigris where they first encircled the castle of Kerkouk. Seeing the helplessness of the situation, the garrison readily surrendered.

Mosul, on the west bank of the Tigris, was next to feel the heavy hand of the Timurids. The Tigris forms a series of loops in this area before coalescing into a main stream. Just across from Mosul lay the ruins of the ancient city of Ninevah where a mosque was built to commemorate the site of its destruction by the Babylonians in 612 B.C.

Both Mosul and the fortress at Erbeil fell from intimidation as the massive armies of Timur presented themselves in full view of the populace. It was now January in the year 1394 and it was time to confront the Sultan of Mardin, Al Malik Azzahiv. This city had become the center for the production of cochineal (from the Kirmiz worm) who were fed on a certain species of oak leaves. The red dye produced from this industry was used to enhance the fabric and brocade industry found in Mardin and neighboring Khoi.

Timur was not interested in the capture of tradesmen or minor artisans but in the ensuing power struggle. In one of his forced marches he arrived in sight of Mardin after five days instead of the normal twelve usually required, "outpacing the birds" in the words of the local poet. The sultan offered himself to Timur in order to spare his city but the inhabitants refused to open the gates of the fortress, the famous "Grey Castle," which was built on a rock promontory to the south of the suburbs.

For three days Timur drew up his army in plain sight and proceeded to display long ladders and heavy equipment in the hopes of intimidating the defenders. On the fourth day he sent a letter to the inhabitants saying: "Let the people of the fort of Mardin know;

they are weak and powerless, destitute and thirsty; we grant pardon to them and give them security concerning their lives and blood; so let them be free of anxiety and redouble their supplication to us."

With only shouts of defiance the defenders dared Timur to attack the walls of the fortress. This challenge was immediately accepted as hundreds of ladders appeared amid the sounding of kettle drums and cymbals. Those that made it to the top of the walls rained arrows down inside the enclosure but were driven off without gaining a foothold inside the walls. This initial attack was followed by five days of cautious siege.

On the night of the fifth day Timur was able to reach the gate-keeper and bribe him with rich gifts and promises of elevation in rank. It was all over very quickly and those that laid down their arms were spared the sword but those that were proven to be defiant, causing considerable loss of life, were beheaded. Sultan Al Malik Azzahiv was treated courteously but sent back to Samarkand as a prisoner along with his courtiers.

The day after the city fell a messenger arrived from Sultanieh to announce the birth of another grandson for Timur. Shah Rukh, still only seventeen years old, had sired an heir who was named Ulugh Beg (great prince) but was also given the formal appellation of Muhammed Teraghay. To celebrate the birth Timur halted all executions in Mardin and even spared the population all tributes that had been imposed upon them. Certainly the invocation of his father's name greatly affected his decision as the great monarch was tired but content.

At age fifty-eight Timur had overcome more territory and population than nearly all great conquerors. In his next few years he would eclipse both Alexander and Chinghis Khan. As a military tactician and leader of men he knew no peer. Yet to be attained was the excellence in governing such a vast empire.

# 11

# The Final Affair with Toktamish

*Deal the Georgian fatal blow.*
*Prepare for war with Mongol foe.*
*From Ural to Dnieper shore,*
*Toktamish banned forevermore.*

The precise time when the sad news of the demise of Omar Shaikh reached Timur is not known. It did take place in the month of January of 1394 as the prince was approaching the castle of Khermautus, near the Persian gulf. The garrison had displayed some hostility and Timur's son was in the process of determining the extent of it when the following account was later given:

"As the prince approached within hailing distance he dismounted from his horse and climbed a small prominence to be seen in person. At this time one of the garrison warriors let fly an arrow, said to be at random, which prompted Omar Shaikh to cover himself with his shield and advance closer to the castle. A second arrow was discharged which pierced his neck and severed the main artery, causing almost instant death."

His body was first taken to Shiraz by Pir Muhammed and placed temporarily in a vault, later taken to Kesh upon instructions from Timur. Having survived for forty-one years, the prince was interred near his brother Jahanghir who had expired some eighteen years before. His epitaph done by a noted historian read: "Alas, where is the plant that flourishes by the side of even the happiest stream, that will not ultimately be laid prostrate by the storm, or where, in the firmament of greatness did that sun ever display its radiance, which was not finally destined to experience an eclipse?"

It was said that Timur received the news in stoical fashion, saying: "God gave, and God has taken away." His grief was more evident in the days to follow as he was prone to give some aberrant orders to his generals. Absorbed with problems at Diarbekir, where a measure of insolence was developing, he once again was able to center his attention on affairs of the day.

Later in 1394 Timur had sent an important convoy on its way to Samarkand which was raided by a certain amir who then sought the protection of the Prince of Jazirah. Of particular importance was the accumulation of rare articles and trophies that were destined to be displayed in the public buildings of the capital. Repeated entreaties to the prince for the safe return of the stolen goods fell on deaf ears. Apparently he felt that his circumstances in a stronghold, coupled with the necessary diversion it would require to effect recovery, was a reasonable risk to assume.

After all avenues of communication were ignored Timur set himself in motion to first cross the Tigris, then on another of his forced marches, hurried toward the province of Jazirah. He met the troops of the prince who was totally unprepared for his sudden appearance, and what followed was carnage of the first order.

Not only was the entire booty train recovered, but further booty, together with large numbers of cattle, were added to the treasures. The enlarged convoy then was taken down river to Mosul where it was off-loaded for transport to its original destination. Having retrieved his valuables and considerably more, Timur spared the life of the prince who in turn, pledged everlasting friendship to him.

One more fortress was to fall before the conquest of Mesopotamia could be declared. The city of Diarbekir had been previously bypassed but now presented a hostility which required immediate attention. The fortress of Hamid, near the city, was built of hewn stone with only one narrow access and an outer wall which completely surrounded the citadel within. Its original foundations were said to date back well over three thousand years and it had only been captured once, at the time of the birth of Islam.

What developed was later called the siege of Hamid. Under partial cover of arrows and catapulted stones, Timur's engineers managed to shield themselves with baskets of earth to arrive under the walls. Three particular towers were singled out for undermining. In the usual fashion a considerable hole was dug under each, followed by timber shoring and later firing. The resulting collapse of the towers allowed the troops to rush in at all sides. The garrison could hold out only briefly and then had to retreat to some subterranean passages. The unfortunate city dwellers were left behind to be victimized by extensive pillaging.

Before leaving Mesopotamia, Timur veered westward once more. Bir, on the Euphrates, was taken without any resistance, whereupon his long delayed move toward home was begun. Two days journey (about sixty-seven miles) from Bir they entered the ancient city of Odessa whose walls extended for a distance of ten miles. Remaining from antiquity were two large columns and a castle. There was also a remarkably clear fountain which had the capacity to irrigate the entire countryside.

Outside the city Timur found a sacred well which was believed to heal leprosy. Those with this sickness were supposed to fast for five days, drinking from the well each day, also washing themselves in the process. After five days they would no longer wash but continue drinking the water up to the twelfth day. Considerable testimony bolstered the claim that the sacred well did indeed, heal the lepers.

As a last gesture while in Mesopotamia, Timur rebuilt the mausoleum of Imam Hanbal, a revered spiritual leader in the area from the previous century. Continuing the northern march, Timur was brought news of a new grandson Ibrahim Sultan, the progeny of his youngest, Shah Rukh. This announcement was greeted by a celebration lasting eight days where toasts were made using the traditional gold embossed cups made from human skulls, a holdover of the Mongol custom.

Shah Rukh's oldest son, Ulugh Beg, was entrusted to the care of Queen Mulkh Khanum, while the newborn was being cared for by Touman Agha, who was still young at age 28. Both wives and their wards followed later on along with the baggage train into Armenia, later in the year, back to Samarkand.

Meanwhile the Egyptian Emperor Barkuk had strengthened his ties with Sultan Ahmed by marrying his niece. In March of 1384 he formed an alliance with Toktamish and Bayazid, the latter head of the House of Othman* and powerful military lord. With this alliance in hand, Barkuk aided Sultan Ahmed in the retaking of Baghdad. For many years the Egyptian Mamluks had claimed a measure of jurisdiction over Syria.

Timur had continued on his northward journey and set up his encampment on the plains near Moush, some 80 miles west of Lake Van. Although it was May, snow drifts hampered the army's progress. Upon arrival in the west of Armenia, Timur was presented a beautiful bay horse as a gift from the Prince of Betlis whose holdings were just east of the encampment. This horse was to become a particular favorite in the years to follow.

The base at Moush was to be the headquarters for the pursuit of the Turkomans under Kara Yussuf, the renegade leader having vacated the area as the Timurids approached. A full division was sent to sound out the fortress of Alanjik on the north side of the large Lake Urmiyah, not far from the city of Tabriz. Meanwhile other nobles were fanning out to scour the countryside for new recruits.

Submission to Timur's authority was now rampant, but the city of Van, on the eastern shore of the lake bearing the same name, held out for forty days of siege. The defending prince finally submitted himself to Timur, who in turn, granted him safety but nevertheless exiled him to Samarkand for some years.

---

* from the province of Othmanly containing Constantinople

Once again, Timur felt the need to make contact with Bayazid, the scourge of the Balkans. This time he chose not to ignore the leader of Anatolia* but sent an ambassador to his court. After numerous gifts were exchanged a pledge of mutual friendship was consummated which was to last for nearly six years. Meanwhile one of the most powerful divisions in the Timurid army was on the move as they proceeded eastward along the eastern slope of Mount Ararat.

With his largest army contingent, Timur appeared on the plains of Kars, still in Armenia, with the intent of intimidating the populace and to receive his amirs who had been making probes into the country of Georgia. Shah Rukh was sent back to Samarkand where he was to assume government duties during the protracted absence of his father. Ladies from the imperial family were sent back to Sultanieh, now the capital of Azerbijan.

Thus prepared, Timur then sought to engage the infidels of Georgia, an idea which had long slumbered in his mind. During the initial thrust most of the inhabitants fled to the hills, the main army then moving on to the siege of Tiflis. The other units were sent to pillage and with orders to exterminate all overt hostility. It was while this was going on that disturbing news came from the camp of his old nemesis, Toktamish.

By the time information concerning the Mongol incursion reached Timur they had passed the straits of Derbent and had overrun the territory west of the Caspian Sea. Upon hearing this, Timur sent a message to Toktamish which, according to his memoirs, contained the following: "What devil is in thee that thou canst keep within thy border? Hast thou not forgotten the last war? Thou knowest the tale of my victories and that peace and war are alike to me. Thou hast made proof alike of my friendship and my enmity. Choose, and send to me word of thy choice."

As an answer Toktamish continued his assault on Derbent and then proceeded to form a defensive line. Timur, once again, had to prepare for war and started his army to intercept the foe. The

* often called Rum, a holdover from the days of Roman occupation

pursuit of Toktamish started in the winter of 1394; the Timurids were on the march through a mountain pass near Mount Elburz where they made first contact with the Mongol army. It turned out to be a battle of hard charging cavalry which remained in doubt for the first few hours.

It was said that Timur was never so near defeat. He was cut off with a few men holding a broken sword in his hand. To ward off the enemy his men dismounted and formed a tight ring around him. It was his faithful friend Nur-ad-din who ultimately saved the day by bringing up captured carts to form a barrier. Timur's third son Miran Shah and the great Amir Saif-ud-din were both wounded in the rescue of Timur's small detachment.

Amir Idaka, a Mongol tactician, had been placed on the left wing of Toktamish's army. He was somewhat coerced into making a break to improve his situation at a feast where the Mongol khan had been drinking heavily. With little warning the khan called loudly to him with accusations of treachery. Idaka countered with: "…let him not destroy a sapling which he himself planted or overthrow a foundation which he has laid!"

He plied Toktamish with humility and submission but managed to slip out during the night to the stables where he procured a fast horse. Before leaving he confided in a trusted friend: "Whoever wishes to come to me will find me with Timur; but do not reveal this secret, until it is certain that I have crossed the wilderness."

Upon reaching Timur he kissed his hands and revealed that no forts or unpleasant surprises stood in the way. He urged a rapid deployment lest conditions change, saying in part: "This is an easy prize in front of your eyes, which you will gain—rich and fine— with the greatest convenience; and why should there be delay, somnolence, hesitation and postponement?"

Since Toktamish had decided to make his stand at Derbent, Timur moved northward to make his primary encampment within one day's march of the ancient city. Derbent, called by many Temircapi, or "gate of iron," was surrounded by five walls with about a mile of beach on the Caspian Sea. Two walls extended from the foothills one half mile away and, at that time, ended in the water to a depth of six feet. The large iron gate which Timur had to breach was purported to have divided Media, the ancient land south of the Caspian from Scythia.

Timur decided to ignore the advice given to him by Amir Idaka to make an early strike against Toktamish and wait out the Mongol's first move. His scribes recorded the remarks made to his commanders on this occasion as: "It is better for the game to run itself into the net than to have to go after it. An old fowl does not fear the bird of prey, and the grasshopper is but big enough to get his wings stained with red, as he can shake off the attacks of the sparrow, blow for blow."

At this time several detachments of Mongols decided to come over to Timur's standard and this, coupled with the arrival of Muhammed Sultan, managed to even up the opposing forces in sheer numbers. During the ensuing battles for supremacy Amir Zadah Rustum, son of the departed Omar Shaikh, distinguished himself in personal combat. During an assault on the barriers Miran Shah had become lame from a fall off his horse but continued to lead his army after being helped back on his mount.

The augmented army of Timur attacked in force with all reserves and managed to push the khan back steadily northward. In a final battle well up on the western shore of the Caspian Sea Toktamish was forced to make a stand without adequate chances of falling back, and with little or no reserves. This significant engagement was later called the Battle of Terek as the Golden Horde was cut to pieces on the banks of the river bearing that name.

Toktamish and a small group of followers fled to the mountains and forests where he would be in hiding for some time until fleeing farther west into Bulgaria. The booty captured by the Timurids was collected to be sent back with Miran Shah who was still handicapped from his fall. The Timurid army moved northward again toward the Volga as most of the Mongol army was still in headlong retreat and were trying to get back to their respective homelands.

News reached Timur while in encampment that Barkuk had returned to Cairo, leaving Ahmed in a vulnerable position holding

Baghdad. The Egyptian emperor's pact with Toktamish no longer held any promise and he had become increasingly suspicious of Bayazid's intentions. His intelligence hinted at a threatened abrogation of the alliance to usurp the command of Irak and Syria.

The tribes of the Volga were dealt with harshly, particularly in the city of Sarai where Timur's army had previously been harassed. The houses and buildings were put to the torch. When Timur arrived to storm Astrakhan at the mouth of the Volga (it was said to have seventy-two mouths in total) he found a unique defense. The inhabitants had placed blocks of ice which froze into a solid barrier when water was poured on them.

With flame and battering, the makeshift wall did not stop the Timurids for long. Most of those that put up a fierce defense were put to death on the spot. As a special punishment the city governor was pushed under the ice in the river. Timur remained encamped on the plains west of Astrakhan for some time as he awaited the arrival of Miran Shah and the heavy baggage train. Concerned with the government of Shiraz, Timur sent Pir Muhammed to that area with six thousand horsemen.

In the presence of a large enemy army Moscow had reason to fear for its future. At that time its population was a little over fifty thousand and was defended by a small army under the grand prince. The people prayed and invoked the ancient image of the Virgin. Lines of kneeling people were hear to cry out, "Mother of God, save Russia!"

Some historians have described Timur's entry into Moscow as one of sacking and pillaging. There is compulsive evidence that this was not the case and Timur's memoirs bear this out. Evidently the entry into the city was uncontested and only a modest tribute was exacted as Timur ordered his army to push only a small distance across the Dnieper before falling back in a southerly direction to cross the Don River on the way to the Caucasus.

From the Russian account* it is evident why Timur stopped at Ryazan with his main army. Prince Vasili had sent some of his

---

* 15th century document called *The Story of Temir Asack*

warriors out to church officials in order to take temporary possession of the sacred icon, the "Mother of God." It was located in
Vladimir and rushed to Moscow in time to deter Timur, who was
known to honor such revered relics. The main army was detoured
toward the Dnieper on the same day that news of the icon reached
his encampment.

In order to ensure continuity of domain for all of Kiptchak
Timur demanded allegiance from a new regime which he appointed
to rule the Mongols. Timur Kutlugh, son of Urus Khan, was installed as the new monarch, thus restoring the old line of Batu
which had previously been deposed back in 1359.

Timur seized upon an opportunity to right a wrong, one in
which he was the precipitator. When Urus Khan, at that time leader
of the White Horde of western Kiptchak, exiled Toktamish, it was
Timur who came to the aid of his protege and personally brought
about the demise of Urus.

The naming of Timur Kutlugh as khan of all Kiptchak
restored the Batu dynasty of monarchs which had reigned since
1226. It also absolved the guilt in Timur for having brought about
the rise to power of the renegade Toktamish. Timur Kutlugh proved
faithful to the great amir as he repulsed Toktamish in his last bid to
return to power in a battle near Sarai in 1398.

This last gasp of Toktamish was launched from his exile in
Asiatic Bulgaria where he had enlisted the help of the Lithuanian
Prince Vitut. After being repulsed by Timur Kutlugh, he was
never a threat again and died in the prince's kingdom of Lithuania
in year 1406.

On his way southward from what was a most successful
campaign Timur tarried for awhile in the Caucasus, pondering what
he could do about the mountain tribes in the vicinity which might
pose a threat to the area between his Mongol empire and occupied
Georgia. Actually it was the challenge of unconquered mountain
areas which piqued his interest—he never tired of seeking out and
overcoming any perceived hurdle.

When a messenger arrived with news that Kara Yussuf was
once again threatening the countryside, Timur was stirred into

action. He felt that he was strong enough to engage both problems at hand. One portion of the army was sent south toward the city of Khoi in the western Karabagh to confront Kara Yussuf, while he kept the other portion in encampment.

Pir Muhammed, heading the army to cut off the siege of Khoi, arrived at Karaderrah (Black Pass) and literally decimated that portion of the Turkoman army on their way to join Yussuf. The few survivors who were able to make it to Kara Yussuf's encampment near Lake Van convinced him to retreat in the face of Timur's wrath. Pir Muhammed chose not to pursue his foe since the threat against that portion of Armenia and the city of Khoi had been alleviated.

At the main encampment in the Caucasus Timur was enthralled with the tales of robber bands and renegade strongholds which had terrorized the mountain area for many years. He was then resolved to bring his own brand of justice to the mountain people, once again in the name of a holy war.

The way through the Caucasus was a perilous one, through gorges and heavily forested mountain slopes. It was necessary to cut a road as they went to provide for the heavy wagons of the baggage train. He was able to recruit volunteers from Kiptchak and nearby mountain tribes to help in the work, from time to time confronting dissidents from the areas they were passing through. While passing through the narrow corridor near Derbent where they had defeated Toktamish's army earlier, it was decided to leave behind a corps of construction engineers to repair and reinforce the fortifications.

While road progress continued through the summer of 1395, the legions of Timur encountered one particular mountain clan which posed a definite threat. They were firmly ensconced on a mountain top protected by sheer rock walls. Timur's scouts reported no good way to the top and advised him to bypass the bastion as not worth the effort.

Timur, in one of his typical decisions, decided not to leave any problem in his wake and ordered long ladders to be constructed. By roping together the units and by means of hoisting them successively from ledge to ledge, they were able to scale the three hundred feet of barrier, in spite of frequent rock barrages.

Some of the Timurids were able to reach the top, and with support by archers who were able to get into position, finally forced the mountain men to surrender. By these means the army literally forced their way through the rugged areas and emerged at the Alburz, a mountain range that separated Georgia from Persia.

There, a grand reception had been planned by the army's advanced units where, once again, it was deemed proper to delve into the wines and traditional fermented mare's milk to celebrate an extended victory. After several days of festivities Timur once again hoisted his horsetail standard and started his army southward.

Miran Shah had been given the task of firming up on his administration of Azerbijan and environs which, at that time, included all the territory between Baghdad and Derbent on a north-south axis and between the Euphrates and the frontier with Mazanderan on an east-west axis. Meanwhile Timur proceeded toward Hamadan, an important city southwest of Sultanieh in the Jibal province of Persia. He planned to discharge certain holy duties during the month of Ramzaun (Ramadan).

Timur had purposely avoided any incursion into Anatolia in accordance with his pact with its monarch, Bayazid. He had long interested himself in the two main tribes of Turkomans who controlled all of eastern Anatolia, the Aq Qoyunlu (white sheep) and the Qara Qoyunlu (black sheep). Their competition with each other had caused considerable unrest and Timur saw an opportunity to bring about his brand of stability and justice at a later date.

Still engaged with his holy obligations in Hamadan, Timur dispatched Miran Shah to deal with one Turkoman resistance spot in his assigned area, the fortress of Alanjik. This stronghold was on the left bank (north) of the Araxes River, northeast of Khoi. From his encampment at Lake Van Miran Shah proceeded to lay siege. There is no account of its final disposition except that it surrendered under somewhat passive conditions at a later date.

Miran Shah was also charged with a siege at Yezd, a semi desert city in the northeastern section of Fars province. This turned out to be a protracted one as Timur was anxious to avoid bloodshed. In the end, many thousands of inhabitants perished from famine, the survivors subsisting on cats and dogs in a vain attempt to tunnel out under their city's defenses.

Timur declared clemency for Yezd because of the suffering that they had endured, ordering that no soldier set foot inside the city walls until the starving population had a chance to recover. Following this incident the armies were divided again to proceed along the Persian Gulf to secure the submission of cities as far away as Ormuz.

Timur spent his 60th birthday in Hamadan where he was engaged in prayer for some days. Having completed a long and victories campaign, he was anxious to return to his own city of Samarkand and attend to affairs of state. On his way back he was joined by his Mongol wife, Princess Tukal Khanum. In her honor he dedicated the summer palace of Dirkusha, or in translation, "opener of hearts."

It was a triumphal return to his capital city, one that a conqueror in the mold of Timur relished, at least for a short time. The nobles of Samarkand presented him with two thousand horses and mules, the latter being curiously one of his fonder possessions. He did not discuss his thoughts with army commanders or even with his close associates, but he left behind one regret—the unresolved problem with Sultan Ahmed and the prize city of Baghdad which loomed like a beacon to tantalize him. He vowed to return and assert his authority at a propitious time.

# 12

# The Way Through the Kush

*Hedonistic days delay,*
*Resolve to find again the way;*
*Subdue the fiercest mountain men;*
*Continue to the south again.*

Samarkand was indeed living up to its name of the "blue city." During the last part of 1396 architects and artisans from all over Timur's empire were at work building mosques, palaces and madrasas*. The blue tile which had become the preferred decor was being enhanced with gold trim in pure white settings to emulate the beauty and symmetry of mideast splendor.

Minarets were topping a honeycomb of intricate scroll work with ribbons of Arabic script. Panels of mosaic tile resembled the designs in lustrous carpets. Placed in strategic locations were lush gardens and sparkling fountains. The majesty of gigantic archways echoed the power of the great monarch, attesting to his devotion to the holy presence of his God, Allah.

Yet, amid this entrancing ambience, Timur remained a study in contrasts. Never far beneath the surface were latent thoughts of conquest where he could impose his will upon thousands of others. His talent for logistics became a chess board where he ultimately

---

\* school or college for teaching the Islamic faith

placed his foes in checkmate. He was constantly tortured by his holy vows which elicited bouts of compassion. In the end his icon became the image of greatness and power.

In February of 1397, in an expansive mood, Timur declared three years of tax forbearance for all Transoxania. He had long envisioned a magnificent palace to endow his progeny with the symbol of an enduring Timurid dynasty. Construction was started for this singular undertaking in a place called the Bough-e-shamzul, or "northern gardens."

In May of 1397 Timur proceeded to take up his residence in the Ak Sarai or White Palace in the suburbs of Kesh. He devoted the entire month of Ramzaun (Ramadan) to his favorite abode. Muhammed Sultan, fresh from his successful occupation of Hormuz, joined him soon thereafter. His grandson reported an aborted assassination attempt on his life while in Shiraz. The would be killer was quickly eliminated as he drew his knife to attack the prince, but was still able to inflict a slight wound before receiving a lethal sword thrust.

For three months, in a rare display of hedonism, Timur indulged in almost unrestrained eating, drinking and in the pursuit of connubial bliss. It can be perceived that at this time of debauchery he closely resembled the call of nature where the cessation of reproductive functions elicits a somewhat frantic innate need to have a last fling.

Emerging from this uncharacteristic period which left him in a sort of withdrawal mode, he ordered a mausoleum built at the site where he worshiped the holy saints in his earlier days. The most respected saint was venerated by placing a sarcophagus of pure white marble over the site of internment. Two years would pass before the mausoleum and all its appointments was completed.

While the many projects in Samarkand were still under way an ambassador arrived from Cathay to establish a permanent embassy to represent the Ming emperor. An Chi, the ambassador designate, and his entire retinue were sent soon after their arrival on a visitation all the way to Tabriz, Ispahan, Shiraz, Herat and other cities, ostensibly to impress them with the expanse of the Timurid empire. By the time they finally returned to Timur's capital six years had passed, an indication of the real purpose for their extended tour. Emperor Hung Wu interpreted this means of detention for his representatives as a rebuke of his regime.

This was a time for indecision in Timur's mind as he pondered the direction for his next move. In his words: "About this time there arose in my heart the desire to lead an expedition against the infidels, and to become a "ghazi," for it had reached my ears that a slayer of infidels is a ghazi, and if he is slain he becomes a martyr. It was on this account that I found my resolution, but I was undetermined in my mind whether I should direct my expedition against the infidels of Cathay or against the infidels and polytheists of Hindustan. In this matter I sought an omen from the Koran, and the verse I opened was this: 'By the order of God and the Prophet it is incumbent upon me to make war upon these infidels and poly- theists....'"

Timur's greatest amirs and commanders were called into council to discuss the logistics of an invasion against his choice of adversaries, the rulers of Hindustan. He pointed out some of the difficulties involved: the crossing of five large rivers, woods and forests which contain interwoven stems and branches, soldiery and land holders, people who inhabit these areas and live like wild beasts and lastly, a reference to their elephants. He described them as having been trained to such a pitch that: "lifting with their trunks a horse with his rider, and whirling him in the air, they will dash him to the ground."

The discussion centered around the problems involved and the outfitting of the army. Timur pointedly refrained from airing the pros and cons in coming to the actual selection of Hindustan as the target for invasion. As was his custom, Timur wrote a letter of intent to the Sultan Mahmud Sarang who, at that time, was residing in the city of Multan. This letter contained certain conditions which made it difficult for a sovereign country to accept, notwithstanding that the consequences of refusal were equally fringing on the foolhardy.

The text of the letter was as follows: "If the rulers of Hindustan come before me with tribute I will not interfere with

their lives, property, or kingdoms, but if they are negligent in prof-
fering obedience and submission, I will put forth my strength for
the conquest of the kingdoms of Hindustan. At all events, if they set
any value on their lives, property and reputation, they will pay me
a yearly tribute, and if not, they shall hear of my arrival with my
powerful armies. Farewell."

Timur's ambassador who bore the letter for presentation to
the sultan was treated with respect and consideration, however, the
answer given was not the least conciliatory. It read: "It is difficult
to take empire like a bride to your bosom without trouble and difficulty and the clashing of swords. The desire of your prince is to
take this kingdom with its rich revenue. Well, let him wrest it from
us by force of arms if he is able. I have numerous armies and formidable elephants, and am quite prepared for war."

Upon arrival back in Samarkand, the answer as borne by the
ambassador brought about predictable results. Immediate orders
went out for all armies to assemble for necessary inspection. The
city's beautification plans, now well along, were put on hold except
for certain completion dates. It was a matter of discussing the
logistics and makeup of the invasion force, not a serious weighing
of consequence attendant to the expedition that filled the deliberation talks. With the blessing from certain passages of the Koran, all
preparations were under way.

Prince Omar, son of Miran Shah, was named viceroy to
administer the government of Samarkand as Timur's other favorite
grandsons were to accompany the southward incursion. In the
spring of 1398 a formidable force left on the ambitious expedition,
first crossing the Oxus to camp at Khulm, some fifty miles east of
Balkh in northern Khorassan. Making up an important part of the
Timurid army was an elite group of 92,000 horsemen, said to be in
conformity with the readings of the Prophet Muhammed, therefore,
a happy omen of success.

Moving to the east, just south of the Pamir range, the army
entered a country which had turned back all invaders since the
eighth century. It had rebuffed Alexander before that and several
Mongol invasions as well. It was the country of the Siyah-Push,

or "men of the black robes," together with the Kators, a fierce mountain group whose very lifestyle was as tenacious as a cornered beast.

Very soon Timur was met by nobles and people alike who lamented their treatment by the Siyah-Push and the Kators. In appeals to the great amir they depicted themselves as "true believers" who had been victimized by having to pay tribute and to endure indignities such as having their women and children captured and put into slavery. When Timur promised to end the tyranny and enslavement, the populace all lifted their hands and invoked blessings upon their liberator.

Ten battalions were selected to serve under Shah Rukh to pursue the two renegade tribes of the Siyah-Push while Timur himself led some ten thousand horsemen to seek out and punish the Kators who had entrenched themselves in the mountains. They thrived in the surrounding countryside where there were large quantities of rice and other grains, along with many varieties of fruits.

At that time the ruler of the Kators was Udashu, and in the pursuit of his rugged forces the Timurids had to dismount and lead their horses and camels over rocky terrain with precipitous cliffs on both sides. The warm weather had melted the residual snow and both men and mounts sank deeply into the drifts. They were obliged to halt and wait for the freezing temperatures of night in order to proceed on their way.

Upon arriving at the highest rise in the region Timur's advance parties reported that the Kators had taken up positions in the caverns and had built snow barricades. The Timurids and their mounts were obliged to slide down the slopes or lower themselves by ropes. Timur made his way down by means of a large wicker basket lined with wooden planks. After a series of several descents he was able to reach the vicinity of the enemy defenses.

When all were assembled Timur raised his scepter-sword and led his men on horseback although the army was still on foot. Their first confrontation with the Kators took place in a fort which was nestled into a mountain side with a river protecting the only exposed place. These defenders were said to be of immense stature and bodily strength, while communicating in an unknown language unrelated to Persian or Hindu.

News of the invaders had reached the fort and most of the inhabitants had fled across the river, taking their valuables with them. Although a key stronghold, the remaining defenders chose to scramble to safety in caves and recesses. Unopposed, Timur entered the fort and leveled it to the ground after taking whatever spoils had been left behind, together with a large number of sheep.

In order to fulfill his promise of reducing the Kator forces, Timur had to separate his army into small bands to root out their enemy. With a shouting of the takbir, or war cry, the process of attrition began. By the end of the day the outmanned defenders were nearly all slaughtered as only a few succeeded in hiding in remote caverns. In the Timurid account, only fourteen of their number perished while ferreting out the Kators.

Those remaining defenders and the ones hiding were offered protection if they promised to embrace the Muhammedan faith. A mass ceremony was held to convert them, followed by the return of much of their personal effects and gifts of clothing from their conquerors. During the night one of the regiments was attacked by the Kators but the commander was vigilant and dispatched the marauders, capturing 150 of their lot. Enraged by the treachery, the officers ordered the prisoners to be put to the sword.

Before rejoining the forces of Shah Rukh, the traditional pyramid of heads was built as a warning of the consequences of opposition. That night Timur dreamed of his sword being bent, an omen which he took as being a warning of possible defeat. The next day he found his regiment had mysteriously disappeared from the garrison left to hold the fortress of Siyah-Push. The commander, under attack by an inferior force, had fled to the mountains in a show of cowardice.

A newly appointed commander with 400 men followed the tracks of the enemy and defeated them with disciplined warriors. The lost horses were retrieved and the errant commander rounded up. Abject cowards were normally dealt with harshly but this one was only banished from the council and reduced in rank. By this time eighteen days had passed and Timur was impatient to get on toward Hindustan.

Between Badakshan and Hindustan lies the Hindu Kush, often referred to as the "stone girdle" of the earth. It was directly in the line of march, but again news of marauding tribes had reached Timur's encampment. He had set up near the Kabul River, the headwaters of the large Indus River which emptied into the ocean to the far south. The marauders proved to be a large group of silver miners who had hollowed out much of the mountainside in their district. They worked by torchlight in their dark caverns, but the scouting parties found them all deserted as they melted into the surrounding hillsides to avoid detection.

When the army had reassembled for the move southward Timur felt the need of sending Shah Rukh back to Herat to assure the continuation of stable government in the Khorassan. He then ordered the crossing of the mountains into the Kush as they started toward the city of Kabul. He paused for a time in the vicinity in order to open a canal which provided continuous water for the capital.

A surprise addition to the army at this time was the sudden appearance of Shaikh Nur-ad-din who had been employed during the expedition of five years with the collections at Fars. He brought with him valuable treasures and personal effects including tents, pavilions, canopies, belts of scarlet cloth, etc. The distribution of all this booty consumed three days and nights.

Soon after this rich offering reached the army two detachments were sent ahead to feel out the enemy presence in Hindustan. Timur then learned of a robber baron in the vicinity who threatened all passage to the Indus River. He enticed the renegade chief to appear near his camp with gifts and promises of rebuilding his fortress.

The ruse went so far as to start the rebuilding process, as promised, but when all the plunderers had gathered, they were summarily disposed of by the local malik and his followers who had suffered most from their wrongdoings. Timur was personally attacked by a small band of would-be assassins but the arrows missed their mark as he easily escaped.

On August 31, 1398, the main army was once again on the move as they headed for the Indus River. By the time they all reached the city of Naghaz, they were informed of a renegade band of Afghans who had plundered part of the booty brought by Shaikh Nur-ad-din. All progress stopped in order to pursue the bandits.

Tracks of the raiders led to the mountains and forests where the pursuing Timurids found signs of their homes after a three day ride. Using a stealthy approach, the soldiers dismounted and fanned out to look for their quarry. A large number of the male population was found and put to the sword. After burning the village, the female population with their children were returned to the local slave market.

Meanwhile the repair party had restored the fortifications at Naghaz. When the march continued Timur was met by one of his generals who had attacked a tribe of hostile Afghans, returning with a great deal of booty to augment their supplies. The general was rewarded and then sent ahead to join Pir Muhammed's army.

Timur was able to join the advance army on the banks of the Indus by the 19th of September, now anxious to move into Hindustan. He ordered the immediate building of a bridge, one that required using grapnels and a large amount of native wood. Pir Muhammed with his forces had already crossed by boats and was moving on Multan. As the main army crossed into the great desert to the east, the expedition to subdue Hindustan was under way.

# 13

## The Conquest of Hindustan

*Turn from thoughts of old Cathay*
*To target yet another day;*
*From mountain Kush to Indus span,*
*Bring terror to north Hindustan.*

Poised on the banks of the Indus River which separates south-east Persia from Hindustan, Timur, the avid historian, must have wondered about the adventure that lay ahead of him. Alexander was turned back by the monsoon but the Mongols had preceded him and left a lingering legacy.

Five days after crossing the river he was met in the western desert of Hindustan by several ambassadors from the local rulers and chieftains. The composite message delivered was one of complete obsequiousness as it read: "We have placed the collar of obedience and submission, in all sincerity, on the neck of our life, and the saddle of servitude on our back; we are anxiously expecting the auspicious arrival of the great king. When will it be that the prosperous shadow of his umbrella will, by its protection, impart felicity to this kingdom, and when will the honor of kissing the sublime footstool be attainable to us?" Needless to say, the lands of these lords and their possessions were never violated by Timur.

On September 24, 1399, the great army started its march toward Multan, an important city on the far side of the desert. Rather than circumvent the crossing by a safe route, Timur chose to provision his army with food and water for a somewhat dangerous direct crossing.

Upon reaching the eastern desert boundary the Timurids were met by several rajahs from the province of Jud who presented them with a multitude of gifts. By the time the army had progressed to the banks of the Jhilam River they discovered their first barrier, a heavily fortified island where a considerable resistance force had congregated. They had hurriedly dug a canal to isolate the urban area with a water barrier. This presented a challenge to Timur who did not wish to leave a threat in his rear.

Most of the army was put to work cutting heavy tree branches which they proceeded to pile into the moat. Two main crossings were completed and on the following day they fought a bitter battle but were unable to penetrate the inner defenses. That night the ruler broke out from the city walls with 10,000 men and attacked the Timurids.

When Timur's lines held and a counter attack was ordered, the tide of battle turned dramatically. Many of the Hindu warriors jumped into the river to save themselves, not a few drowning in the process because of the weight of their armor. Shahab-ud-din, the ruler, had set aside 200 boats for this contingency and managed to escape down river. As Timur's archers pursued them on horseback along the banks, many were cut down. Most of the rest were slaughtered by the army of Pir Muhammed who was positioned along their escape route.

Considerable booty was left behind which was gathered up before putting the torch to all wooden buildings. At the confluence of the Jhilam and Chinab Rivers, the army was obliged to halt to consider means of crossing. The swift water prevented bridge building and so they had to fall back on the commandeering of small boats.

Coming to the city of Tulamba, some seventy miles from Multan, a ransom was set for the citizens in order to spare them a forced entry and to offer protection from any army looting. In turn, the nobles of the city were given presents and Arabian horses. When more reinforcements arrived there was a shortage of food among the Timurids and the specified ransom in coin was changed to food for the soldiers. When the city's inhabitants balked at any ransom the army helped themselves so that the plunder exceeded any barter price agreed upon.

Meanwhile part of the army under Pir Muhammed had exacted tribute in the surrounding countryside but found that the same people had soon after armed themselves for war. In Timur's words; "They planted their feet on the highway of contumacy and rebellion…" In the battle that followed the Hindus fled to the jungle where two thousand of them were slaughtered. Booty taken from this encounter was removed to Timur's encampment. A certain local ruler next came to the attention of the invaders as word of his assembling a resistance army of some several thousand made its way into the ranks.

Nuskrat Khokhar had sent words of defiance and positioned himself in a fortress on the banks of a small lake. In hot pursuit the Timurids found themselves on swampy ground where heavy equipment would soon bog down. The infantry regiment made up of Khorassaners pressed to the attack and suffered considerable losses in the process. A second attempt with the help of reinforcements broke down all resistance into a headlong retreat of Nuskrat Khokhar and his troops.

Following the entry and sacking of the fortress, it was discovered that the lord himself had fallen in combat. Following the loading up of all useable plunder the army moved on to cross the Bijah River on its way to Janjan. That evening a messenger, arriving from the Khorassan, brought assurance that all was well there.

Pir Muhammed sent word that his army, after six months of siege, had finally captured the city of Multan. It was a matter of starving out the inhabitants as the ruler sued for peace (Sultan Mahmud had long since fled to Dehli). A peaceful entry ensued where no punishment was meted out for the long resistance. During the last days of the city's resistance the full force of the Barsh-Kal (monsoon) hit all of the northern provinces and Timur was obliged to replenish his supply of horses that had perished in large numbers during the heavy downpour. Its severity had been unfortunately underestimated and Timur hearkened back through the centuries to the failure of Alexander to cope with this phenomena.

A semipermanent camp was created at Janjan, only eight miles from Multan, to wait out the heavy rains. While there, Pir Muhammed presented his grandfather with jewel embossed girdles, single jewels of priceless value, gold articles, Hindu coins, together with plates and dishes, hand wrought urns, etc. so many items that it required two days for the court scribe to inventory them all. This entire treasure was distributed to the amirs and other nobles.

Pir Muhammed had also lost many horses in the extreme flooding while at the siege of Multan. Timur rewarded him with 30,000 chargers to supply every horseman with at least one mount. It was increasingly evident that his grandson was becoming a close second to his most trusted youngest son, Shah Rukh. The years were beginning to weigh heavily upon Timur as he had developed a decided eye droop and his hair was in the process of turning white. His old ankle wound had long since caused some articulation collapse with the foot bones and made his lameness more apparent. His horse was always tethered to his tent so that the troops could not observe him with his sensitive frailties.

Wearying of court life once again, the great amir was anxious to move on. He dispatched a Turkish regiment under Musafir Kabuli to attack Dilalpur. Still in the rainy season, the outnumbered Turks were defeated and their leader, through a series of treacherous moves by his nobles, was lost in the melee. As a result of this rout the Hindu army first put to death over one thousand of the captives, then retreated to one of the most renowned fortresses in all of Hindustan. In recorded history Bhatir had never been taken by an enemy force.

Ten thousand of the elite cavalry then descended upon Bhatir as retribution was pledged for lost comrades. On his usual reconnoiter of the attack area, Timur discovered that a single reservoir of rain water served the entire fortress. He cut off this supply but was not content to wait out the results. With all his forces assembled, the kettle drums, trumpets and cymbals signalled the start of an all out attack on the stronghold.

Storming the walls at all points was not a normal procedure for Timur, but in this case, he determined it to be his best choice. Even with the population doubled from refugees, the superior ability of the Timurids reduced the fortress to a hopeless situation within hours. The ruler, Rao Dul Chand, sued for peace and was given immediate cessation of hostilities pending a formal surrender to take place on the following day.

True to his word, all of Timur's troops left the city and bivouacked outside the walls. The next day they found the gate barricaded and no overtures of surrender being offered. The Timur action, as anticipated, was to set the engineers to work undermining the walls at strategic points. This was accompanied by a barrage of arrows and Greek fire lobbed over the walls. With some difficulty, the engineers were able to undermine several of the towers, but before they could be set afire, the defending prince decided that his gamble had not paid off and his officers were sent out from the fortress to beg for mercy.

For some time Timur pondered his response, then remembered the old adage that "Clemency is better than victory," as he once again withdrew. The following morning brought the ruler himself to Timur's pavilion where he announced that he was prepared to kiss the royal footstool as a sign of homage. He brought with him 27 Arabian horses, gold mounted harnesses and sporting hawks. Timur, in turn, presented the prince with a gold brocade robe, other richly decorated garments and a gold embossed sword. All of the inhabitants of Bhatir were spared except those responsible for the slaughter of Musafir Kabuli's prisoners.

In dismay, the prince protested this treatment and withdrew once more into the city to show his defiance. When a fresh assault was set into motion, Rao's brother and son took matters into their own hands and laid the keys to the fortress down before Timur. For this act they were honorably treated, however, there was to be no chance for another act of treachery by the prince himself. The Timurid army entered the city and burned all that could be put to the torch.

Instead of the ransom that had been asked for, it was now a complete sacking, yielding an immense amount of booty. Those nobles who fought bravely were handsomely rewarded and the remainder of the spoils divided up among the ranks of the junior officers. The tendency to resist overwhelming odds against his best trained fighters throughout all of Hindustan would continue to dog Timur's expedition everywhere he went. Undaunted, the drums of departure sounded as the composite army moved to their next bout with destiny.

Passing by the fort of Firoz which was not defended, Timur moved next toward Sarsuti, a city which surrendered by default when word came of the numbers in the invading force. Just before entering the jungle country, one more city surrendered by default, however, in the next encounter, the village along the line of march tried to pass themselves off as Musulmans. When the ruse was exposed, they were overrun by a small force, but not before two hundred of the pretenders were slain.

On November 11 Timur arrived at the Khagar River, stopping two days to allow time for his heavy baggage train to catch up. The army crossed over the Firoz-Shahi bridge and regrouped after a day's march to prepare for the eventual approach to the capital city, Dehli. The Timurids discovered a magnificent palace built by the late Sultan Shahi which had been constructed on the banks of the Jumna and only seven miles from Dehli. It was decided to spare the palace in *toto* in order to conserve the decor for succeeding populations to enjoy.

Before a final regrouping for the assault on the capital Timur had, once more, to deal with bands of marauders. These fierce tribes, calling themselves Jatts, had been plundering and terrorizing the countryside for years. At this time they had retired into the scrubby forests and thorn bush to wait out the invader's incursion into their territory.

Timur accepted the challenge of rooting them out by personally leading his most experienced warriors. The baggage train was sent ahead as he envisioned the upcoming experience to resemble a sort of game drive, where the quarry would resort to the cunning of hunted animals. His first move was to encircle the area of the tribes and then carefully work inward from the perimeter. The marauders were then systematically put to the sword as long as they offered any resistance. All of the neighboring villages were put under the protection of the imperial army until their tormentors were eliminated.

Back on track toward Dehli the army found excellent forage, therefore, they paused long enough to refresh their horses and livestock. Meanwhile the fortified city of Louny was the last obstacle before Dehli and needed to be neutralized. The defenders put up only a moderate defense before giving up as a direct result of sapper* activity which undermined their resolve. It was then time for Timur to reconnoiter the defenses of the capital in order to devise a plan to conquer it with the least possible loss to his forces.

With the selection of a battlefield which suited him, Timur was next engaged in enticing his foe to react to his plan. His first move was more of a probing action which required the Hindus to engage him and expose their defense mode. The forces of Sultan Mahmud took the bait and appeared outside the city walls with a body of four thousand cavalry clad in mail, and five thousand foot soldiers, accompanied by twenty-seven elephants with their mounted archers.

Using a vanguard of just 300 Turk horsemen, Timur sent wave after wave of cavalry and archers but pulled back after killing the first elephant. Because of considerable losses the Hindus opted to also withdraw to regroup within their city walls. In the council of war which followed, Timur laid out his plan of action. The first part was to convey the idea that the initial charge by the elephants caused considerable dismay and that the withdrawal would extend for several days.

Keeping the sultan's army bottled up with quick forays up to the city walls, Timur's army was busy scouring the countryside for

---

* an individual trained in destruction

water buffalo and bundles of straw. Meanwhile the engineers were busy digging a deep ditch around their position but leaving several escape routes. The ditches were filled with brush and camouflaged with plain grass—the trap was ready to spring! As Timur had hoped, the Hindu army appeared outside the city, this time with 120 elephants, ready to crush the opponent that they felt was showing undue weakness.

As anticipated, the elephants led the charge. This was the signal for the bundles of burning straw and cotton, now tied behind the horses and camels, to be drawn transversely across the path of the lead elephants. In the panic that followed many of the beasts turned and stampeded back into their own ranks, however, a goodly number were controlled by their drivers and continued to charge forward. When the Timurid ranks opened up in these sectors many foundered in the ditches as all of the water buffaloes were tied together to divert their headlong rush.

The main army of Hindus consisting of 4,000 horsemen and 5,000 foot soldiers, anticipating a break through in the center, were quickly outflanked by fast charging Timurids. Although the decimated army of the sultan fought valiantly, they were cut to pieces and defeated by sheer strategy. A battered remnant of the large force which took the field made it back to within the city walls where they tried to build up temporary defenses.

In the original battle plan a number of caltraps* were to be strewn on the field to impede the elephants and horses. This need never developed as the air of victory hung over the exuberant attackers. Ghyas-al-din later wrote of this engagement in his *Habeeb-us-siyer,* in part: "Sahib Keraun (Timur), of pure belief, according to his usual practice, came down from the swift horse and offered two special prayers out of humility, and having rubbed the forehead of sincerity upon the ground, he begged for victory and success from the bountiful God, and the mark of acceptance of his petition having been perceived in his brilliant and right thinking mind, he put his auspicious foot in the blessed stirrup with a strong heart and with a large hope...."

* a steel ball with four sharp prongs

*Elephant Charge at Dehli*

In the city of Dehli the mood was most somber as the court of Sultan Mahmud assembled. They pondered the possibility of further resistance, then considered the manner of repentance where it was no longer available to them. In the end they took the option of flight which they accomplished during the night, each of the nobles leaving by a different gate. Their departure, however, was noted by the alert guard and the several amirs of Timur's court were sent in pursuit.

Having a better prepared exit, both the sultan and his commander of the armies, Mullou Khan, were able to out-distance their pursuers. Nevertheless, the two sons of the khan were captured along with some lesser nobles who were not privy to the internal plans. The gates of the city were then secured so that no more escapees could leave. This prompted a mass capitulation to the imperial army as the remaining nobles returned to the city to rejoice in their successful efforts to prevent a sacking. The gold embroidered standard of Timur was displayed on the terrace of the blue colored domes.

The magnitude of this victory would have certainly become one of the greatest in Asiatic history had it not been marred by an incident which has been touted as evidence of pure bestiality. Having a reputed 100,000 prisoners in tow, the war council decided they presented an inordinate amount of risk to their rear before a big battle, given the number of guards available to contain them. It was generally known that although Timur gave the final order, he was privately revulsed and left the council without full accord.

Although the actual count was closer to 60,000, the disposition of this many prisoners as a matter of pragmatism, has transcended the mystique of the great amir to prompt the scribes of later generations to condemn him as inhuman. There are many examples of prisoner massacres in history, notably Richard I of England who did the same in 1190 on the third crusade. It was the sheer number put to death which produced the shock, although there was some mitigation of this when the renowned historian K. S. Lal claimed that the final count was closer to 50,000.

Of the captured elephants, several became gifts to the army commanders, with ninety being singled out to be sent back to the homeland for future use. A formal dedication of the city was made from the largest mosque where Timur was declared heir to the throne of all Asia. There followed this ceremony, a series of festivities and "social enjoyments" which lasted for several days.

What happened next was seen to add to the aura of inhumanity that has cloaked Timur in the minds of many. It followed the taunting of the city's inhabitants for their inability to defend themselves, at the precise time that an alarm was sounded from an unknown source which was construed as a call to arms. As the population poured into the streets in answer there was mass confusion, resulting in a self igniting melee which left thousands of citizens slaughtered near their homes.

On the following morning much of the eclectic army, now out of control from a drinking euphoria, stormed through the city to plunder and destroy as they went. The ban against drinking was ignored by so many of the warriors who did not ascribe to the laws of Islam that it was quite impossible to control. Those that sought shelter in the great mosque of the old city fared no better as they were sought out in the fury and put to the sword as well. No conqueror since Chinghis Khan ever left so much carnage in his wake.

This was too much, even for Timur, as he confided to his holy men that he had reached a state beyond satiation. He longed to be back in his beloved Samarkand, but having gone this far, he concluded that his leadership must be continued to finish the expedition's initial goals. Meanwhile, one of his most learned followers, Moulana Nas-ru-din had already withdrawn from the court in shame.

Fifteen days passed and the inertia from shock had to be broken. Timur rode out of Dehli on the last day of the year 1399 on his way to the River Ganges. Several of his amirs were sent to investigate the fortress of Muttra which lay on the route northeast of Dehli. The defenders were asked to capitulate peacefully but the answer came back clearly defining an open hostility.

Several chieftains had recently occupied Muttra and they felt secure in their fortifications. In a note to Timur they pointed out that no less personage than Termasherin Khan, back in 1327, had tried and failed to conquer the fortress. This, of course, was a challenge which could not be resisted and helped to mitigate the shame of Dehli. At the head of ten thousand horsemen Timur appeared outside the gates, stopping only long enough for his engineers to dig two trenches toward the walls from opposite directions.

With their usual efficiency the engineers undermined and then shored up sections of the wall with props ready for firing. The defenders lost heart when sections collapsed but held out until the main gate was breached. The defending prince and his son were both captured, and those that resisted to the last were summarily executed.

The governor of Lahore, some distance to the northwest, paid homage to Timur by appearing at his court with his entourage. He presented two white parrots in the manner of Hindu subservience, kissing the carpet before offering a number of gifts to the great monarch. In good graces, the governor's city and province were spared any invasion and he continued to rule as before.

A few days later the Timurid army reached the upper Ganges River as the heavy baggage train with all the encampment supplies was sent to the main branch called the "Black River." Divisions of the army fanned out to cover the several tributaries. Intelligence brought news of a flotilla of forty boats with armed men heading down river in their vicinity. Archers, posted along the banks on both sides, ambushed this expeditionary force and allowed only two boats to escape their lethal attack.

Other units of the Hindu chieftain bands were attacked and decimated in the hill country, until there remained only token resistance. At this time Timur was becoming increasingly weary and was suffering attacks of weakness, particularly in his knees. He ordered a final sweep of the surrounding hills before declaring the area secure, then started his exit westward toward the territory of Jummou, the last possibility of resistance.

Agents of Timur had been sent into the large country of Kashmir to the north to demand tribute. An ambassador from

Kashmir appeared at the encampment and asked for a reconsideration of what the governor had thought was an exorbitant amount to demand. Now in a more expansive mood, the triumphant monarch apologized for evident excesses in the requests and settled for a much more modest tribute.

Pir Muhammed was selected to lead a peaceful incursion into Kashmir while the main force proceeded westward through the area known as the Punjab, then on to the Jummou and its city of the same name. Intimidation was running high in Jummou as the elders and children fled to the mountains when they learned of the impending invasion. The army succeeded in securing a bountiful supply of grain and some cattle from the city administrators before ostensibly leaving the area in a fanfare of kettle drums.

Timur, once again in his favorite mode of misdirection, had secreted warriors in the hills the night before, and when the population in hiding returned to their city, they were pounced upon and held in bondage. The rajah of Jummou and fifty of his nobles were made prisoners but the rest of the inhabitants were released. The rajah, wounded and completely subservient, appeared before Timur and agreed to be converted to the Muhammedan religion. After attending to his wounds, he was honored with a special robe and restored to his office once more.

Curiosity about the country to the north permeated the Timurid court and it was decided to make a visit before leaving Hindustan. Timur's engineers had brought back stories about multi-storied buildings and of the large population in a city near present day Srinigar. It was a city divided by an extensive river which changed names as it flowed down country. Timur became overcome by home sickness after a short while and was content to turn his legions westward once more, this time to continue through the desert country and start the long trek back to Samarkand.

As the army encamped in the western desert close to the Indus River, the amirs and commanders brought the finds of their conquest spoils to lay in front of their sovereign. Timur, feeling magnanimous, distributed all of these treasures among his courtiers, keeping none for himself. On the 27th of March, a day set aside for dispersal, the commanders were given a special personal jewel and sent to their respective areas of the empire. Crossing the Indus River on a boat bridge, Timur was in the best of humor with the prospects of home strong in his mind.

Once more in the vast expanse of the Khorassan, the great monarch reveled in the success of his expanded empire, at that time being able to deliberately put out of his mind the carnage left behind. Plans of administration swirled through his head as he was intrigued by the notion of expanding justice and tranquillity to all of the conquered lands.

Several days after his arrival back in Samarkand Timur's captured elephants arrived and became singular curiosities to the populace. Two of the governor's from Hindustan who had accompanied the army were escorted through the extensive gardens and imperial palaces before being sent homeward. The aging monarch was content—all was well in his homeland.

# 14

## The Troubled Empire

*Trouble in the empire's span,*
*From Baghdad to Mazanderan.*
*Your engineers will breach the wall:*
*Sivas and Aleppo fall.*

For some time it had been one of the fondest hopes of Timur to build the ultimate monument in honor of his holiest pursuits, a cathedral mosque. On the fourth of Ramzaun, the day fixed by his principle astrologer, he saw the first portion of the foundation laid. For some time he had been importing the most skilled workmen in Asia, and now he was to realize the culmination of his plans.

Two hundred workmen were employed in the foundation work and five hundred in the mountain quarries. It was here that he had envisioned the employment of his many elephants; the transport of heavier than normal blocks. Each of the princes, amirs and highest ranking generals was to have a pillar, arch or pinnacle dedicated to them. There were to be 480 pillars alone, all of hewn stone and seven cubits high.

Four lofty minarets were planned, each on the corner of the main cathedral. Inscriptions from the Koran were planned in bas relief, together with many decorations in gold. Throughout the decor the colors white, blue and gold were almost exclusively dominant. When completed it was to have several attendant buildings, all contained within a large courtyard featuring fountains and flowers.

Years later the fame of this cathedral–mosque was to carry a legend which, after many repetitions emerged in the following form and was called the Mosque of Bibi Khanum: As the legend goes Timur was away during the Hindustan expedition and his wife, Mulkh Khanum, envisioned a tribute to her monarch in the form of a magnificent mosque. She engaged a famous architect who was to complete the job using four hundred pillars and four minarets.

In order to finance its construction she sacrificed her gold and jewels which, unfortunately, ran out before the completion of the building project. The architect then admitted to being in love with the beautiful "Bibi" and would only consent to finish its construction if she granted him a kiss. This she refused to do but said that she would substitute her most attractive handmaiden instead. Bibi then illustrated her offer by displaying before the architect several different colored eggs, then broke them to show that all were the same inside the shell.

Refusing her offer, the architect used an illustration of his own to prove a point. He presented two cups of clear liquid; one, he said contained water; it will satisfy the thirst but it is not long lasting. The second cup, he said, contained a pure white wine; it will tingle when swallowed and have a long lasting effect within.

It was only when Bibi learned that Timur would be on his way home soon that she agreed to the architect's conditions, however, when he bent to kiss her she suddenly turned her head and placed the back of her hand in the way. The fervor of the architect's kiss was so intense that it burned through her hand and emblazoned a lip print on her cheek.

Although tricked, the architect saw the effect of his kiss as a permanent mark, which had turned fiery red, and did indeed, finish his work as promised. When Timur called upon her to give his heartfelt thanks for the beautiful mosque, she was unable to disguise the telltale mark.

Forced to confess the details surrounding the incident, Timur became enraged and ordered the architect arrested. Now a fugitive, he ran into one of the minarets where his pursuers reached the top only to be told by a young man that their quarry had left through a secret exit and was already on his way to Persia.

In order to disguise what could be a monumental humiliation, Timur decreed that all women should thereafter cover their face with a black veil. This legend was given as the start of the custom which prevailed in the orthodox tenets of the Prophet.

Back in Samarkand it was a time of rest and deliberation for the affairs of state. While in Damascus Timur had made sketches of the building domes which so intrigued him. This style was used in the Bibi Khanum cathedral mosque and also in the mausoleum for his sons and grandsons—the Gur Amir. It was used during the Moghul era in India and later appeared in the building of the Taj Mahal.

A matter of great significance presented itself to Timur at this time. His third son, Miran Shah, had fallen off his horse in the autumn of 1396 and a persistent aberrant behavior had surfaced from time to time since then. At first it manifested itself in the sentencing of certain casual criminals to death. Later, it was the refusal to take into account accurate intelligence, substituting instead, his own sometimes capricious ideas.

When carrying out his orders to subdue the cities of Sultanieh and Tabriz, Miran Shah proceeded with acts of whimsy. Several years before he had cut off the head of the son of the Prince of Herat, explaining that it was an act caused by excessive drinking. His nobles were heard to say: "He is afflicted of Allah—did he not strike his head upon the earth when he fell from the saddle?"

Coupled with this problem of his errant son were overt acts of unrest bordering on rebellion in several parts of Timur's kingdom. Some chieftains had defaulted in Asia Minor and there were ominous signs coming from Georgia. Timur sent word to his commanders to prepare for a long campaign, then provided for an interim government at Samarkand.

This was not a journey to his liking and Timur rankled at having to be deterred from his grand purpose, that of challenging the emperor of Cathay. He did have one distinct advantage over those that dared to oppose him—they were divided forces who were to meet up with proven veterans under a single command. It was the problem of logistics that bothered him as his potential foes were far away with hostile territory in between.

Before leaving for this uncertain expedition he took the precaution to send a letter to his chosen one, Timur Kutlugh, to insure that the khan of all Kiptchak would maintain complete neutrality. The army leaving Samarkand was indeed a formidable one with a number of elephants, a camel train and many extra horses.

Timur's first destination was Hamadan in western Persia but he first had to settle the matter with his son, Miran Shah. From his encampment just outside Sultanieh he reviewed a number of transgressions perpetrated by his errant offspring. There was evidence of plundering of the imperial treasury and the destruction of a number of mosques and fine houses.

According to a court scribe, when Miran was confronted by a group of concerned nobles he shouted out to them: "I am the son of the greatest man in the world. What deed shall I perform in these cities that I may be remembered after I am dead?" At first Miran Shah was reluctant to appear at his father's pavilion but was persuaded by his erstwhile friend, Amir Suliman, son of the monarch of Anatolia, to present himself in penitence.

Timur at first refused to see his son but preferred to have him wait for a full day before giving him an audience. Miran immediately prostrated himself at his father's feet but was received with cold politeness and reminded of his sins against the empire and the holy order. He was also brought to task for his licentious lifestyle with excesses of drinking and delinquency. In the end Timur did not exact any physical punishment but relieved him of his command, largely on the advice of his own council of nobles.

News of the death of Egyptian Sultan Barkuk reached Timur while he was still busy near Sultanieh. The sultan had died in June of 1399 and had been replaced by his son Malik Faredje, then not quite twelve years old. Previously Timur had learned that his ambassador to Cairo had been murdered as a last gesture of defiance by the ailing sultan.

A messenger was dispatched to the young sultan demanding satisfaction for the demise of the official ambassador and also, for the release of Atilmish, his appointed governor of Avenik in northern Armenia. Since being captured by Kara Yussuf and delivered to the Syrians, there had been no word as to where he was being confined. Apparently the Turkoman Yussuf was anxious to stay in good graces with both the Egyptians and their vassal-protectorate of Syria.

The new monarch, with the same tendencies as his departed father the sultan, proceeded to hold this new messenger in the castle of Aleppo, then the primary stronghold of western Syria, located not far from the shores of the Mediterranean Sea. Timur was not set into action by this turn of events but decided to winter over in the Karabagh near the banks of the Araxes River. Although this was a cautionary move there were pieces of news filtering in which tempered any decision of import.

The mongol leader of northern Cathay had died, leaving a vacuum which could lead to the Emperor Hung Wu extending his control to all of Cathay. In Egypt the Mamluks (literally the "slaves"), who had long been elevated to a position of control, were vying for favorable positions in the court of the young Sultan Faredje. This, in turn, affected the country of Irak. When news came of the demise of the monarch of Jettah, Khauja Oghlan, Timur felt a sense of relief. Although his old nemesis had been violently murdered he could expect some respite from the unrest which was sure to follow.

Soon after this series of events transpired came news which again changed the balance of power in Cathay. Emperor Hung Wu had died, leaving the celestial empire to his sixteen year old grandson. Earlier, the four sons of the deceased emperor had been dispatched to distant parts of the kingdom in order to forestall an imminent power play. Nevertheless, the youngest son had marshalled his forces and was setting himself in opposition to his nephew. Timur anguished at his lost opportunity to make his long delayed move eastward, however, there were too many distractions in all of Asia Minor.

When the winter season was waning in the Karabagh, Timur made some changes in the government of Georgia, then hurried to the banks of the Kur River where he was joined by two of his satellite princes. These rulers of the provinces of Shirvan and Shekky were anxious to prove themselves in the seek-and-destroy mission, one which would carry them to the thick forests to the east where renegade bands were terrorizing the inhabitants.

Even with heavy snow the army under Timur was able to root out the enemy and inflict heavy losses on them. The intransigent Georgian leader escaped to a section where the free use of wine extended to even bathing the dead in it before burial. Timur sorely objected to this departure from Muhammedan orthodoxy and paused long enough to destroy all vestiges of the grape vines. Satisfied that he had punished the renegades to the fullest practical extent, he then retired to his cantonments in the Karabagh.

While in winter quarters Timur dictated the beginnings of what would separate him from a common overlord, a treatise on logic and fairness, coupled with a doctrine on common law. One of the first considerations was to exempt payment or barter from any land owner without substantial cause and to declare a civilian's house his place of privacy. Land left without heirs reverted to the throne, where it was to be reapportioned to loyalists.

Timur fancied himself through the sublimity of his mission as the emissary between the Prophet and mankind within the confines of the Koran. It came upon him as a sort of gestalt through the conditioning of years of success and flattery. This self serving mission carried through into improvements throughout his entire empire.

He saw to it that certain mosques and holy places were restored with elegance. The old Khorassan road to Persia, Hindustan and Badakshan was modernized with guard stations and rest houses placed at strategic intervals. These post houses were disposed to protect and care for horses and camels with a fixed toll rate. Commerce between the cities of Bokhara, Taushkend and Samarkand going to and from countries to the south and west was thriving as the old Khorassan road was extended to the Black Sea.

Some of the yams or post stations had fountains that were served by water brought in from a considerable distance through aqueduct and pipeline. Timur, ever in readiness, decreed that the stations were to report by courier at regular intervals. These messengers, called elchis, rode their mounts often to exhaustion. It was said that a common sight along the roads was the bodies of horses that had been discarded. Elchis had the right to fresh horses, even from those of higher rank.

Having taken into account all affairs of state from his winter quarters, Timur was then anxious to settle military accounts with those that were threatening the stability of the empire. Baghdad had never been freed from the Egyptian incursion which placed it in the hands of their designated governor after the limited garrison had been forced out. There was concern in Timur's court that his two grandson's expedition to free the City of Khalifs (Baghdad) was bogging down. News came that Pir Muhammed was stalled in the area of Nouhendejaun, north of the city, where he was said to have feigned sickness. The other army under Meerza Rustum had reduced Dizful, some 250 miles to the east, but was moving slowly westward toward Fhuzi in old Babylon.

In a continuation of strange behavior, Pir Muhammed retired back to Shiraz where he had apparently abandoned his disposition to attack Baghdad and was instead, showing signs of instability. When this behavior developed into gross mismanagement, Timur was apprised of his grandson's predicament.

Trouble was also brewing in Baghdad at the court of the Sultan Ahmed, he who was still referred to as the "protector of the faithful." Amir Shirvan, Timur's appointee as administer of Khuristan*, had been plundering his subjects for riches and putting to death those that resisted. He suddenly appeared before Sultan Ahmed to offer allegiance, bringing with him a column of one thousand fully equipped horsemen.

---

* small province of southwest Persia

After establishing himself firmly in the sultan's court Amir Shirvan proceeded to use his vast fortune to bribe the courtiers. If it was not for one family member, Ahmed's aunt, the plan to dethrone the sultan might have succeeded. Having been forewarned, Ahmed dispatched the amir on a special raid and instructed his trusted followers to eliminate the threat to the monarchy. The expedition returned with the head of the amir, an act which triggered one of the bloodiest retributions in Mesopotamian history.

All members of the court suspected of bribery collusion in the service of the murdered amir were put to the sword. The sultan then proceeded to select the most egregious individuals for punishment but, in turn, selected succeeding possibilities with the same stigma until many of the remaining courtiers were beheaded. The count eventually topped the two thousand mark in the city alone. Informers were rewarded but one intended victim called out; "Excellence, as long as you and I remain alive, it matters not what becomes of the rest of the world." This statement caught the sultan's fancy and the man was spared.

What followed these acts of violence could only be attributed to one who was deranged. Not trusting anybody, even his own kitchen crew, he at first lived the life of a recluse. Then, one night, he fled across the Tigris to join his trusted general Kara Yussuf, the Turkoman, who proposed to team up with him to pillage his own city. At the last moment, however, he repented these base plans and called off the raid just before launching it.

It was now summer of the year 1400 and the threat to Baghdad by Timur was becoming more imminent. When the reclaiming army of the amir reached northern Mesopotamia Sultan Ahmed panicked and decided to leave Baghdad altogether. Once again he joined up with Kara Yussuf and retreated toward Aleppo. Timur's army met opposition from the Mamluks of Egypt and Syria but managed to defeat them, forcing a temporary refuge within the walls of Aleppo.

By the time Sultan Ahmed had continued onward into Anatolia a rift appeared between himself and his Turkoman ally. Ahmed went to join the great Bayazid while Kara Yussuf followed at a later date to the Turkish court where he enjoyed a dispensation of his own in Anatolia. Timur, now sensing a need for his presence in the south quickly wound up his expedition in Georgia with the extermination of many of the Christian churches and with a final accommodation with the rebellious Malik Gurguin, Prince of Georgia. By the time Sultan Ahmed had decided to flee Baghdad he was moving through Armenia on the last leg of his extended campaign.

In the city of Calmarin, said to be the first city to be built after the great biblical flood, Timur was welcomed as a deliverer. A nearby castle called Egidas had been held by a large robber band, representing an always threatening presence, but no match for the Timurids. The lord was immediately put to death as his followers deserted him en masse, scattering throughout the land and becoming fugitives. The castle was then conferred to the robber's wife but as an afterthought, all the doors were removed. This was so that no malefactors could again use it as a base for plunder.

Near the foot of Mount Ararat Timur came upon a castle called Vasit-Calaside. The siege of this fortress was short lived as the lord offered tribute to Timur in order to spare the lives of himself, his court and warriors. The next castle in line, that called Maca, withstood a one day siege but then sued for clemency in order to spare its destruction. The lord sent his son of twenty years with horses and presents to the invaders. Timur was so impressed by the son that he was asked to accompany the army and later live with his grandson Omar Meerza, then residing in Sultanieh.

First contact with the influence of Bayazid, "the thunderbolt." was in the Armenian province of Erzeroom. A demand had been made by the House of Othman (Ottoman Empire) for tribute and warnings of reprisal for lack of compliance. Since both monarchs were on the same track for the elimination of Christianity, it came to mind that a sort of compromise could be worked out. With this thought in mind Timur sent a note to Bayazid with diplomatic overtones.

Bayazid's answer came directly to Timur; one that would normally have enraged him enough to instigate immediate action.

It read: "Know, O bloody dog named Timur that the Turks are not accustomed to refuse shelter to friends or to shun battle with foes, or to resort to lies and tricks of intrigue."

Timur's reply was a cautious one. It was a reminder that Bayazid could lose influence in Europe and that he stood a chance of losing against elephants which could crush him. In a brief return note Bayazid was contemptuous and referred to Timur as "Timur the lame," while threatening to violate his favorite wife, Mulkh Khanum.

The exchange of threats stopped at that. Timur controlled his rage and forced himself to postpone the thought of confrontation and turned another direction—to the south.

After waiting for favorable weather, Timur sent his main divisions into Asia Minor by way of the upper Euphrates River. By the time summer had started he had taken several cities and laid waste to the countryside. His next move was to subdue Malatiyah, a stronghold which consumed nearly a month of his time as he shied away from a frontal attack. When he arrived at Arrum he pondered his time table, then decided to bypass it. Considering it as quasi-sacred, he qualified his decision by saying; "Allah, when he established it, set it apart and chose it for Himself."

Arriving near to Sivas which is at the junction of three provinces, Timur paused for a few days. Controlled by the House of Othman, it was ruled by none other than Amir Suliman, son of Bayazid. Although still on friendly terms because of his relationship with Miran Shah, he felt threatened and sent a messenger to seek help from his father. Bayazid was fully involved with the siege of Constantinople and needed all of his warriors in this effort. Amir Suliman was notified that he must deal with his emergency on his own terms.

The actual siege of Sivas began on the 21st of August and Timur quickly noted that he was confronted by steep walls and a ditch on three sides. The first problem that presented itself was the depth of the water table only a few feet below ground level where many springs were found. It appeared that only the western approach was feasible for a conventional attack. Once again the engineers employed their undermining technique at a point which minimized the fusillade of arrows and stones they had to deal with.

This was perhaps the most formidable job that Timur's special units ever tackled. According to records of historical significance the fortress walls were ten cubits* in thickness at the base and six cubits at the top, reaching an average height of twenty cubits. Nevertheless just eighteen days after operations started, several of the towers collapsed, much to the surprise of the defenders. Just as Timur's warriors were about to storm the city its governor, after the flight of Amir Suliman, sued for surrender terms. An agreed ransom was subsequently paid but only the Musulmans were spared punishment.

There seems to be some disagreement as to the disposition of the remaining citizenry. All agree that the Christians were sent into slavery but some historians have as many as nine thousand virgins being sent back to Samarkand. Since Timur promised no bloodshed as part of the surrender terms, his treatment of Suliman's warriors who inflicted many casualties on the Timurids were punished in a unique way—they were herded into a large pit and buried alive. Almost to a man these were members of the Armenian corps.

As the challenge from the Mamluks continued, Timur diverted his attention away from Baghdad and to the subjugation of Syria and possibly Egypt. Against the wishes of his amirs who sought the time to recover from the rigors of the recent campaign, the army moved due south with Shah Rukh's division leading the way. Their first encounter with the Syrians was at Behesna, seen as a fortress of singular strength which was nestled in converging mountain passes.

When Timur set up his observation on a promontory just above the fortress he was met by rocks catapulted from within, one of which fell almost at his feet and rolled into his tent. The manjeneiks, or large catapults, were placed near to the wall to commence their destruction. In the interim reinforcements had arrived from Shiraz under Meerza Rustum.

---

* cubit = approximately 18 inches

As before, the sappers and engineers were able to undermine the massive walls. Sensing the inevitable destruction of his fortress, the governor dispatched messages asking for mercy. The reply from Timur was that he would consider this entreaty only after entering the city by force. Very likely it was the challenge of invincibility of this particular fortress that prompted his answer, together with the considerable energy already expended on the assault.

Firing of the wooden props under the wall was done on the 26th of September, and as they collapsed in several places, panic extended through all of the ranks of the defenders. The governor then ordered that all known valuables be turned over to Timur as a palliate for his intentions. As a result of this offering, together with complete subservience, the entire city and its inhabitants were spared further reduction.

In the Syrian city of Aleppo the governor, now thoroughly alarmed at the news from Behesna sent for immediate help from the young Sultan Faredje of Egypt. In response a large army was sent out from Damascus with orders to give complete support to the threatened fortress. In order to play both sides, some emissaries from the Syrian general Shedoun were sent to Timur to explain that any ensuing actions on their part was ordered by the sultan alone.

Having covered themselves with a mantle of shared responsibility, they chanced a meeting with Timur's army on the plains outside the city. Timur was aided by intelligence from spies he had planted in the synagogue disguised as Jews who were capable of quoting from the Talmud. On November 8th the first encounters were with small advance units which established a firmness of purpose. On the second day there was a passive confrontation which ended with both armies retiring to their respective camps.

Day three dawned with a forceful charge by three sections of the invading army numbering some 12,000. With Timur in the center, as usual, advancing with his elephants, leaving in reserve a division of 10,000 horsemen on a low rise. This advance was accompanied by the traditional din of kettle drums, trumpets and cymbals.

By sheer force the defending Syrians were driven back and sent into retreat to within the walls of Aleppo, leaving behind a large number of dead and wounded. With the impedance of the city's inhabitants who were crowding the gates, many of the would-be escapees were cut down without gaining entrance. The city's ditch was said to be overflowing with bodies of the unfortunate victims of the ensuing melee. Detractors of Timur report the incident as a deliberate burial of those who fell in battle as they wished to illuminate his unyielding attitude and innate brutality.

To add to the confusion outside the city entrances, Timur's machines went to work lobbing naptha fire onto the mass of soldiers and civilians. Meanwhile General Shedoun, with as many warriors as he could muster, entered the fortress and secured the gates. Because of the nature of the stone escarpments, having been built on an artificial mount, the Syrian defenders felt that the walls were unassailable by any normal means.

Having gained access to the city environs, Timur's pavilion was within sight of the fortress, as his archers were keeping up a steady assault over the parapets. While the sappers and engineers were busy draining the moat, others started working over the granite blocks at the base of the wall with bars and pickaxes.

Nizam Shami, Timur's primary scribe, had been on his way to Hijaz when he was detained in Aleppo. Located on a rooftop opposite the citadel, he was an eye witness to the lowering of five armed men down ropes to the area of the undermining diggers. They proceeded to hack the attackers to death but were then promptly attacked by the squadron of protecting soldiers. He noted that the five men were hauled up soon after being riddled with arrows.

When a message was sent from the defenders concerning the futility of trying to undermine the walls, a feat that had never succeeded in the past, it was understandably ignored. It was only a later entreaty to desist in favor of promised submission that caused the laboring at the wall to be halted. With princely liberality Timur allowed the entire garrison to leave without incident. He did, however, confiscate all the treasure found in the fortress and favored his amirs and commanders with most of the booty.

In the wake of a formal surrender the governor and nobles of Aleppo assembled in Timur's presence who initiated a dialog with the following text, in part: "…Let none reply to me except your most learned and most eminent man, to whom I am greatly devoted and in whose company I delight and I have the ancient zeal for learning." It was a holy man whose father lived in Samarkand who stepped up to carry the conversation, at which time a discussion of what constituted a martyr took place.

At the conclusion of the conversations and negotiations it was time for the hour of prayer. The entire assemblage entered into the ceremony as Timur prostrated himself among his former enemies. While in Aleppo, Timur stayed in the house of the governor as he pondered over his fate, for he was not to be left unpunished for putting to death the envoy sent to him. In the end the governor's life was spared but two amirs were placed in charge of the administration and were housed in the college of the sultan, situated opposite from the protective fortress.

Edward White, much like Christopher Marlowe, writes in Elizabethan prose his account of the life of Timur. That portion which deals with the fall of Aleppo is shown in part: "Renowned emperor, and mightie Callepine; God's great lieftenant over all the world. Here at Aleppo with an hoste of men, lies Tamburlaine, this king of Persia. In number more than are the quivering leaves, Ofidas forrest where pour higheffe hounds, with open crie pursues the wounded stag: He meanes to girt Natolias walles with siedge; fire the towne and over-run the land.…"

With his soldiers now exhausted, Timur called a halt to all activity except tending to the wounded. He himself, could not sustain the vigor of his younger years. He increasingly had to delegate authority in matters he normally personally pursued and he found the need for longer rest periods. The many years in the saddle, added to the vicissitudes of a series of cold winters, were becoming most evident in the sagging of his facial muscles. He found himself drifting off into the musings of how he would continue to administer a larger empire than any other conqueror in history had been called upon to do.

# 15

## The Three Year War

*Your weary army trumpets call,*
*Portenders to Damascus fall.*
*History may yet deplore*
*Pursuance of the Three Year War.*

Early in November another entreaty had been sent to Damascus while Timur's army was still in a recovery mode, yet in Aleppo. Failing to get an answer, the next move was to send an emissary directly to Cairo (Kaherah in Syrian phonetics) with the news that both Shedoun and Timur Tough were prisoners and that the next target would be Damascus if the previously detained emissaries, now in Egypt were not released.

In the interim period the army of Pir Muhammed was sent to place a siege on Hama, on the edge of the great Syrian desert. His grandfather had marked time with the hope that his previous problem with military lassitude was now behind him. At Hama, as with Aleppo, the city fell fairly handily but the inner fortress was holding out. Timur himself showed up soon after and his presence was enough to intimidate the garrison into submission. All of the defenders were spared, but were forced to give up their valuables.

Even Timur, filled with feigned energy as he was, had to admit that the army was fatigued to its limit and the livestock presented a nearly starved appearance. They then proceeded to the plains of Tripoli* for the purpose of rest and renovation. These were days of restlessness for the great amir as he chafed at the delay and longed to be on his way to his eventual destination—Anatolia.

Some days before three nobles from Aleppo presented themselves at the court in Damascus and addressed their council with a warning: "O assembly of Muslims, to fly from evil which cannot be overcome is among the counsels of the prophets; let him who can't fly seek a way of safety and let him who can, gird his loins and not stay a night in Damascus or deceive himself, for rumor is nothing compared with what we have ourselves seen."

There was much confusion and indecision in the wake of the news from Aleppo. Some left for the holy land, some to Egypt, others felt secure in hiding themselves in an inaccessible place. Pleas for help were sent to Egypt where they reached a responsive ear. The Sultan Faredje agreed to send an army to help in the rescue of Damascus.

Once again the Timurid army was on the move. They first overran Hems** where they found only token resistance, then presented themselves at the ancient city of Baalbek. Here Timur paused and sent other divisions to Seydah (Sidon) and Beirout. Turning his attention back to Baalbek, the entire army was amazed to see the gigantic blocks which formed the city wall, said to have been erected by supernatural powers in prehistoric times.

Nevertheless, the city fell without undue exertion and the army was rewarded by an abundance of fruit and grains. By now it was late in the year 1400 and the cold season was closing in on the soldiers. On December 20 they started down into the more fertile valleys, in particular those leading to Damascus. By the time Seydah and Beirut had been secured, along with Phoenicia, the army was once more at full strength.

When news reached Egypt that Timur had conquered Asia Minor, destroyed Sivas, and had returned to Syria, Sultan Faredje

---

* Syrian Tripoli
** in present day Lebanon

felt he had to act. He gathered up his armies, opened up the Bureau of Stipends and announced to his troops that they were to march to Syria. The army first reached Gaza, then on to Damascus in time to forestall a preemptive strike by the Timurids by setting up camp in nearby Shakhob. By the time they reached Damascus, Timur had conquered and left Baalbek.

To the relief of the Damascus defenders the sultan of Egypt had fulfilled his promise as his army arrived with a great deal of pomp and splendor on December 23. Another plan developed in the minds of the Syrians, however; that of assassination as a means to dispose of their illustrious adversary. A particularly ruthless ruffian was picked for the job and sent as part of an envoy group by the sultan. This perpetrator was joined by two others, all being equipped with poisoned daggers.

The entourage, together with the assassins, readily gained admission to Timur's presence but found little opportunity to get close enough to perform their foul deed. Before long their suspicious behavior betrayed them and they were seized and searched. Upon being certain of their mission, all three were hacked to death and burned to ashes. The rest of the envoy group were sent back to Damascus—alive, but without their ears.

Needless to say, this prompted an almost immediate response as Timur moved with full strength on Damascus. While observing from a neighboring hill, a full attack followed when the defenders ventured out of the city with vengeance driving them to furious action. Timur's forces easily drove back this foray with considerable losses as they once again retreated to the protection of the city. Prisoners were shown no mercy in light of the treacherous plot that had been exposed. General Shedoun, brought with the army from Aleppo, was executed but Timur spared the lives of others who had given him good intelligence information.

That night of December 30 in the encampment, a most unexplainable incident occurred. Sultan Hussein, grandson to Timur, defected along with a few aides who were said to have decided on this rash adventure following a drunken orgy. They made their way directly to the city where the Syrians and Egyptians received them as royal dignitaries. Their presence in Damascus was construed as a harbinger of success.

Perhaps an inkling of this attitude, or by shrewd design so often attendant to Timur's campaigns, he also did the unexplainable by making a general retreat well away from the city. Back on the road to Canaan and Egypt he proceeded to dig a ditch around his encampment with breastworks of stone. Then, in another atypical move, he sent one more envoy to Damascus to ask for the release of those who had been detained earlier.

The Syrians and Egyptians not only received Timur's envoy with cordiality, they put on a display of what was known in those days as Greek fire. After agreeing to return the entire envoy entourage, they seemed disposed to feel superior to their attackers. When, after a period of ten days, Timur was forced to move into a new forage area to the east of the city, its occupants then felt sure that it was a sign of weakness and that the Timurid legions were preparing to retreat toward the Euphrates.

All available warriors were assembled within the city of Damascus to take to the field for an attack on their tormentors in the weakest spot, their rear. Their emergence onto the field was likened to a flock of locusts feeding on the crops. Timur countered this move by pitching his tents in front of the advancing army with stones and articles of baggage as barricades. Time was then taken on a neighboring hill for obligatory devotions before mounting horses for the upcoming battle.

The army made up of Syrians and Egyptians which came out against Timur was formidable. A Persian poet sings its praises in this way:

> *"Lions, when they charge; stags when they stand erect;*
> *Mountains when they stand firm; seas when they advance;*
> *Suns when they shine; moons when they appear;*
> *Winds when they are aroused; clouds when they move;*
> *Hawks, when they swoop; leopards when they leap;*
> *Thunders, when they crash; thunderbolts when they fall."*

At the last moment the main army of Timur quickly divided in two with the swiftest horsemen leading each side in a flanking movement. When the maneuver was under way the center unit waited until the ranks of Mamluks and Syrians were forced into a rapidly diminishing space, then struck with all their force, elephants leading the way. Timur's ruse worked to perfection as the slaughter continued all the way to the city gates. The defector, Sultan Hussein, was captured on the left wing and brought to the monarch's pavilion.

At the insistence of Shah Rukh, the deserter was released but never again during his lifetime given a command. As the son of Timur's daughter he could appear in court but never was to assume a place in the ranks of his peers. The fateful battle was fought on February 3, 1401, and decided the fate of the city of Damascus. To solidify their gains Timur drew up his entire force with all the machines of destruction and line of elephants on the following day. The inhabitants were terrorized, having never imagined the extent of the forces arrayed against them.

The Sultan of Egypt then called a council to determine what their next step should be. It was the Syrians who presented the compelling argument that their defenses were still in place and that they were still a fairly strong army, even with the heavy losses sustained in the field. The plan finally agreed upon was to send a message of friendship to Timur to stall off any attack, thereby allowing time for the Egyptians to steal away in the night, leaving the Syrians to make the best of the situation.

In a note sent by the sultan it disavowed any intention of violence toward the Timurids and, together with a number of valuable presents, agreed to whatever terms were forthcoming, to be carried out on the following day. After agreeing to this proposal, Timur withdrew and ceased hostilities. In the meantime the sultan and his chief amirs learned that some of the other amirs were engaged in a seditious plot to bring about a revolt by suddenly returning to Egypt in order to stage it, thus isolating Sultan Faredje in a foreign land.

They had to agree that a possible overthrow of their government was more important than the siege of Damascus and that they must act accordingly. On the night of January 6, the sultan and his entourage left secretly for Cairo; the remaining troops and inhabitants were left to their own devices. News of the escape reached Timur earlier than was expected as a defector in the march southward left at a propitious moment and reported to the Timurid camp. The first counter move was to surround Damascus to prevent further escape and then the faster units were sent in hot pursuit. Rear guard action by the Egyptians was a matter of sacrifice as they were promptly cut to pieces. In the process of continuing the pursuit the Timurid horses gave out and the chase had to be abandoned.

Back in the city it was an apprehensive time as the inhabitants did not know what to anticipate. Following the first shower of arrows coming over the walls it was apparent that they were in an untenable position and sheer terror dictated a capitulation as soon as possible. As the gates were thrown open to signify unconditional surrender, they assumed that their best hope for survival was in offering ransom.

Within the castle, however, the governor decided to resist. He was said to be a man of violent disposition and resisted any approach to the walls with catapults using Greek fire. With the gates closed it was a matter of waiting for the defenses to slacken, at which time Timur's engineers rushed to drain the moat and approach the walls. Their attack method included heating the foundation stones followed by a dousing in vinegar to cause spalting, followed by pounding with heavy hammers. After several days the walls were showing signs of giving way and finally the heaviest section did start to fail. Meanwhile, in their well rehearsed manner, the engineers were ready to fire the propped sections. On this occasion, in an unpredictable collapse, nearly eighty attackers were buried in the rubble.

Soon after this incident it was all over and the keys to the storage vaults were given over on February 25. There they found an immense quantity of grain that was destined for Mecca and Medina. For his belligerence, the governor was put to the sword, all others being released upon providing suitable ransom. The more unfortunate ones were reduced to slavery with their particular skills being implemented by a move to Samarkand. Nearly all of those transported were employed in the elaborate building program still under way.

One of Timur's first administrative directives was to replace the base metal currency with that of gold and silver. He was appalled by the condition of the descendants of the Prophet's tombs, particularly those of the women. These were restored with the choicest of marble. Before leaving the area, Shah Rukh, accompanied by a full division, was sent to root out any opposition along the shores of the Mediterranean all the way to that territory held by Bayazid.

One of the first nobles on the Egyptian negotiation team was Cadi* Ibn Khaldun, a native of Tunis, who made the final arrangements as he went on to become a conversant with the great amir. Over a period of the next twenty-five days they discussed many things, primarily Timur's favorite subject—military history. This extended conversation into polemics so endeared Timur with his Cadi that afterward he extended protection to him and his dependents (numbering some 2,000) and showered them with presents. The Cadi gave his host a mule as a gift, but upon returning to Cairo later, he received payment for it by special messenger.

The Cadi, likely in preparation to receive amnesty for his friends, addressed Timur in the following manner: "May Allah aid you today—it is thirty or forty years that I have longed to meet you." Timur was said to ask what the reason for this was, to which the Cadi replied: "Two things: the first is that you are the sultan of the universe and the ruler of the world, and I don't believe that there has appeared among men from Adam until this epoch a ruler like you...." The second reason which has led me to desire to meet you is concerned with what the prognosticators and the Muslim saints in the Maghrib (southern coast of the Mediterranean) used to tell of the conjunction of the constellations...." He also added: "I have written your tarjumataka (biography) and I wish to read it to you so that you can correct the inaccuracies."

---

*a special title given to eminent scholars

After the departure of the Cadi, on the 15th of March, fires broke out in Damascus which were beyond extinction where many valuable buildings were razed. Timur rushed to the aid of the fire fighters to preserve the principal mosque but found it too late upon arrival at the scene. Before leaving the countryside Timur granted clemency to the people by releasing all the slaves other than the few that had already been sent to Samarkand, and setting in motion a rebuilding program to reclaim that part of the city destroyed by fire.

Claims that Timur ordered the burning of the mosque have been summarily discounted. Arabshah, his primary denouncer, believed that the Raphadites (Shiites from the Khorassan) were the arsonists. Built by the 6th Caliph at the start of the 14th century, it was a marvel of architecture and elegance. Only the marble pavement survived as the gold ceilings, with their ornate pillars studded with gold and precious stones, were destroyed as a result of the intense heat.

Soon after the fall of Damascus, Timur fell ill and word was sent to "the princes of the blood" (Miran Shah and Shah Rukh) to return from their winter quarters in Canaan. Timur made a speedy recovery but had to be helped on his horse for some time thereafter. The two armies then continued on to Canaan.

In a parting gesture to the lands of Syria, Timur dispatched Shaikh Nur-ad-din to root out a renegade tribe and restore order to the neighborhood of the desert city of Palmyra. Soon after crossing the Euphrates, Timur decided to stop at Mardin. It was the Prince of Mardin who, after a short imprisonment at Sultanieh, was allowed to continue his government after solemn oaths of allegiance. There was evidence since that time that he no longer felt bound to that oath.

When Timur invited Sultan Eissa* to his presence the prince turned a deaf ear to a proposal of collaboration and chose to hide himself in the fortress. It was not a propitious time to lay siege to the home of Bayazid's son, and there was a paucity of grazing land for the livestock which prompted Timur to leave after

* one of Bayazid's five sons

leveling every structure capable of providing a blockade in the months to come.

About this time he received a letter from the Sultan of Egypt which was quite curious in content from one who was forced to flee. It read in part: "Do not think that we were seized with fear of you and fled from you;… The good man, when two diseases appear in the body, heals the more dangerous and we thought you a slight and mean affair… but by Allah! we will leap upon you with the charge of an angry lion and make our thirsty spears drink from you and your army deep draughts from the springs of hatred and mow your army down like hay and trample upon you as dry ground is trampled, and the millstone of war will drive you in every direction, vexed by dense stabbing of spears and close packed blows of swords, as milled flour is expelled; and we will block for you the ways of escape and you will cry out, but there will be no time to escape."

The bearer of the message was not a regular envoy and Timur dismissed him with no reply. There were important matters to terminate, none the least was to lift the siege of Alanjik and to return to Georgia, where riots had recently broken out. By the time he had crossed the Tigris at Mosul word had come that Sultan Ahmed had instituted another uprising in Baghdad and that he was seeking the help of Bayazid to consolidate it.

For the second time in his long career Timur was torn between two major and very conflicting ideas. He had been weighing the diversion of having to storm the massive walls of Baghdad again and the time table he had set for the handling of the Turkomans. Sultan Faredje, having been given the government at Baghdad with the admonition to fight to the last man in its defense, now obviously had a change of heart. Timur's two advance divisions were certainly not adequate to reduce the city's defenses should the sultan's army prevail. In the end he decided to head back south with most of his army by way of the "Golden Bridge," on the lower Tigris near the Malik Canal.

Arriving in the vicinity of Baghdad Timur took up a position below the city, on the left bank. The sappers and miners were sent to work on what was most familiar to them. In an important council of war the various amirs and commanders were all given extended orders to cover any expected contingencies.Malik* Faredje then thought it to his advantage to send an officer in his confidence to seek out Timur's intentions and to contemplate a possible counter offer.

Although the malik's agent was treated cordially and given the usual gifts, he returned with the dreaded word of no conciliation. Knowing that the population needed to be insulated from the impending full out siege, the agent was put into isolation as the malik thought out his very few options. Already random arrows had killed two of his chiefs.

With the prospect of reducing the massive walls in the pursuit of siege plans, it was necessary to call up Shah Rukh with the heavy machinery who was, at that time, on his way to Tabriz. When the formidable army was arrayed in plain sight of the city's inhabitants, it was cause for considerable alarm. Before the actual placement of the newly arrived equipment to be used, there was a need to build a bridge across the Tigris for better logistical purposes. Before this operation was commenced all possible escape routes from Baghdad were cut off.

At the precise time of maximum decision making, a present arrived from Timur's grandson—a gigantic single ruby taken from the mines in Badakshan which weighed 120 methkols (about 2,400 carats). This was not only a most gratifying gift but, in the monarch's mind, an omen of great significance. Although the engineers were succeeding in bringing down sections of wall by their usual means, the desperate defenders were repairing them almost as fast with round-the-clock masonry work.

The August heat was now an all consuming force, making it almost intolerable to exert a full day's work. Timur's commanders were trying to persuade him to move up the time table for a massive attack in order to bring the matter to a head. Once again Timur ignored his generals' pleas and the troops were reduced to suffering in the heat, as the battering rams continued to work around the

* Malik = "king' used interchangeably with sultan

clock. Several days later, at the height of the noon heat, Timur chose the moment of attack. When the defenders had only a token force on the outer wall, the engineers suddenly appeared with hundreds of ladders.

To the roar of drums, trumpets, and cymbals, the warriors, crazed with the heat, attacked with little or no thought of personal danger. Nur-ad-din, said to be the first to gain the parapet to plant the horsetail standard, recounted that thousands were swarming up behind him. The seasoned veterans under Shah Rukh, together with the legions of five amirs, continued to pour into the city with raised swords.

Timur had taken up his post on the river bridge where a number of inhabitants had elected to jump, favoring drowning to being beheaded. Many tried to escape by boats and were assailed by a hail of arrows. Malik Faredje, along with his daughter and a few followers, were among the boat people able to escape. Most of the unfortunates who plunged into the Tigris were picked off by the alert archers. Once again some misinformed historians reported that the malik was compelled to jump into the river where his body was later recovered.

Nizam Shami, the only scribe to recount the exploits of Timur during his lifetime, was dwelling in Baghdad during the final days of resistance. He was the first to come out of the city and pay homage to the conqueror, by whom he was graciously received. In his description of the aftermath he describes the Tigris as alive with the victorious army swimming across it, so filled with warriors that the plain and river blended in a solid mass of humanity, making it difficult to distinguish the boundaries of each.

The order, once before given, was for each warrior to account for an enemy head. Accounts of the carnage vary, but the stifling heat after a most taxing siege crazed the assaulters to perform bestial deeds. What became a shock to the foes of Timur was the head count of dead at about 90,000. There were a reported 120 pyramids of gruesome heads adorning the city in the aftermath.

Only the mosques and a few buildings of significant value survived the onslaught. This razing of a major city was accomplished on the 20th of August in the year 1401. Timur, after leaving the ruined city, stopped at the mausoleum of a revered holy man, that of Imam Moussa-al-Kauzem located some twenty five miles north of Baghdad. It was his usual measure of atonement, brought about by a belief that he had indeed served the tenets of Islam, and the cause of his Sunni sect in particular.

The order went out for all the troops to offer alms and perform the necessary pious prostrations at the shrine of Ali-at-Nudjet, the most holy of their Muhammedan precursor in the area. This then, set the stage for a long delayed visit to Tabriz, the capital of Azerbijan in order to confront the challenge developing in Georgia.

One detachment of the army came upon the treasure of Sultan Ahmed, strictly in a serendipitous manner. They were to attack the fortress of Aligny, only six miles northeast of Baghdad on the Nahrawan Canal. Finding it difficult to approach the fortress, they lowered the water in the canal and exposed three large chests which proved to be a large part of the elusive sultan's treasure, containing mostly gold and silver coin which had been placed there for safe keeping. The fortress itself proved to be an easy conquest as only a token force remained in its garrison.

The complete destruction of Baghdad brought to an end to what is generally called the "Three Years War." It was an exhausting one for both Timur and his hard driven army. Attrition had worked its way throughout the ranks and replacements had been sent for, to come from Samarkand. Their arrival some time later were both welcome to the tired veterans and invigorating to the entire corps.

Kara Yussuf had been plotting for a return to power and was distancing himself from Bayazid's court in order to act on his own. He was able to recruit a number of Arab followers who could be described as soldiers of fortune. Ahmed Jalayr, the appointed governor of Baghdad, was uneasy about retaining his hold on the city and decided to ask for the aid of Kara Yussuf when he perceived that his own son was plotting to overthrow him.

Seeing an opportunity for aggrandizement, Yussuf sought out and attacked the wayward son where he was defeated and lost his life in the Tigris River when the weight of his armor dragged him down under the waters. Once disposed of his obligation, Kara Yussuf then appeared at the city and proceeded to take control from his solicitor, Ahmed Jalayr. The governor became a virtual prisoner in his own city and finally ended up going into hiding. A faithful follower spirited him out from the walls during the night and he was able to make his way to the city of Takrit, some thirty-five miles up river from Baghdad.

Kara Yussuf deigned to ignore his departure and set about to conquer Arabian Irak with his band of mercenaries. Hearing of this treachery against his appointed governor, Timur sent two amirs with their respective armies to settle the matter. In forced marches they came down from the north to surprise Kara Yussuf who had just traveled a little below Hillah on the lower Euphrates. The pretender to the throne of Baghdad found himself outnumbered and outmaneuvered. He elected to flee toward Syria with a small band of followers, leaving behind a great number of sheep and cattle. Baghdad, once more without direction, was given to Abu Bakr, Miran Shah's oldest son, to administer and rebuild.

Timur was not present when his two amirs discovered the remains of the tomb erected in memory of the revered holy man Mashad Ali. As the story goes, Mashad was stabbed in the Kutah Mosque located near the Tigris and immediately gave orders for the disposal of his body. When the "breath was out of my body" he was to be put upon a camel and the beast turned loose—at the place where the camel knelt down, he was to be buried.

For some years the burial place was kept a secret but when all chances of violation had ceased, a shrine was built at the spot where the camel had stopped to kneel. A home for the Saids, descendants of Muhammed, was built near the shrine which gradually spread into a settlement, then a town which was called Mashad Ali. The Babal Hadrat (Gate of the Presence) led directly to the shrine. It had been reported that cripples were healed of their infirmities upon praying at the site and hanging a lamp of precious metal near the crypt.

In his *Tamburlaine the Great,* written in 1580, Christopher Marlowe's tragic play calls upon a great deal of imagination.

Written in old Elizabethan blank verse, he finds the true Timur only in the results of his deeds. His cruelty is depicted as unusual in its severity with brilliant tactics and intrigue pointedly removed. Below, in part, is Marlowe's characterization of Timur's introspection, his *raison d'etre*.

*Nature that fram'd us of foure Elements,*
*Warring within our breasts for regiment*
*Doth teach us all to have aspyring minds:*
*Our soules, whose faculties can comprehend*
*The wondrous Architecture of the world:*
*And measure every wandering plannets course,*
*Still climbing after knowledge infinite,*
*And alwaies mooving as the restles Spheares,*
*Wils us to weare our selves and never rest,*
*Until we reach the ripest fruit of all,*
*That perfect blisse and sole felicitie,*
*The sweet fruition of an earthly crowne.*

At long last Timur could turn his attention to the thorn in the side of many Europeans and, of course, to his own pride. The taunts of Bayazid had long been fermenting in his mind; now was the time to reckon with this powerful lord whose ambition was to be the greatest conqueror of all times. What would transpire was to dramatically change the direction of history in both Europe and Asia Minor.

# 16

## The Fall of the House of Othman

*Oh crafty monarch turn your gaze*
*Upon the fraught with danger phase:*
*The time has come to make your bid:*
*Confront the mighty Bayazid.*

Focus was now on Tabriz, just twenty five miles east of the large lake of Urmiyah and principal city of Azerbijan. There were rumors that Bayazid himself had shown an interest in it, a possibility which was anathema to Timur. After suffering considerable destruction over the years it was now under restoration, however, certain irregularities in its administration were evident. The finance minister having been accused of mismanagement, made a half hearted attempt on his own life as an answer to the scandal. In the inquiry which followed, more embezzlement evidence was found and one of the principals was hanged as a result.

One of the best descriptions of Tabriz in its best days comes from an Italian merchant who noted that: "Two beautiful streams flow through it and underground aqueducts bring water to fountains at several mosques and to the great palace. This palace is very lofty and seems solid half way through. The entrance leads to a very lofty long hall, on one side of which is a solid cube, intended to be a hiding place, sustained by four large columns paces apart and about twice the grasp of my arms in girth. The capitals of these are wonderfully carved; the cement is a certain mixture of stone like fine jasper...."

Timur made a routine inspection of Tabriz before continuing through the Karabagh on his way to the goal of the moment, the review of fortifications at Alanjik, now a key to the defense of northern Azerbijan. From Timur's encampment at Nuksheven, just across the Araxes River from the base of Mt. Ararat, good news arrived from Kiptchak. The khan had pledged his continued loyalty in answer to Timur's letter some time before. This was a matter of great import in the pending conflict with Bayazid.

Many miles to the east came disturbing news concerning his grandson Eskander (the Turki–Mongol name for Alexander). Omar Shaikh's younger son, at only fifteen years of age, had been made governor of the city of Andijan, but was now on a pillaging spree through the Moghulstan cities of Khotan and Kashgar. Timur was most distressed that another member of the imperial family should act in an aberrant way.

Muhammed Sultan was summoned to handle the entire affair as his grandfather wanted to clear his mind for the fateful campaign into Anatolia. Eskander was brought before the council who, cognizant of his royal heritage, set him free but stripped him of his command. Later he was given a partial command by Timur but his other grandson Meerza Sultan, the deserter, was never given an imperial pardon and remained in disgrace as a lowly courtier.

Charles VI, King of the Franks, had been feeling out Timur for some time as the possible savior for halting the Balkan invasion by Bayazid. All of Europe was alarmed with the Othman successes and feared for their own countries. After Charles VI sent an ambassador in the form of a bishop to Sultanieh, Timur felt obliged to return the favor with a letter of friendship. In it he listed the many areas of cooperation and agreement but did not commit any thoughts to the problem of the Balkans.

An eventual confrontation with Bayazid was in the forefront of Timur's long range plans. The Turkish monarch's courage and cunning was well known in Asia Minor and Europe, particularly his ruthlessness which was well established after the episode in which he strangled his own brother. Bayazid had become the titular lord of Constantinople and followed up with the conquest of most of Greece in the Battle of Nicopolis back in 1396.

Only Timur could offer a threat to Bayazid's hold on Constantinople as the great city was at low ebb. The nearly deposed Emperor Manuel II (of Greek origin) was in the process of trying to raise men and supplies but found little assistance from the neighboring monarchs who were absorbed in political realignments. His own nephew was already drawing up terms of complete surrender pending Bayazid's return from the Balkans.

There was a problem requiring an internal resolve with Timur at the time, that his principal adversary was also engaged with in a war against the infidels. He, therefore, hesitated for a time before launching an expedition into Anatolia. It was of particular concern also, that Bayazid had reached the peak of his strength and elements of doubt as to the eventual outcome were of practical significance. There was also a factor of physical and mental fatigue throughout his army of which his generals had made him acutely aware.

By the time the army arrived at the border of Georgia and Armenia it was at full strength. When he reviewed this vast array of warriors Timur felt confident that success was in the offing. A message was sent to Bayazid asking for a peaceful surrender of the fortress of Kemaukh, a request that was only a formality in view of its absurdity. One piece of news was most heartening—Kara Yussuf had quit the court of Bayazid in a dispute which left him with only a few followers.

Early in 1402 Sultan Ahmed returned to Baghdad where he intended to rebuild the city. At the same time detachments were sent to the areas surrounding the city to regain control of the countryside. When news of this reached Timur's encampment he sent four cavalry units toward Baghdad, each to approach the city from different directions.

As these detachments closed in on Baghdad in the dead of winter they had to first confront the Kurds who had come down from their mountain strongholds to escape the seasonal snows. It was Abu Bakr who arrived first outside of Baghdad, only to find that the sultan had fled along with his son and courtiers just minutes before. When the other three units arrived they fanned out to consolidate the entire area, then left to join the imperial army, leaving only a small garrison behind to administer the government.

While the army of Timur was encamped in Armenia a messenger arrived from Samarkand with the news that a son had been born to Shah Rukh. Given the honor to name his new grandson, Timur decided on Muhammed Jouky. The birth at this time was taken as a good omen, but it was the sighting of a comet that appeared in the sky for several months which prompted the astrologers to become jubilant. Called the "Lampbearer" by the Greeks, this sighting convinced Timur and his nobles that the time to invade Anatolia was at hand. Note: This was not Halley's Comet, as it appeared in 1456 on a 76, plus or minus, year return cycle.

There was a diversion that presented itself as the army was engaged in foraging for food and livestock pasturing. The fortress of Tertoum, held by only a few hundred Turks, had been an extreme annoyance but posed no real strategic problem. It was assigned to Shaikh Nur-ad-din who was able to reduce it in a period of six days. Meanwhile nearly two months had passed without any reply from Bayazid and the army had to make its move. No possibility of a quasi friendly relationship could be expected in any event.

Kemaukh was a fort whose reputation for invincibility was known throughout the land. It had been described to Timur in the following manner: "Truly this fort is firm like the knowledge of God, and as fortified and invulnerable as the faith of the devout worshipper. The arrow of imagination would not cross the ditch of its inaccessible strength and the javelin thrower of ingenuity would not find a way to reach it. Divine providence, like an architect, set its strong foundations on inaccessible cliffs and the Creator built its towers geometrically like a builder,... Truly this thing is most wonderful."

At Erzeroom, near the headwaters of the Euphrates, the army found a garden spot where the pasturing was ideal. Plans went ahead for the attack on the fortress of Kemaukh, some thirty miles away, as previously announced in the message to Bayazid. It was the army of Muhammed Sultan which was assigned to prepare the siege but later other units were also sent to aid in its reduction.

After draining the moat, ladders were placed against the wall in the dead of night with the strongest warriors assigned to scale the escarpments. On the first assault the defenders scored telling results as they were prepared with large stones to shower down on the attackers. As the sun rose the next day a concentrated effort followed the shower of arrows and catapult missiles. This time the troops were able to gain the summit and with overwhelming numbers, soon secured all of the fortress area.

Before returning temporarily to Erzeroom, Timur installed Amir Tahertan to govern the Turkish fortress and then decided to clear out the cave dwelling natives who had been a menace to their neighbors. At Sivas he paused long enough to receive the long awaited message from Bayazid.

Bayazid had been seized with anger upon receiving Timur's letter saying to his nobles: "Shall he frighten me by this folly or drive me to flight by these fables? Does he suppose that I am like the armies of Syria or its mixed horde like my army? Or does he not know that I know his affairs and how he has treacherously deceived kings and in what way he has always weakened one after another?"

Accompanying the envoy were gifts which Timur refused as the message contained the threat of complete desolation in his empire if he insisted on war. It also contained acrimonious defiances and, of course, refusal to give up the fortress that had already become *fait accompli.* The messengers had engaged themselves in groveling at Timur's feet with every expectation of reprisal.

With the assurance of safe passage back to their monarch, Timur gave them the following message, in part: "Tell your master that since he has thought fit to disregard the counsels of good will and experience, and to reject the demands of justice on my part, if he be, what he would persuade the world to believe him, a man of undaunted courage, to take his ground with firmness; for He* was

---

* Allah

at hand to assail him, whose power it would require his utmost energies to withstand."

A review of the entire army followed the dismissal of the Turkomans. It was said to pass like waves of clouds with each division displaying a particular color, the most recently arrived division from Samarkand being particularly magnificent in their accoutrements. From Knolles *History of the Turks* the army was said to consist of three hundred thousand horse, and five hundred thousand foot soldiers, coming from all parts of the empire.

What awaited this formidable army was well known. The road to Anatolia lay through gloomy forests where, from time to time, it would be necessary to constrict movement through narrow defiles at the foot of Mt. Tauros. With the city of Kayserai as the rallying point each commander was warned not to advance beyond it under any circumstance. This was also a place for the accumulation of more food supplies. They were, at this time, nearing Angora (Anguriyah in Persian).

When Timur learned that Bayazid had taken the desert road, he had chosen to pass through the more developed countryside where choice fruits were available. A Persian scribe writes of the passage of the army this way: "And they crossed not to delight in crops and pastures and udders, amid sidras* without thorns and tall trees set in order and spreading shade and flowing water and gentle breezes and health-giving delights, in security, tranquillity, abundance and amplitude, without fear, journeying at their convenience, confident of prosperity and victory, promising themselves wealth and spoils, bending Fate and Providence to their will."

Bayazid's lightly armored troops were already within a day's march and each unit was warned to be on the alert at all times and to watch their quarters at every step. When first contact was made the Turkish commander upbraided his units for not immediately attacking a numerically inferior detachment. At sunrise the next day he ordered his entire army to move against their adversaries.

---

* genus of cedars, now spelled Cedrus

At this juncture Timur was concerned with lack of intelligence and sent out his most distinguished followers with the securing of prisoners to this end. The patrol made a successful raid on the enemy's right wing and returned safely. Early on the following day, in an address to his amirs and generals, Timur's most often quoted utterance was delivered: "There are," he told them, "two courses to follow now. We can wait here, refresh our horses and stand against the Turks, or we can push on into their country, laying it waste and compelling them to follow. Their army is mostly infantry, and marching will tire them." Then, with only a few moments pause he added: "That is what we will do."

As the army started to move against the Turks, one division shifted to the right to insure that no surprise hostility would be coming from the vicinity of Angora. Also a contingent of engineers was sent to filter along the line of march to dig wells. The entire army then veered northward and arrived without incident near the former city of Angora. Their only contact at this time was with a column headed by Bayazid's son who was attacked but managed to escape with only moderate losses.

From the Turk encampment there was some dismay; they waited — two days, three days, a week. When word came back that Timur had gone, the commander was furious at being outflanked. They had been confident because of the way they had rolled over the defenses in the Balkans and defeated the Serbians in the Battle of Kosovo. They also held a defensive position where they could enjoy the benefit of their foot soldiers. Bayazid's main army had pulled out of the Balkans and was encamped at Brusa, near the Sea of Marmosa*. It had conscripted a number of Greeks and Serbians to fill the need for replacements.

First in line for concentrated attack by the Timurids was the fortress at Angora which was considered a difficult siege target. Once again the sequence of events in the attack covered the draining of the moat, temporary filling, bringing in the ladders, etc. The primary assault on the walls had just begun when intelligence

---

* connection with the Black Sea near Constantinople (now call Marmara)

reported Bayazid's main army within striking distance. The time had come for correct and perhaps intrepid logistics.

Timur then proceeded with one of his uncharacteristic acts. He donned full armor and made a complete circuit of the field of battle that would decide the fate of one of the world's greatest warriors. He discovered only one source of water and an idea occurred to him which could turn the tide of battle. He immediately called in his suppliers to fill every container with water and then ordered the spring to be rendered unfit. His sappers spent the entire night filling the crystal spring with everything rotten and loathsome that could be obtained.

On the following morning the Turks arrived from their hillside on a forced march. When they found their supplies low and no source of water, they had no alternative but to attack. Bayazid found that he had to do what was tactically incorrect— launch his inferior cavalry against Timurid horsemen. The battle was lost just as one might lose the match in the first few moves on a chess board.

The order to mount was given, Timur placing himself in the middle of a gigantic crescent of men and horseflesh with some forty thousand horsemen in reserve. Those elephants that had survived the previous campaign were placed near the center, each with several archers and naptha throwers of Greek fire.

The army of Bayazid was similarly aligned with the great sultan near the center. Most of the armored warriors were dressed in black and covered with as much protection as they and their horses could bear. First to be attacked was the right wing of Timur's army where daring and ferocity allowed the Turks to break through, however, it was the better disciplined Timurid warriors which made it possible to hold their ground.

On the other side of Bayazid's army the horsemen broke through into the middle of Timur's forces but they were immediately outflanked like a resilient spring which reacts when the pressure is reduced. This army, under the command of one of Bayazid's sons, seeing its best warriors failing, suddenly decided to retreat. With concern that the first breakthrough on the Turk's left might run into a trapped pursuit, Timur sent Muhammed Sultan's army in the gap as a protective measure.

There was a time of uncertainty when a Serbian general at the head of a number of European cuirassiers* rushed laterally to the right in an effort to prevent the collapse of that side. It was only after a bloody battle that the ranks of the Serbians were thinned out enough to recover from the threat. It was then that the reserves were called up to fill in the right and left wings to present a solid front once more.

One of the pursuing horse units was attacked by Bayazid in person and he was able to rout them. It was not until he mounted a hilltop and was able to view more of the countryside that he realized the peril of his deployment. The Turkish troops tried to rally around him but successive waves of the more disciplined imperial troops succeeded in a game of attrition. It finally became a fast moving coil of seasoned warriors closing in from all sides like a constrictor.

Accompanying Timur's army at this time was a grandson named Sultan Ahmed Meerza whose Timurid mother had married Sulyman Meerza of Teheran. This grandson was sickly and was ordered not to enter into the fighting. In the hurry to return to battle after confining his grandson, Timur lost his headpiece and was obliged to fight without replacement for the balance of the day.

It was late afternoon when Bayazid decided that his only recourse was to try and break out. His army fought a defensive holding action and then in one gigantic charge, managed to break through amid a shower of arrows. The terrible losses in Bayazid's army were now aggravated by lack of water as the heat of the day was taking its toll.

One detachment was dispatched to pursue the fleeing Turk army and they were able to run them down in spite of a fierce rear guard action. Timur had returned to his pavilion when the great sultan himself was brought in with his hands bound. The victory celebration was suddenly halted at this piece of good fortune.

---

* conscription from Bayazid's victory over Serbia in 1389

*Capture of Bayazid*

Probably only legend, but certainly a plausible story, was what has been alleged to have followed. Timur was engaged in a chess game with Shah Rukh and looked up with a smile at the entrance of the famous captive. Bayazid was said to have made a contrite admission by volunteering: "It is ill to mock one whom God hath afflicted."

Bayazid's bonds were ordered removed and he was seated in the pavilion. Timur relished the idea of being able to dictate terms but was quite courteous to his captive. Bayazid asked that a search be made for his sons. Only one of them was found. Later it developed that Mustafa had been killed on the field of battle but his other sons apparently escaped.

Of Bayazid's five sons, it was his eldest, Amir Suliman, who was able to retreat to Brusa with a partially intact army. His remaining brothers Eissa, Muhammed and Musa were able to hide in the fort of Kharshanal, called the Baghdad of Anatolia because of its invulnerable nature.

Eissa later presented himself at Timur's court, bringing with him a substantial tribute. With Shah Rukh pleading his case, he was reinstated in good graces and given the governorship of the city of Mardin.

Intrigue and treachery followed their later lives as Eissa was murdered by his brother Amir Suliman; Musa then killed the eldest as a matter of revenge for the death of Eissa. Musa was able to survive as the last of the family for a few years, only to die from poisoning by his ambitious courtiers.

This greatest of all battles during the time of Timur was important to him because of the immense satisfaction it gave in light of the risks taken. During the quick attack the Serbian King Peter was killed and news was brought to the imperial camp that Prince Muhammed, son of Jahanghir, received severe wounds. The prince was removed to his encampment where he was treated by the most skilled of doctors.

Officially the battle took place on July 20, 1402 but there has been a disagreement as to the losses sustained. Knolles had placed Bayazid's losses at two hundred thousand and Timur's at not too considerably less. The lowest of estimates placed them in the tens of thousands Timur at twenty thousand and Bayazid at nearly twice that. In the memoirs Timur claims to have been at the head of some 400,000 warriors.

It is definitely known that Bayazid was ordered unshackled and that he expressed remorse for his rash decisions in the conflict. His greatest concern was his fall from power, as he had always planned to be the greatest conqueror in history.

It would seem plausible that the account by Johann Schiltberger would be authentic. An Austrian citizen, first captured by Bayazid, then by Timur, he travelled with both monarchs and had a penchant for historical accounts. Although much of his biblical chronology and interpretations are somewhat fanciful, his close encounters at the Battle of Angora were from first hand knowledge and deemed valid.

Schiltberger states that Timur, employing thirty two elephants, had isolated Bayazid on a mountain side, the one he left to engage the Timurids in desperation on the 20th of July. He details the losses only as "heavy" with Bayazid losing considerably more than Timur. Before the battle Timur noted in his memoirs that his legions stretched out a distance of fifteen miles and consisted of 400,000 men.

The events that transpired later are in accord with all eastern and Byzantine accounts, therefore, can be construed as accurate. The Timurids were concerned for the welfare of Prince Muhammed whose wounds developed into a mortification which confined him to his bed where he was kept under day and night surveillance. When it appeared that he would be unable to travel with his army it was decided to leave him near the battlefield. Some time later he was able to be moved by litter to Ak Shahr where he was confined for his convalescence.

This was a serious blow to Timur and it was said that he had become morose at the contemplation of his grandson's possible demise and of the Timurid dynasty itself. Pir Muhammed, then ruler of Hindustan, would be his remaining heir as Omar Shaikh had died several years before. Not only was Prince Muhammed

Sultan his grandfather's favorite, he was also idolized by his army. At age sixty-seven Timur was showing more signs of aging and his limp was more pronounced as he was less able to disguise his infirmity. It must be noted that Shah Rukh was his chosen and direct heir, but it was tradition to select a member of the second generation to carry on the dynasty.

Ak Shahr was an oversized village near the south shore of a very pretty lake where the climate was said to favor healthful living. Soon after Prince Muhammed was taken there for a team of doctors to care for, the ailing monarch Bayazid was also taken to the same place by litter. In Marlowe's *Tamburlaine the Great* Bayazid was said to have been humbled by confinement in a cage and paraded around the area. This is very likely pure myth as Marlowe's handling of the life of Timur was one of contention, particularly in the Chaghatay lord's alleged cruelty. The litter carrying the defeated monarch had some restraints on the sides, perhaps somewhat resembling a cage.

For some time the conquest of Angora had been forgotten in the wake of the siege of the fortress which was perched on a rock promontory overlooking the old city which was in partial ruins. The name had persisted since the time of its founding by King Midas many centuries before, and still has been retained to identify a breed of goats, later cats, which came from the area.

Timur seemed to be unwilling to pursue the surviving Othman heirs as they retreated to Brusa, just across the Sea of Marmosa from Constantinople. With no longer any compulsion to resist in a lost cause, Yakoub, the governor of Angora presented the keys of the fortress to Timur. The area was secured by a garrison of Timurids in the event that it might be threatened some time in the future. The old city of Angora eventually was rebuilt and later became the thriving capital called Ankara.

Following the regular route through Anatolia, Timur led his army to Kotauhiah, only two days distant from the scene of the big battle and fairly close to Prince Muhammed's confinement at Ak Shahr. He found Kotauhiah a beautiful city where he elected to extend his stay, treating the inhabitants as friends. While there he dispatched one segment of his army to push northward all the way to the Black Sea and another to move southward to the Mediterranean as far as the land portion opposite the island of Rhodes.

Close associates of Timur noted that the extended stay in the city of his choice was a manifestation of his satiation with warfare and a longing for a period of relaxation. Meanwhile Bayazid's son Eissa had been captured and placed out of harm's way. After a period of time, having satisfied himself that all necessary administrative duties were behind him, the supreme monarch then set the stage for an appropriate celebration.

All of the princes of his family, the amirs of his court and the generals of his army had assembled amidst the splendor of long accumulated wealth. For four days they exhilarated with goblets of gold, the juice of the grape and the tunes of hundreds of minstrels. Although devout in his chosen religion, there was always a time set aside to eschew orthodoxy in the pursuit of a spirited drink.

This was a time of anguish for the courtiers of the former Turkish conqueror. Many of them had taken what treasures they could lay their hands on and fled the country, mostly to Europe. Others went to the seacoast and managed to hide for the duration of the customary sweep of the countryside. Two of Bayazid's daughters, together with one of Sultan Ahmed's, were captured and kept in seclusion. Kara Yussuf, feeling that his break with Bayazid was not sufficient protection for him, fled into Arabia where pursuit was almost impossible.

Later it developed that the surviving Prince of Serbia, having been captured with much of the treasure of the House of Othman, was brought to the imperial quarters. With a magnanimity of a courtly person, Timur reunited the prince with his wife and allowed the entire retinue to return to their homes at will. At the same time one of the Turkish princes, Mahomman Beg, was released from prison, given lavish presents, and returned to the sovereignty of the province of Kermiyan in central Anatolia.

Weariness setting in with Timur had left him with diminishing vigor and resolution. He was given a lift in spirits when Malik

Faredje arrived from Cairo to pay his respects at the court. The ruler of Egypt realized that he had counted on Bayazid to be the endowed world conqueror and was left without any choice except subjugation to the great amir. Upon arriving at the court, the malik knelt to kiss the throne and proceeded to express himself in the most conciliatory terms. When he asked for the privilege of being the mediator between Sultan Ahmed and Timur, his wish was granted as the great monarch had been in deep thought as to how he might prevent an unpleasant incident.

After receiving all the envoys and from each a remonstration to preserve the sanctity of Mecca and Medina, Timur dissolved his court and once again turned his attention to his homeland. He recalled the old hostilities that he had experienced since his boyhood, particularly the despot Jengueiz who had ordered the extermination of all the male population, even to the infants at their mother's breasts, in the area bordering Cathay.

Although his first experiment in transplanting populations had been a dismal failure, he now conceived a plan to do the same with the more pastoral population around Sivas in southern Armenia. Their destination was to be in close proximity with the Jettahs where they could serve as a neutralizer for any possible threats to Transoxania. The difficult task of transporting twenty thousand people across central Asia to the southeast of the Kiptchak expanse was left to the ingenuity of the amirs and generals.

Each family was to receive a bribe of clothing and other personal valuables to dissuade their expected hostility. They were also promised safe passage with the imperial armies and complete protection from the Jetes in their new homeland. Finally they were to be guaranteed prosperity for the remainder of the initial group's lifetime. With the background of the kettle drums sounding and the hoisting of the imperial standard, the horsetail topped by golden half moon, the strange caravan was set into motion.

Looking back on his campaign in Anatolia, Timur reflected on his many conquests and singled out the defeat of Toktamish as his most satisfying one. It would seem that history would remember the Battle of Angora as the most significant one affecting the large population of Europe. The monarchs of Europe were all beholden to Timur for deflecting the powerful ambitions of the Ottomans. Each one sent letters of thanks and conciliation, the latter consideration to deflect any thought of conquest in their direction. Timur was consumed with plans in the other direction.

# 17

# The Last Reaches of the Empire

*Compassion at the Golden Horn,*
*The House of Othman is reborn;*
*Then on to conquests of renown;*
*Add jewels to the empire crown.*

By now a month had passed and Timur felt he must be on the move again. First it was westward where he entered the new city of Shehernou and waited for the arrival of the army division under Abu Bakr, Miran Shah's son who was named after Timur's lifelong friend. With the expanded army he then proceeded in a southwesterly direction. From his encampment near what was called the "Golden Rock" he issued orders for the execution of the governor of Thrace, presumably for former treachery.

Timur had temporarily put aside thoughts of a punishment for the thorns in his side, the Sultan Ahmed and the young Sultan of Egypt, Malik Faredje. Before renewing plans for these two, an ambassador was sent to Constantinople to demand tribute from the Greek emperor. It was he who had previously asked for Timur's help in restoring the city from Bayazid's control, and now his entreaty had been granted. As a parting gesture in the matter of tribute, the name of Timur was to appear on the coinage of Egypt and Syria henceforward.

With the armies of Timur on the move they were likened to a spreading scourge by the historian Ahmed Ibn Arabshah as he says in his usual disparaging tone: "And a heavy cloud of dust went forth, from which a mist covered the eye of the sun, and the sea of the Tatars raged like that which God swelled into seven seas; and it advanced entering no town without laying it to waste nor did it descend upon a city without destroying and removing it; and it crossed no place without damage and no neck submitted to its bond but was broken, nor did the top of a high fort resist it without being overthrown."

During this time attention was diverted to the court of Amir Suliman, eldest son of Bayazid, who had retreated into the European side of the Bosporus at Gallipoli. Timur felt obliged to enter Constantinople but lingered on the Asiatic side and decided that other matters were more pressing than the pursuit of the last remnants of the House of Othman. While there he chastised the Greeks for double dealing; that is, providing boats for the evacuation of Turkish nobles while paying tribute to him for the liberation of Angora. Eventually the Genoese did ally themselves with Timur but the Venetians never did.

While in Constantinople he was lavishly entertained by the emperor and sought out by several of the Greek princes for tribute. Five or six days were spent in the imperial entourage with inspection of garden spots along the sea coast. Timur finally took leave in the midst of many expensive gifts and a special group of thirty horses with all their furnishings.

Before leaving Constantinople Bayazid's son sent a number of gifts to Timur including animals of the chase and a myriad of curiosities to seal his pledge of friendship. Adding to this was a considerable number of florins which represented a handsome tribute. Amir Suliman did not forget to note that his father's humane and liberal treatment after being captured prompted much of his tendered loyalty. Timur then congratulated himself for his decision not to press his expedition into European Anatolia.

It later transpired that Amir Suliman made a play for control of Constantinople by employing Greek sailors to arrive as a fleet and anchor at night in coves not easily seen from the Asiatic side of the straits. The sailors and their accompanying Turkish warriors hid in the holds and attacked the Christians when they boarded the ships. In the end there were enough of the inhabitants of the great city to prevail and defeat this undermanned force.

Among the events of the time was the death of Sultan Mahmud Khan, the titular head of Transoxania. Timur mourned his loss because he had been his closest adherent from the dynasty of Chinghis Khan. He once again quoted from the Koran: "We came from God, and to God we must return."

By autumn in the year 1402 Timur was lodged near Tanghouzlig, a place about sixty miles distant from Smyrna*, having passed through the sites of Troy and Ephesus. Many of his warriors had become sickened from the waters of a tainted spring and the army was obliged to recover at this encampment. Each division, at this time, was seeking a suitable place for winter quarters.

One pocket of defiance remained in the area of Smyrna, a fortress of hewn stone and masonry with the sea on three sides and a deep ditch separating it from the peninsula of land. At that time it was in the hands of Franks who were remnants of the crusaders of the order of St. John. It had long been a place of sanctity and a terminal point for certain pilgrimages. The knights of this fortress felt quite content to defy Timur because they had held out previously against Bayazid for a period of seven years. This, of course, was an intriguing challenge for Timur that he felt he must address.

There had been considerable hostility for years between the Christians within the fortress and the Musulman community of the countryside. Several replies to messages taken to the enclave were answered with rudeness and defiance. In reaction to these rebuffs the heavy equipment was moved up close to the walls on December 1, 1402. Timur arrived to survey the scene and to make his plan of attack.

With the only feasible access from the land side being a deep moat, it presented the first problem to be solved. On this occasion

* present day Izmir

it could not be drained in the usual manner because it was sea water, therefore, Timur came up with one of his ad hoc counter plans. Under cover of a shower of arrows, catapulted rocks and Greek fire, he proceeded to build a breakwater to close the narrow entrance to the bay.

While this was going on the engineers had succeeded in removing some of the masonry and had installed the wooden props ready for firing. At a given signal the dry brush and naptha was lighted and soon after large sections of the wall dropped, carrying some defenders with it. At this time night was falling and some of the defenders were able to lower themselves by rope into waiting boats that had been hidden in reserve.

By the next day it was all over. Even the townspeople joined in by swarming into the formerly impregnable fortress to help in the disposition of those still resisting. After all valuables had been removed, the remaining walls were reduced to rubble. In two weeks Timur accomplished what Bayazid and his father before him were unable to do in many years of siege. A relief fleet of boats from Rhodes was driven off as the final act of conquest.

Henry IV of England, together with Charles VI, king of the Franks, sent messages of congratulations to Timur. The Greek Emperor Manuel II was once again installed in Constantinople where he promised continued tribute to the monarch of all Asia. Messages of submission were received from the Sultan of Egypt and from John VII (coemperor of the Byzantine empire with Manuel II). From across the Golden Horn the horsetail standard of Timur now flew in the European city of Pera.

The attack on Smyrna was the one and only time that Timur destroyed a bastion of Christianity as he strived to maintain friendly relations with the princes of Europe. He refrained from attacking the holy cities of Meshed, Mecca and Jerusalem. He was also tolerant of other religions, notably in Tabriz where Jews, Nestorian Christians, Malakites and others were left as undisturbed as possible. He even made use of a Christian bishop as his envoy to King Charles VI. As a result he was considered as a "half-Muhammedan" by the Sultan of Egypt and the House of Othman.

Before retiring to the plains of Ayazlik, the Ismeer of the Moslems in Smyrna was given ample stores of war supplies to enable him to defend himself against any Christian incursions that might result from their expulsion. Additional support was sent to Angora to insure its security and then Timur moved on to the vicinity of the Meindar River in preparation for crossing to the east where several fortresses had still not yielded to imperial control.

The army came upon the large fresh water lake called Gul, some 250 miles east of Smyrna. One fortress was located on the lake and another on one of the two islands within the lake. The town of Egridur was subsequently attacked and fell without much concentrated defense. Many of the inhabitants had fled to the lake fortress. This, in turn, was assailed when every available boat was commandeered for the trip to the island fortifications. There was a treasure trove of valuable effects which had been brought there for safe keeping. The population, now swelled to above normal, used these accumulated properties as ransom to save their homes from being sacked. While this peaceful submission was in progress, Timur received alarming news about his grandson Muhammed Sultan.

When the troubled monarch arrived at Ak Shahr after a forced march of over seventy five miles, he was met by doctors who had been treating his grandson. The patient was not responding to their medication and his rising fever had addled his brain. When Timur arrived at the bedside his speech had already slipped from one of slurring to an almost loss of communication. The litter was moved to a different spot, one with purer air, in the hope that this would effect a recovery.

Timur spent most of his waking hours by Muhammed Sultan's side and sadly witnessed the slow ebbing away of his life. On March 11, 1403, his favorite grandson and fondest hope to continue the dynasty, expired quietly. In the custom of the Tatars, the prince's war drum was sounded for the last time, then destroyed. His body was embalmed and sent to Avnik in Armenia, to be later transported to Samarkand for final entombment.

Meanwhile Bayazid, also confined in Ak Shahr, had been gradually losing ground in his battle with severe asthma coupled with quinsy, and died just three days before Muhammed Sultan. Ak Shahr was located just south of a large lake named by the Byzantines as the "Lake of the Forty Martyrs." The great castle of Kara Hisar, some fifty miles to the west, was left undisturbed by Timur as he was overcome by the loss of his future heir apparent. During his grief Timur saw to it that Bayazid's body was returned to Brusa where he was buried with full honors at the royal mausoleum.

After the sad ceremony with his grandson Timur clothed his army in black garments and word was sent ahead for all to do the same upon arrival of the body. It was a sad journey back to his army, but Timur has sent word ahead that he deplored all expressions of sympathy. Having secured nearly all of Anatolia and received ambassadors from Egypt pledging eternal loyalty, it was time to move on.

Members of the royal household who had wintered in Sultanieh moved on to Avnik as Timur pushed eastward with a small detachment. Most of the troops were left behind to seek out and destroy pockets of Turks who were hiding out in caves and other secretive places. Upon arriving at Avnik Timur was soon after met by his family; first to greet him were the three young sons of Muhammed Sultan. As they ran to meet their grandfather he could not contain himself and broke into tears.

At the funeral feast nobles from all over Asia Minor attended, after which the embalmed body of the prince was sent in procession to Sultanieh. Before leaving Avnik Timur conferred the kingdom of Irak upon Abu Bakr, son of Miran Shah. Undaunted by the loss of his grandson, Timur mounted his horse and directed his army to the northeast, once more heading for Georgia.

The Prince of Georgia, Malik Gurguin, had failed to live up to his agreement, first, to supply troops to Timur and second, to appear at his court of nobles. For the sixth time an invasion of the Caucasus became necessary.

Several of the most diplomatic envoys from the prince's court were dispatched to reach Timur at the earliest moment. In his message Malik Gurguin characterized himself as being mean and insignificant, that he was already the most dutiful and obedient of subjects. He added that if tribute is called for, he was ready to empty his treasury and agree upon an annual revenue. When Timur received this entreaty he was not to be deluded. The prince was given two choices: 1. to appear in court and immediately embrace the tenets of the Koran or, 2. pay a regular tribute to insure against seasonal invasion, after which he could retain his titular head of country.

When harvest time arrived and still no answer from the malik, it became evident that he was counting on supplying his storehouse before taking any action. Shaikh Nur-ad-din was given the commission of entering all of Georgia to take charge of the crops and return with most of the harvest. As suspected, the Georgian army was making plans to withdraw to their most unassailable fortress with all the supplies they could muster.

In the deepest part of the mountains between Tiflis and the Armenian border was the fortress of Kurtin, a lofty rock with only a small bit of table land on top. Accessible by a single narrow pathway, it was surrounded by steep crevices as if designed by a master of defense. No expense had been spared to make it as formidable as possible, even beyond nature's endowment. A cistern excavated in the rock provided an adequate water supply, together with livestock crowded into the small mountain meadow.

Timur's commanders knew better than to try and dissuade him from the attack. In any event, they were too well acquainted with his ability to cope with any adversity to doubt his inherent capacity to respond. When the attackers advanced on their first foray they were met by volleys of arrows and stones. Orders were given to surround the rock mountain and occupy areas that offered some protection. Timur then set about to construct three redoubts or counter forts to make their presence more tenable.

In the next phase a tower of masonry and timber was being erected on the only blind side of the fortress. With rams and catapults in place, they proceeded to be activated in order to promote uneasiness in the defenders and to keep them from normal rest periods. Meanwhile Timur had sent for the most intrepid mountain climber in all of Tatary who, during one night, explored a way to the top which in turn, had an access possibility to the topmost peak. Using goat's blood from one captured on the meadow he marked his route down to the bottom.

Under cover of darkness on the following night the climber and three companions managed to drop silk ropes which, in turn, were attached to rope ladders. After a series of these were made fast, a party of fifty Turkomans and Persians were able to reach the plateau by daybreak. They managed to overpower the sleepy guards and with some losses, fought their way to the gate and opened it from within.

Like a dam bursting, the attackers poured in from the pathway with superior numbers and secured the lower level within hours. When the chances of survival at the higher level were deemed hopeless, the entire garrison collapsed. Many of the defenders were put to the sword as the women and children were sent to the countryside as virtual slaves. Back in the encampment the climbing team was given the greatest of rewards in treasures of all kinds. Before moving on Timur placed the most valorous of the Khorassan chiefs as administrator of Kurtin.

Leaving two divisions to make a sweep of northern Georgia, Timur retired to his encampment to spend several days in hunting the local game. While there he was petitioned by the Mufties, interpreters of the law, to no longer commit hostilities against the advocates of the true faith, the Prince of Georgia being so classified. Timur took this at face value and spared Malik Gurguin retribution that would normally been in store for him.

Promised gifts from the prince then arrived. Among them was a perfect ruby having roughly the equivalent of 432 carats. As further tribute the prince's agents presented Timur with one thousand gold pieces, all struck bearing his name. On his march back to Tiflis many Christian monasteries and churches were destroyed. The Mufties declared these acts as lawful because no individual was involved in violence.

For some time the rebuilding of the city of Beylekaun* had been in Timur's mind. Having been thoroughly destroyed by the Turkomans, it required restoration from the ground up. He spent

---

* lying between the Rivers Araxes and Kur in the eastern Karabagh

several weeks in the vicinity to oversee his engineer corps and group of architects. It was a monumental accomplishment as cold rain hampered their efforts. When completed the walls measured a little over a mile in circumference and thirty five feet high. As a final touch a canal was dug to bring water from the Araxes River, a project requiring about twenty one miles of difficult digging.

As he often did, Timur wintered over in the Karabagh. One uprising in the Mazanderan was put down by the army stationed at Rei. News of the treachery involved in the death of Nur-ul-werd (the splendor of the robe) reached Timur at this time. As the son of Sultan Ahmed, it once again set the area around his territory in some turmoil.

By the end of this latest campaign many prisoners had accumulated and had become a burden upon the fluidity of the army. After much deliberation it was decided that the most expedient act was to send them all back to portions of Persia where they could be of help in the repatriation of areas under the imperial standard. Little is known of the success of this move because all of the attention was directed to the east, particularly in the capital city of Samarkand.

When Timur departed from his homeland for the expedition to the west he had anticipated being gone for a period of seven years. In his absence the many captive skilled workers were directed to beautify the capital city in all attainable ways. His eclectic army also contained many captives who were battle tested and had pledged loyalty to him. All of the nobles and officers had been asked to bring their wives and/or concubines on this protracted expedition.

In the deep recesses of his mind Timur had been formulating his last great battle plan, the invasion of Cathay. It was first brought to his mind forcefully back in 1399 when the Emperor Hung Wu was succeeded by his grandson. His decision to first conquer northern Hindustan set these plans aside, and the events in the western reaches of his empire had further postponed the incursion to the far east. Now in the year 1403 the new Emperor Yung La had sent an insolent message to Timur which prompted a renewed pledge of power extension.

The message of tribute as demanded by the young emperor of Cathay had been started on its way while Timur was still engaged in Anatolia. The town of Yarkand on the extreme western frontier of Cathay was considered a journey of five months and from the newly established capital in Pekin, somewhat longer. From Yarkand to Samarkand was normally a trip requiring several weeks in addition. Timur was caught up in the details of planning for the thousands of workmen who were engaged in making Samarkand the physical capital of the world.

Early in 1404 Timur decided to put into motion some ideas which were intended to strengthen the empire, among them the appointment of his old friend Shaikh Nur-ad-din to administer all of southwest Persia with headquarters in Baghdad. While still encamped on the Oghluk River he received his grandson Khalil Sultan who reported that there was excellent stability in Samarkand. Restless with inactivity, Timur took his army first to Ardebil, near the Caspian Sea, and then to Sultanieh, where he arrived on the last day of April.

Soon after arriving in the city he received a request from his veteran commander Shaikh Nur-ad-din asking that his disgraced son Miran Shah be allowed to join him in Baghdad. Timur did not honor this request but did recant and install his son back in charge of Sultanieh along with a large sum of money to keep him in a comfortable lifestyle. His head injury seemed to have long since failed to inhibit his behavior.

Now, wishing to return to Samarkand, Timur sent most of the baggage on ahead before starting eastward. The army passed by the ruins of the fortress near Demavund, located at the foot of a mountain bearing the same name. After putting his engineers to work to restore it he left Mazanderan and went on to Feyrouzkouh, in the Khorassan. Here he came across a fortress that had never submitted to his rule, having been passed by on several occasions. By this time his reputation paved the way for an easy surrender.

Leaving a protective garrison behind, the army continued eastward and Timur sent on the remainder of his imperial family with them. Shah Rukh had been laboring under a lingering sickness and was sent to Herat to be tended to by his own physicians. Timur reluctantly postponed his return to Samarkand in order to follow up on the defection of his grandson Meerza Eskander who was hiding out near the Caspian Sea. Omar Shaikh's third son eventually outdistanced Timur who had to withdraw in a continuing rain storm. He then sent Meerza Rustum, the older brother, to track down the errant amir and headed eastward once more.

Shah Rukh, once recovered from his illness, met his father near the city of Merv to assure him that he was ready to assume his full duties. As Timur neared Balkh he was met by a stream of magistrates who were anxious to present themselves in his presence. By the time the imperial army reached Ak Serai, Timur, feeling the strain of the extended campaign, decided to tarry for awhile at the White Palace.

Once again on its way the army accelerated their march in order to arrive at the capital as soon as possible. Timur was met by his great grandson Meerza Keydou, first born of Pir Muhammed and now eight years old. It took many hours for all of the courtiers to pay their respects and give thanks for his safe return. One of his first official acts was to visit the college erected in the memory of Muhammed Sultan.

Again the strain of administration was telling on the great monarch as he was seized by an attack which was now becoming more frequent This time he was taken to the house of Princess Touman Agha and was nursed back to health in a little over a week. Returning to his own favorite garden he spent several days in supervising the gardener's work. On the third day news was brought to him of the birth of a grandson who was named Hussein, the son of his daughter Aukia Bekki.

At this time Timur called his primary scribe, Nizam Shami, and dismissed him to return to his place of birth in Tabriz. Having completed the historical work in a style dictated by Timur up to the year 1404, it was the monarch himself who gave title to this famous tome; he declared it should bear the name *Zafar Namah,* or *The Book of Victory.*

Once more involved with the memory of Muhammed Sultan, Timur directed his architects to start building a mausoleum in conjunction with the college. They were commissioned to use white marble, to be inlaid with gold and lapis lazuli. This building was then to be surrounded by an extensive garden area. He also ordered an enlarged gallery at the large mosque built after his return from Hindustan. This structure, erected in honor of his favorite wife Mulkh Khanum, became part of the large group of magnificent buildings commonly known as the Bibi Khanum.

While in Angora Timur had sent a message to the King of Spain requesting diplomatic relations. On May 21, 1403, Ruy Gonzalez de Clavijo left from Seville with some attendants to journey to the court of Timur. Don Henry, King of Castile and Leon sent a message which only arrived with his ambassador in August of 1403. One of the attendants had perished on the long journey. When ushered into Timur's presence, de Clavijo was asked to come closer in order to be recognized. The great amir's eyesight was increasingly failing and he had to view people through drooping eyelids.

When the pleasantries were exchanged Timur asked the ambassador: "How is my son* the king? Is he in good health?" Later continued with "Behold! here are the ambassadors sent to me by my son, the King of Spain, who is the greatest King of the Franks and lives at the end of the world. These Franks are truly a great people and I will give my benediction to the King of Spain, my son. It would have sufficed if he had sent you to me with a letter, and without the presents, so well satisfied am I to hear of his health and prosperous state."

In the letter from Don Henry to Timur which accompanied the gifts the greeting was directed to: "The Lord of Mongolia, Northern Hindustan, the Khorassan, Persia, Media, Derbent, Armenia, Land of Khwarazm, Arzingan, Erzernam, Kurdistan, Damascus, Aleppo, Babylonia, Baldes and Anatolia." It was quite clear that all of Europe was well acquainted with the exploits of the great monarch and were anxious to pay tribute to him.

---

* an endearing term only; Timur has apparently confused the two kingdoms

The first version of the mausoleum Gur Amir, completed in 1404, was not grand enough for Timur. He had it rebuilt on the scale of the Bibi Khanum in a purported two weeks flat. The outer dome was thirty-two meters high and the inner one eighteen meters. It carried Kufic inscriptions ten meters high which read: "There is no God but Allah and Muhammed is his prophet." Under this was an octagonal hall with two cenotaphs of white marble and one of jade. They included Timur's oldest son Jahanghir, his second son Omar Shaikh and his grandson Muhammed Sultan.

Timur little knew that his own sarcophagus would be the central point of interest in a few years to come. On my visit in 1995 the Gur Amir had been restored to its original grandeur, with all its blue, gold and white decor in magnificent splendor.

# 18

## The Samarkand Years

*A weary warrior mounts his horse,*
*As years of strife have run its course;*
*Back home with all your tired band,*
*To your beloved Samarkand.*

Comprehensive improvement of Samarkand was always part
of the grand plan for the empire. After the completion of the
beautiful blue and gold tomb built for his sons and grandsons,
Timur set about to tear down much of the residential section in
order to widen the streets and upgrade the houses. Also in the
expanded plan was a provision for an extensive market area to
accommodate merchandise coming in from all over Asia and the
Middle East.

As houses were pulled down consternation followed closely
behind. There was an urgent compulsion involved as work was
ordered to progress day and night. Many of the owners whose
houses were being razed complained that they were not being
compensated properly. Upon hearing this Timur first flew into a
rage, then became quite temperate as he said: "This city is mine as
I paid for it with all my possessions, and I have the letters for it
which I shall show you tomorrow, and if it is right I will pay the
people as you desire."

This declaration was closely followed by the appointment of a holy man called Cayris who was to evaluate each claim and make appropriate allotments of land and money to the deserving. That portion of the city which was set aside for an international market was covered with a vaulted roof, all containing fountains and gardens at regular intervals. Having completed his project in record time, Timur was so pleased that he rewarded his architects and primary builders with handsome gifts.

When the emissary of Don Henry, King of Castile, arrived in 1403, his prosaic description of Samarkand became the classic version for historians to follow. Ruy Gonzalez de Clavijo writes in part, as follows: "The city is so large and so abundantly supplied, that it is wonderful; and the name of Samarkand, or Cimesquinte, is derived from the two words "cimes" (great), and "Quinte" (a town). The supplies of this city do not consist of food alone, but of silks, satins, gauzes, taffetas, velvets and other things.

"The lord (Timur) had so strong a desire to ennoble this city, that he brought captives to increase its population, from every land which he had conquered, especially all those who were skillful in any art. From Damascus he brought weavers of silk, and men who made bows, glass and earthenware, so that, of those articles, Samarkand produced the best in the world. From Anatolia he brought archers, masons and silversmiths. He also brought men skilled in making engines of war; and he sowed hemp and flax, which had never before been seen in the land.

"There was so great a number of people brought to this city, from all parts, both men and women, that they are said to have amounted to one hundred and fifty thousand persons, of many nations; Turks, Arabs, Moors, Christian Armenians, Greek Catholics and Jacobites, and those who baptize with fire in the face (Brahmins), who are Christians with peculiar opinions. There was such a multitude of these people that the city was not large enough to hold them, and it was wonderful what a number lived under trees, and in caves outside.

"The city was also very rich in merchandise which came from other parts. Russia and Anatolia sent linens and skins; Cathay sent silks, which were the best in the world, (more especially the satins), and musk, which was found in no other part of the world, rubies and diamonds, pearls and rhubarb, and many other things...."

When Timur returned from his winter quarters with the bulk of his army he declared that a festival of two moons duration be prepared. He was to receive the ambassadors from twenty countries, even the Moghuls. Upon arrival, each in turn had long talks with Timur, followed by an exchange of precious gifts.

The description, again by Don Henry's ambassador, is the most comprehensive as he writes: "Lord Timur was seated in a portal, in front of the entrance of a beautiful palace, and he was sitting on the ground. Before him was a fountain where red apples floated, and which threw up the water very high. The lord was seated cross legged on silken embroidered carpets among round pillows. He wore a robe of silk with a high white hat on his head on the top of the hat a spinel* ruby with pearls and precious stones round it."

The princes attended their amir and were obliged to lead each ambassador closer to him because of his failing eyesight. One bit of protocol ensued which Timur quickly corrected. When he saw that the envoy from the Emperor of Cathay was seated above the others he changed their places declaring: "The envoy of Cathay is a thief and a bad man." This pronouncement paved the way for his last expedition—the ambitious move to confront the Ming Emperor.

After the ambassadors had left his court Timur longed for one more incursion into the southern Khiva desert. This time it was not to put down a rebellion but to make inspections. That part of the Khiva and Khwarazm to the west was peopled largely by Turkomans of the Sunni sect. They were conspicuous by the armaments they carried; a ten foot spear, longer than normal sword.

It was customary for these people of Turkish extract to use bright embroidery on their saddles which were also embossed with silver. They used tents by choice, ignoring more permanent homes by saying: "A coward builds a tower to hide in." They often kept

---

* actually one of the world's largest red magnesia spinels of 361 carats

trained hawks for hunting tied to their tent poles and usually housed dogs in their felt shelters for company.

Perhaps their most unusual custom was to drink spirits from the skull of a conquered foe. Some of these were heavily decorated and were treated with considerable deference, sometimes weeping during a toast to a departed companion. Their favorite drink was mare's milk laced with spirits. Although they revered their horses it was often their source of meat, together with expendable camels.

This sect also was known for their tireless journeys which often exceeded eighty miles in a day. Their foes feared to be captured by them because they habitually tied prisoners to their saddle bows and tortured them. Just short of death, they would finally cut them down, only to be taken to the slave markets.

It was on another expedition to the south when his compassion surfaced again as Timur came upon a family while returning to Samarkand in July of 1404. He had stopped at Salugar Sujassa, a desert town near Merv, where he discovered that the Caxis (lord) had died and left two small children. He wasted no time in seeing that they were brought back to Samarkand as his wards, to be placed in special education so that they could be given the opportunity to lead the life of their choice.

During early September, Timur spent some time in the gardens that he had dedicated to several of his wives, this time at one called Baghi Ginar. He had ordered a feast to be prepared on the 15th of the month to which all ambassadors in residence were invited. The gardens had been outfitted with wooden terraces which were covered by awnings of red cloth and varicolored silks. In the center of each courtyard was a pond shaded by elms and poplars where jets of water motivated crimson and gold balls, as in suspension.

The royal architects had designed a beautiful house in the center of the garden which was built in the shape of a cross. Its walls were lined with glazed tiles fashioned by Syrian artisans and a special high dais in place near the entrance where Timur was seated on gold embroidered silks. On each side of the vaulted doorway were rich trappings mounted on canted poles.

The ambassadors arrived very late but were escorted through the rooms of the regal house and then dined at a tardy hour. The main feast had terminated long before as the meerzas in charge of invitations and selected interpreters had failed to have their guests arrive on schedule. Timur was understandably enraged and threatened reprisals which were later ameliorated to merely verbal chastises.

To make up for the misunderstanding the ambassadors were again invited a week later, this time arriving at the appointed time. This second feast was held at a different location outside the city proper and was in a garden setting called Baghi No (new garden). This one featured four high corner towers and high walls, a more austere setting than the one of the week previous. The central house, however, was decorated as before in ebony and ivory to give the event a festive setting.

The meal consisted mostly of roasted horses and sheep served with au jus rice and accompanied by spicy tarts. As soon as the feasting was concluded one of Timur's meerzas arrived with a heavy basin filled with silver coins which were scattered over the attending ambassadors and nobles. After this ceremony the ambassadors were given new robes of embroidered cloth. This was the plan that had to be postponed because of faulty courtiers.

Toward the conclusion of this celebration and feast Timur ordered wine served to all by servants on bended knee. As per custom they did not allow any of the guest's cups to become empty in spite of the normal prohibition as laid down by Islamic law. It was felt that no proper feast could be successful if the participants did not end up in a drunken state.

The expected amenities at an end, Timur felt free to pursue his inspection once again. After a brief excursion northwest of the city he returned to Samarkand where he visited the chapel which had been built for Mulkh Khanum's deceased mother. Apprised of a new group of envoys, Timur hosted them in the ornate setting of special houses located near the chapel.

His obvious ploy was to accentuate the proffered good will of those who could be most helpful for his forthcoming grand campaign. Timur had been casting about for a replacement from the Chingisid line for a traditional new khan. He had been advised that the people's favorite at the time was the grandson of Toktamish. Those that had come to Timur with this petition in mind were kept in their quarters outside the city for a period of two days, a dictate of the old Mongol custom. On the third day he received them with all their offerings.

Once again a feast was prepared, this time on the plains of Kani Gil (Rose Mine) where the entire contingent was encamped. The centerpiece was a large red pavilion supported by twelve large poles decorated in gold and blue, topped with copper balls and Islamic crescents. The floor was also carpeted in red with many streamers hanging from the roof to accent the large assortment of gold embroidered silken drapes.

Eleven royal tents with expansive awnings were set up for the household of Timur. They were decorated with colorful tapestries and shag velvet, some lined with ermine and squirrel pelts. Mulkh Khanum's special pavilion was fronted with double doors taken from Bayazid's treasure at Brusa, high enough to allow a mounted horseman to pass through. A tree of gold decorated with many precious stones and animated by golden birds in various poses was on display.

When all had assembled there were emissaries from Cathay, Mongolia, Hindustan, Muscovy, Irak, Syria, Mesopotamia, Egypt, Spain, Anatolia and Byzantium. Timur was able to count thirty four princes and sixteen princesses from his immediate family of two generations. In order to take advantage of this unprecedented gathering a mass wedding was to take place, some with the scions of Timur and their families. All were ritualistically dressed and undressed nine times, in different adornment according to custom. During each change they were sprinkled with gold coins and/or gem stones which were allowed to fall to the floor, to be picked up at the end of the ceremony.

After the feast was concluded Timur's close friend Shaikh Nur-ad-din presented him with a number of silver strands where presents were offered in groups of nine, the traditional number.

Nearly all the gifts were given in turn to the nobles, followed by the ubiquitous shower of coins.

After the departure of the envoys Timur presided over his council of lords at which time he was also to celebrate marriages of two grandsons, Ulugh Beg and Ibrahim Sultan, to selected brides of nobility. This more private celebration lasted for several days where the women attendants were dressed like goats and fairies to entertain the council with frivolity and cavorting. Tradesmen demonstrated their particular skills as others dressed as lions and foxes to add to the nonsense aura of the occasion.

A more somber theme followed the feasting as gallows were erected to punish a chief magistrate who had vacated his post for over six years, neglecting his duties in the process. Other officers of the state were hanged for various offenses ranging from embezzlement to cheating their fellow citizens. Those of lesser status who had broken the law to an extent that merited them the death penalty were beheaded. The pall cast over the festivities because of these events was quickly forgotten when the court resumed with another round of feasting.

Timur chose this time to present his obviously favorite grandson Pir Muhammed to the council. The apparent heir to the throne dressed himself in blue satin embroidered with gold symbols. His hat was adorned with pearls and precious stones, topped with a brilliant ruby. The prince was described as of dark complexion and clean shaven. At twenty two years of age he carried himself in a regal manner and appeared to have managed his post as governor of North Hindustan in a wise and even handed manner.

During the ceremony Timur's wife Mulkh Khanum cut such an imposing figure that historians were able to describe her finally in some detail. Long ago she had been given the title of queen, even though her husband had never assigned himself one beyond that of amir. When she was presented to the assembled nobles she wore the traditional red silk robe which was sleeveless but long and flowing, requiring a bevy of attendants to hold up the train. Over her veiled face she wore a crested headdress adorned with pearls, rubies and emeralds which was topped by a miniature stylized castle. Her shoulder length jet black hair was largely obscured by the nature of the adornment.

Although attended by a number of eunuchs, it was the number of court ladies which attracted the most attention. Following behind the canopy holders were some 300 of them. After Mulkh Khanum was seated the lesser wives filed in and took their seats in rank order. All of the court ladies were given a cup of ceremonial wine before being finally dismissed.

At the end of the feasting and wining the amirs, governors and army commanders were convened in a grand koureltay of state. The only high ranking amir to be exempted was Shah Rukh. The reason given was that he was considered too important to his government, however, it was significant that he had already opposed the under-lying movement to annex Cathay into the empire. The importance of this particular meeting was underscored when even the Malik of Egypt was a prominent attendee.

Positive statements on the need to invade Cathay brought mixed emotions from the assembled top level koureltay members. Most of the doubts centered around the health of Timur and his ability to personally see it through, but this feeling could not be expressed in light of his previous exploits and dominant spirit.

Those in favor of this master plan followed two separate trains of thought. The young Malik Faredje of Egypt, together with a few others from Asia Minor, could foresee a possible failure which would strengthen their hand or even restore their autonomous rule. Princes from the imperial family sided with Timur in the hopes that this final jewel to be added to the empire would place them in a superior power structure. The top echelon from the army voiced only a few apprehensions but all were short of any expressed caveats.

As it transpired, Timur had already made his decision to prepare for war, the departing council members painfully aware that they were to be called upon for maximum support. The great conqueror seemed to have been inspired by the prospect as he hastened off to put into effect the many logistic plans that had long been in the recesses of his mind.

Timur's first move was to evaluate each division of his vast army as to their precise numbers and accoutrements, down to their individual supply needs. When all preliminary arrangements were made he sent Pir Muhammed by way of Herat and Kandahar to the Goug Sarai, or Blue Palace, to set up headquarters. His generals were sent out in all directions to recruit from the empire. They were charged with proselytizing in the Khwarazm, Turkestan, Balkh, Buddulestan, Mazanderan, Khorassan, even the tribes transplanted from Anatolia.

Long before the recruiting started to materialize Timur was pleased to find that the head count exceeded 800,000. The various armies were assembling in their winter quarters which ranged from Taushkend in the north to Kabul in the south.

An incident arose at this time which was kept somewhat of a secret because of family prestige. Miran Shah's son Khalil Sultan had found a desirable concubine from the harem of the late Saif-ud-din which he favored to the exclusion of his wives. When she turned up among the courtiers a formal complaint was made with a recommendation that she be put to death. Timur believed that this would settle the matter quickly, but it was only after she went into hiding and Khalil pleaded with his grandfather to spare her, and after a promise of discretion, that the order was rescinded.

Impatience was overcoming Timur as he discarded the advice of his generals and some nobles to precipitate the march eastward as the winter weather was threatening to close in. His eldest sons and several grandsons were already in their stations to govern while he was away. He felt it necessary to address a special assembly of two hundred, a sort of development of his reasoning, in order that he would receive the maximum of support for this most ambitious of undertakings.

The die was cast. Timur's indefatigable spirit would not dictate otherwise. His entire life had been defined by reaching distant goals which were a part of his destiny as the "Lord of the Grand Conjunctions." As in the case of the dedicated mountain climber when asked why he pursued such a dangerous activity; the classic answer has been; "Because it is there."

# 19

## The Fateful March

*A winter wind blows hard and cold;*
*The flesh is weak, tho you be bold.*
*Life's hourglass has all run out*
*And you have stormed your last redoubt.*

Since the dynasty founded by Chinghis Khan had been expelled from Cathay, Timur felt that it was his duty, indeed his Tatar honor, to reinstate the Chingasid line back into power. His family elders were given their respective kingdoms and the younger members an imperial wedding ceremony, all in preparation for his extended absence from Samarkand.

Timur's favorite scribe preserved his speech to the assembly of nobles, later translated as follows, in part:

"He had not been able, he observed, to effect the vast conquests he had made without some violence, and the destruction of a great number of true believers, but he added, 'I am now resolved to perform a good and a great action, which will be as an expiation of all my sins. I mean to exterminate the idolaters of Cathay: and you, my dear companions! you who have been the instruments of many of my crimes, shall share in the merit of this great work of repentance. We will proceed to this holy war; we will slay the infidels; mosques shall everywhere rise on the ruins of their vile temples: and the Koran has told us, "that good works efface the sins of this world." ' "

Timur, dressed in his winter garb, rode out from Samarkand on November 26, 1404 at the head of his favorite division of Tatars. That night they encamped at Karabulauk,some forty five miles from his capital. After two days of regrouping they moved on to Tablik as the winter snows were already setting in. Blizzard conditions forced the army to halt at Auksulaut where cantonments had already been put into place. This storm was to be the vanguard of one of the fiercest winters to hit Transoxania in decades.

The governor of the fortress of Aspora had been ordered to grind grain into meal on a round-the-clock basis but the freezing weather had stalled the wheels into an inert state. As the advance army had to halt, supplies kept coming from Samarkand which were sent forward when progress was possible. Reports of men and horses dying did not deter Timur as he wished to push his legions as far to the northeast as was physically possible. The element of surprise could only be achieved if he could launch the attack the following spring from well inside Cathay.

Timur ordered outer coverings to be prepared for the felt tents and double breastplates to be forged. When his commanders revealed their increasing disquietude he summoned them saying: "Do not be anxious about the injuries of winter; truly this is refreshment and safety." Five hundred wagons armored with iron had been assembled, some of which were filled with seed corn to be sowed when the snow melted to supply his warriors on their return through barren land. Thousands of foal camels accompanied the army so that they could provide milk when needed.

When the order came to push ahead there was considerable unrest but the massive army responded with blind faith. Advance units were sent ahead to trample the snow so that the cattle and reserve horses could proceed at a somewhat normal pace. Most of the supply wagons and heavy armament followed at a slower rate in the rear.

By the time the main army reached the Jaxartes River reports of losses in the horses and livestock reached an alarming state. The river was frozen to a depth of three feet and was easily crossed with the heaviest of wagons. There was adequate housing and relative safety in Taushkend for the top echelon of officers, while the amirs and nobles found refuge in the imperial buildings.

The court had set up in the governor's palace (Berdi Bek) as Timur set out almost immediately to see about his army's comfort. Upon his return to his headquarters he was given the news that Khalil Sultan's concubine had arrived in the city some time before and was settled in at a comfortable site. She was ordered to be bound and brought to him as he vowed to settle this troubling matter once and for all. Upon discovering that she was several months pregnant, he was forced to relent and placed her in the care of a trusted court lady. In the meantime Khalil Sultan was still far behind with the heavy baggage and was not due to arrive for over a week.

At this time Kara Khoudjah, the envoy of exiled Toktamish Khan, found his way to the imperial court. He was pleading for atonement and stating that enough suffering had resulted from being made a fugitive. Timur's answer was a tentative one which postponed any decision until his return from the great expedition.

It was well into January when the decision to push on to Otrar was made. This principle city was down river some 150 miles near the junction with the Pamir River. Only advanced units made the trek as most of the army was to follow when the roads became more passable. Reports of snow depths up to two spear lengths did not deter the elite units from plunging on.

Timur's several divisions reached Otrar on January 13, 1405. He was housed in the palace where he developed a severe chest congestion followed by a rise in body temperature. He nevertheless made the rounds of his men's quarters to try and bring them a bit of cheer. With the reduced number of men he was able to house most of them in more permanent quarters. A fire which destroyed part of the palace roof was interpreted as a bad omen, however, Timur shrugged it off.

Perhaps the most colorful description of Timur's plight in the throes of an exceedingly severe winter came from the pen of Gonzalez de Clavijo as he fancied the thoughts of the elements themselves. The following account of this was later presented by Timur's greatest detractor, Ahmed Ibn Arabshah, as he paraphrased it in the following manner: "How long shall hearts be burned by your fire, and breasts consumed by your heat and ardor? If you are one of the infernal spirits, I am the other; we are both old and have grown weak while destroying countries and men; you should take, therefore, an ill omen for yourself from the conjunction of two unfavorable planets*; if you have slain souls and frozen men's breath, truly the breaths of my frost are far colder than yours; or if among your horsemen are men who have stripped the hair of Muslims by torment and pierced them with arrows and deafened them, truly in my time by the help of God there was that made more deaf and naked. Nor by Allah! will I use pretense with you; therefore, mark my warning and by Allah! the heat of piled coals shall not defend you from the frost of death nor shall fire blazing in the brazier."

Several physicians were in attendance at all times to treat Timur's rising fever. At first he was given arrack, a spirit made from the fermentation of coconut derivative with sugar and various spices. He drank copious amounts of this liquor but other disturbing symptoms were developing, all of which were lumped together and described as the ague. For the first time Timur showed signs of realizing his predicament was life threatening.

Timur's favorite physician Mevlana Fazlullah finally declared the monarch in a near hopeless state. The ranking amirs were advised that time was running out for their lord and that they should make appropriate preparations for his eventual demise. They reluctantly approached the ailing monarch with admonitions of providing for the continuity of the dynasty. To their surprise he did not protest but called for his scribes to come to his side. Timur had assured himself that his soul would "pass from its terrestrial mansions of pride to the heavenly paradise of eternal delights." He had conveniently ignored the conjunction of unfavorable planets to pursue his last wish of conquest.

---

* the baneful portent in the conjunction of Saturn and Mars

When the amirs were assembled in his presence Timur departed from his normal straightforward manner and became an enigmatic conversant. He held up two fingers and asked how this should be interpreted. One amir suggested that he would be on the road to recovery in two days and another opined that two successive treatments would be required to effect a return to more robust health.

Timur gravely shook his head and announced that he had but two more days of life. There was an immediate response of grief as all of those present fell on their knees with protestations of disbelief. From the attendant scribes the following translation accounts faithfully for his actual words on this occasion:

"I know for the bird of my soul will soon leave the cage of my soul and that my refuge lies by the throne of God, who gives and takes life, when he wishes so. I entrust you now to his mercy. It is imperative that you do not shout and moan about my death, because they will not have any use. Who do ever deflect death by shouting? Instead of tearing your clothes and running like madmen, ask God to have mercy on me and read from the holy book so my soul can rejoice. God was kind to me and allowed me to establish good laws upon my lands, and now in all states of Persia and Turan* nobody can hurt another, the rich cannot prosecute the poor, and all this gives me hope, that during my reign I did not allow the mighty to suppress the weak, at least I was not told otherwise. Although I know that this world is volatile and will not be true to my wishes, but nevertheless I do not advise you to willfully leave this world, for this will cause unrest among the people and threaten safety on the roads and hence disrupt peace amongst our people. And on Judgement Day we'll be asked to be responsible for it."

On the following day Timur was attended by his queen, Mulkh Khanum, and several other family members. There was a clarity of destiny which penetrated the throes of the rising fever. He was immersed in a reverie of the yesteryears and was said to have deplored some of his earlier actions. For those transgressions he

* the old name for a portion of northern Khorassan and part of Transoxania

implored the forgiveness of Allah and asked that portions of the Koran be read to him. At times he silenced his attendants and quoted sections on his own which had long been embedded in his memory. From time to time he drifted off into periods of incoherence as his voice lowered to the extent that those at his bedside strained to hear every word.

Once again the scribes and amirs were asked to attend the failing monarch as he wished to make his final proclamation and bind his closest nobles to swear final allegiance. In a labored voice he dispatched the following:

"I pronounce my grandson Pir Mohammed, son of Jahanghir, absolute heir and successor to my throne, and to the imperial dignity. To him, therefore, it behooves you all to submit yourselves with zeal and fidelity, cautiously abstaining from these contentious animosities, which must compromise the peace and welfare of so many nations, and finally subvert to the foundations, that superb fabric of government, which it has cost me so many years of painful exertion to erect. I demand that all present shall pledge themselves to confirm to these arrangements of our common faith; and that the generals of the troops that are absent shall bind themselves under the same solemn obligations, not to defeat the object of these, my last commands."

All of the nobility present then crowded around his bed with tears streaming down their cheeks, each in turn, pledging their confirmation to the end that every day of their lives would be sacrificed to the preservation of their venerated sovereign's wishes. They then sought to bring Khalil Sultan and the other generals in the vicinity to Timur's presence that they might all pledge to keep the words of his last wishes inviolate.

In his kaleidoscope of fleeting memories Timur was apparently reliving his varied life; his escape at birth from the vengeance of his uncle Hadji, the brush with death in his youth when rescued by nomads, his wife Aljai and her stoical resistance when prisoners in the desert of Khiva, his crippling wounds in the Seistan followed by a tortuous way back to health and power, his continued trouble with the Mongol khan Toktamish, his point of no return and subsequent victory in the Kiptchak, his satiation with carnage in the conquest of Hindustan, his crowning achievement with victory over Bayazid, his loss of loved ones and the return to his capital, Samarkand, it was all slipping away....

Timur, realizing that his moments of life were rapidly diminishing, reminded his nobles that the presence of the missing commanders was not of such material importance and that they would meet again in the hereafter. While he was still able to speak lucidly he said that he had nothing more to wish for in the world other than the opportunity of consoling his eyes with the sight of his wonderful son, Shah Rukh.

In the waning moments of his life Timur brought himself to advise the princes about their future conduct, in particular, the wisdom of a fraternal union where they were to carry their swords in honor. There were then periods of time when his voice would trail off and then in his final moments he seemed to be quoting from the Koran. He was also heard to say in a halting manner: "I lost my senses, and resigned my pure soul to the Almighty and Holy Creator. I desire that this, my testament, and whatever I shall say to the last moment of my existence, shall be written in my memoirs as if proceeding from my own mouth." According to some, his last words were said to be a gesture of humility: "Only a stone and my name on it."

The Mullah Heibetullah performed the dying rites in the early evening of February 17 as Timur breathed his last, amid clouds of incense and weeping attendants. Several priests behind the door were intoning: "There is no God but Allah." Timur left a prodigious number of sons, grandsons and great grandsons—thirty six in number, thus fulfilling the prophecy of the old khizr he met in his youth. The dynasty that he founded was so far flung that only a strong willed ruler with an indefatigable constitution and endless tactical abilities could hold it together. This high tide of empire has never been matched since Timur's time and likely never will again.

With great sorrow the carpenters built a coffin of simple wood and the body was embalmed with resins and herbs. News of his demise was not dispatched to the populace and army as the nobles debated the impact of the dreaded news. After several days Amir Shah Malik and Shaikh Nur-ad-din sent out the word to all the members of the imperial family.

The body arrived in Samarkand after a forced march on February 25 and was taken to the Madrasa Mohammed Sultan, having covered over 300 miles in the dead of winter. Hadji Yussuf, in charge of the body, requested that family members not wear somber clothes for the first day after arrival in order to perpetuate security on the dismal news. The actual religious ceremony at the place of temporary burial was shortened to preserve the clandestine nature of the affair. The madrasa was not in use as a scholastic building at that time and it was to serve as an interim mausoleum until the Gur Amir was suitably prepared for its illustrious occupant in 1409.

Sensing Timur's last wishes, although not clearly stated, the generals and amirs present at the last rites set the army in motion toward Cathay. Their first encampment was only four miles from Otrar where Sultan Hussein, son of Aukia Bekki (Timur's daughter) sent immediate word to disperse the army. Second in command, Ibrahim Sultan, and the rest of the amirs were very much relieved for they had no stomach for the invasion. At that time Pir Mohammed was far away at Shiraz and was not able to participate in any decision making.

This was a time of confusion as two pretenders to the throne were on their way to Samarkand. Sultan Hussein, who gave the order to withdraw, and Khalil Sultan, the second, who was closest to the city of Samarkand as he hurried from his headquarters at Taushkend. When Shah Malik arrived in Samarkand after leaving Shaikh Nur-ad-din to stopover at Karajek, he found the gates barred against him. The forces of intrigue were already set into motion.

Khalil Sultan, the first to return, had coerced the governor Argha Shah through promises of support to yield to him. Entreaties to the governor by the two imperial envoys were ignored, and the amirs of the army under Rustum Toghai Bougha (son of Omar Shaikh) decided to support Khalil in his bid for the throne. The two armies of the north were forced to withdraw to Bokhara and prepare for a possible attack.

Even though apprised of Timur's last wish to elevate Pir Mohammed to be his successor, Khalil had built his power base carefully enough to defy organized resistance. When the keys to Samarkand were turned over to him, fear of reprisal brought enough of the amirs over to his side to assure a successful coup. As a token to bolster legitimacy, Pir Mohammed was named Prince of the Chaghatays in absentia.

Shah Rukh, upon hearing of these proceedings, immediately proclaimed himself sovereign of all of the Khorassan and found quick recognition with the populace. To this he added all of the Seistan and Mazanderan. This transfer of power was consummated by the end of March, 1405. Back in Samarkand it became the lot of the two faithful amirs to enter Timur's old pavilion and break his standard—the horsetail surmounted by a half moon. His great kettle drum which had sounded many a battle cry was also broken in the solemn ceremony.

It was the mistress deplored by Timur who was said to be the downfall of Khalil Sultan. The citizens of Samarkand saw, with disgust, a woman of low birth and dissolute character passing in eminence the numbers of high born. She was paraded through the streets in chains as insults were shouted from all sides.

When Shah Rukh was raised to the sultanate in 1408 he sympathized with his nephew Khalil and reinstated the concubine Shadulmulk as a bona fide princess. When the deposed monarch died in 1409 his princess struck a poniard to her heart to join her lover. Khalil and his princess were buried in the city of Rei, just north of the Great Salt Desert.

Pir Mohammed had indeed challenged the authority of Khalil Sultan to install himself as Timur's heir. Through internal treachery Pir Mohammed was assassinated by order of his own minister in 1407. Miran Shah had been residing in Azerbijan when he died in 1408. Shah Rukh continued to rule the shrinking empire until his demise in 1446. He was a brave and generous ruler but preferred to revert to the penchant of his youth, the science of learning. His son, Ulugh Beg, succeeded to the throne, to be later known as the "astronomy king." He became known also as the person responsible for the Persian calendar.

The vast land holdings that Timur had slowly built faded away in the wake of uprisings and personal intrigue. Only that portion consisting of north Hindustan survived well into the fifteenth century as the nearly pure heritage of the great conqueror. History has placed a veil over the terrors that spread from Egypt to the expanses of Siberia during Timur's time. The statue of the great warrior on his horse that stands in the park at Tashkent cannot reflect the dynamics or penetrate the glory that was Samarkand when it was the capital of a large part of the known world.

Timur's Memoirs, written in the Turki language (Chaghatay) were translated into Persian by Abu Talib Husaini between 1628 and 1637. Thirty years after Timur's death Sharaf-ud-din Yazdi wrote the celebrated *Zafar-nama,* or *Book of Victory.* He records that: "The third recommendation of this, my work, is its truthfulness, the exactness of Timur's life, both at home and abroad. Men of the highest character for learning, knowledge and goodness, were in attendance at the court of Timur, and a staff of them under the orders of the emperor wrote down an account of everything that occurred. The movements, actions and sayings of Timur, the various incidents and affairs of state, of religions and the ministers, were all recorded and written down with the greatest care. The most stringent commands were given that every event should be recorded exactly as it occurred, without any modification either in excess or diminution...."

Perhaps a feeling of mystique better serves the memory of Timur in light of his unusual innovations and occasional bursts of compassion. Without doubt, much emphasis should be placed on his ability to lead men and to command their absolute devotion, to overcome superior forces and to rise to every occasion without negative compunctions. It is fitting that he was to join the other three great men because of sheer magnitude—those who were also given the title of "Lord of the Grand Conjunctions."

# Epilogue

A dynasty that Timur envisioned never materialized. The three Amirs who always attended their lord were powerless to withstand the claim of Khalil Sultan, son of Miran Shah, and only twenty-two years of age. He was the only one in residence when the embalmed body of Timur was brought back to Samarkand. By methods of intrigue he consolidated the nobles to secure the army and the commanders were obliged to fall into line.

When Khalil ordered the deaths of the three faithful amirs to eliminate the last vestiges of opposition, two managed to escape to the Khorassan to be under the protection of Shah Rukh. Amir Botudo was beheaded and the remainder of the court assembled for the pretender's ascension to the throne.

The crowning of Khalil Sultan was consummated in March of 1405. His plundering of the treasury and dissipation of it to what was described as the "basest of profligates" thoroughly disgusted the remaining amirs and the deceased Timur's old friends. It was not until 1408, however, that the rightful heir to the throne was able to restore order and dignity in Samarkand. Under Shah Rukh there were a few years of stability while the empire gradually slipped away. Without the dynamic Amir of Tatary its destiny faltered and its dynasty eroded.

Unlike Caesar, the good was not interred with Timur in the eyes of many. Perhaps the best comprehensive, albeit tinged with goodwill, comes from Sharif-ad-din in his *The Book of Victories of Lord Timur the Splendid,* where he says, in part: "Courage raised him to be the Supreme Emperor of Tatary, and subjected all Asia to him, from the frontiers of Cathay to those of Greece...he governed the state himself, without availing himself of a minister; he succeeded in all his enterprises. To everyone he was generous and courteous, except to those who did not obey him — he punished them with the utmost rigor. He loved justice, and no one who played tyrant in his dominion went unpunished; he esteemed learning and learned men. He labored constantly to aid the fine arts. He was utterly courageous in planning and carrying out a plan. To those who served him, he was kind...."

In retrospect I am once again standing in the domed Gur Amir with the shafts of sunlight striking the ornate walls but failing to reach the slab of dark green nephrite jade which covers the sarcophagus. Below it lies the remains of what the world has come to know as Tamerlane, by any criterion, the ultimate warrior. Once again I recall his final words: "Only a stone and my name on it."

# Chronology

| | |
|---|---|
| 1204 | Crusaders capture Constantinople |
| 1211 | Chinghis Khan invades Cathay |
| 1215 | King John of England signs the Magna Carta |
| 1220-21 | Chinghis Khan invades Transoxania and Persia |
| 1227 | Death of Chinghis Khan |
| 1234 | Mongols overthrow the Sung Dynasty of northern Cathay |
| 1237 | Golden Horde invades northern Russia |
| 1250 | Death of German Emperor Frederick II |
| 1260 | Khubilay becomes great khan |
| 1261 | Byzantines recapture Constantinople from Crusaders |
| 1265 | Clement II named holy Roman Pope |
| 1275-92 | Marco Polo visits Cathay |
| 1279 | Khubilay Khan establishes the Yuan Dynasty in Cathay |
| 1307 | Edward II becomes King of England |
| 1322 | Charles IV becomes King of France |
| 1326 | Beginning of the Othman (Ottoman) empire |
| 1327 | Edward III crowned King of England |
| 1336 | Birth of Timur Beg in Sheri-Sebz, near Kesh |
| 1337 | Start of the 100 Year War between England and France |
| 1341 | Approximate time the "Black Death" reached Asia |
| 1342 | Uzbeg Khan of the Golden Horde dies |
| 1346 | First major battle of the 100 Year War |
| | Amir Khazagan takes over as king maker of Transoxania |
| 1355 | Timur marries Narmish Agha and Abjaz Turkhan Agha |
| 1356 | Timur's first and second sons born |
| | Timur's mother, Takhina Khanum, dies |
| 1357 | Ottoman Turks invade Europe |
| 1358 | Tugluk Khan threatens Transoxania |
| | Assassination of Amir Khazagan |
| 1359 | Timur joins Amir Hussein in invasion of Khorassan |

| | |
|---|---|
| 1361 | Timur's father, Teraghay Nevian, dies |
| | Timur gains leadership of his Barlas tribe |
| 1362 | Wounds sustained in Seistan cripple Timur |
| 1363 | Ilyas Khoja is defeated - Timur regains his homeland |
| 1364 | Charles V, from the House of Valoir, becomes King of France |
| 1365 | Timur's only defeat at the "Battle of the Mire" |
| 1366 | Abjaz Turkhan Agha dies |
| | Birth of Miran Shah, Timur's third son |
| 1368 | Birth of Shah Rukh, Timur's fourth son |
| | Yuan dynasty overthrown in Cathay — beginning of Ming |
| 1369 | Timur deposes Amir Hussein and is crowned ruler of Samarkand |
| 1370 | Timur proclaimed sovereign of the Chaghatay |
| | Roman throne restored |
| | Gregory XI becomes Pope |
| 1374 | Oldest son of Timur marries Khan Zada |
| 1375 | Defeat of the Jetes in Moghulstan |
| | Timur defeats army of Urus Khan of the White Horde |
| 1376 | Timur's oldest son and niece die |
| | Timur disbands the Jalayrs |
| 1377 | Young King Richard II placed on throne of England |
| 1378 | Yussuf Sufi lays siege to Samarkand and dies in battle |
| | Capture of Urganj by the Timurids |
| 1380 | Charles VI succeeds his father as King of France |
| | Toktamish becomes khan of Golden and White Hordes |
| 1381 | Destruction of Herat and further conquests in the Khorassan |
| 1382 | Timur invades the province of Mazanderan |
| 1383 | Conquest of Persia begins - Seistan again subdued |
| | Timur's wife Dilshad Agha and oldest sister die |
| 1384 | Invasion of eastern Persia — Urganj is sacked |
| 1385 | Capture of Tabriz in western Persia |
| 1386 | Timur invades Asia Minor |

| | |
|---|---|
| 1387 | Capture of Ispahan and Shiraz |
| | City of Van pillaged |
| 1388 | Timur returns to Transoxania to battle Toktamish |
| 1389 | Persia becomes part of Timur's empire |
| | Expedition to the Irtish and Yulduz |
| | Ottoman Turks defeat Serbians at the Battle of Kosovo |
| 1390 | Timur defeats Qamar-al-din and pursues Toktamish |
| 1391 | Toktamish defeated at Battle of Kunduzche |
| 1392 | Timur extirpates the Ismaelites of Persia |
| 1393 | The Muzaffars are defeated in Persia, Irak falls |
| | Omar Shaikh, Timur's second son dies in southwest Persia |
| 1394 | Birth of two grandsons; Ulugh Beg and Ibrahim Sultan |
| 1395 | Timur again invades Kiptchak |
| | Toktamish is defeated in the Battle of Terek |
| 1396 | Timur defeats the Georgians and returns to Samarkand |
| | Ottoman Turks defeat Crusaders at battle of Nicopolis |
| 1397 | Rebuilding program in Samarkand and Kesh |
| 1398 | Timur invades the Hindu Kush, enters Hindustan |
| 1399 | Capture of Dehli and Multan |
| | The famous mosque is built in Samarkand |
| | Henry IV becomes King of England |
| 1400 | Timur invades Syria and takes Aleppo |
| 1401 | Damascus and Baghdad occupied |
| 1402 | Invasion of Anatolia |
| | Destruction of Bayazid's army at the Battle of Angola |
| | Capture of Smyrna |
| 1403 | Timur sacks rebellious cities in Anatolia — Ephesus falls |
| | Timur's grandson and heir apparent, Muhammed Sultan, dies |
| 1404 | Timur deposes the Sultan of Babylon and Persia |
| 1405 | Cathay invasion begins |
| | Timur succumbs to illness and is entombed in Samarkand |

Khalil Sultan assumes rule of Samarkand and
Transoxania
Shah Rukh holds on to Khorassan, Seistan and
Mazanderan
1408    Khalil Sultan is deposed, Shah Rukh installed as ruler
of the remains of the Timurid empire

# Appendix A

## The Reconstruction of Timur

Through the newly developed science of forensics we learn of the physical details which handicapped Timur during his days as a mighty warrior. M. M. Gerasimov headed a team which exhumed the body of Timur in 1941 to discover the anatomical features which the body could disclose to the best clinicians in the U.S.S.R. Actually this same group also examined the remains of two of his sons, Miran Shah and Shah Rukh, along with two grandsons, Mohammed Sultan and Ulugh Beg. Details of these four are not pertinent to the historical accounts of Timur.

The Russian team described the crypt beneath the floor of the Gur Amir as being encased in grey sandstone with a carved monolith bearing symbols of the empire. Mortared stone slabs sealed the sarcophagus which contained a simple wood coffin. It was covered by a dark blue cloth, still emblazoned with embroidered quotations from the Koran.

An odor of embalming materials (described as conservatives) emanated from the coffin when it was unsealed. Timur's arms were placed alongside his body and his right cheek tilted toward Mecca. Mummified muscle tissue was still evident in the area of the head, neck, arms and legs. The head showed signs of having been heavily waxed, for it preserved his Mongol features in some dessicated detail.

Tall for his day, Timur's remains still measured 170 centimeters in length. His hair was uncommonly long, which would have been consistent for a particularly severe winter at the time of his death.

Although nearly all grey-white in the head area, his beard still displayed the brown tinged with reddishness that historians of his time ascribe to him.

Evidently the damage to Timur's right knee cap during the purported brush with a nomadic tribe during his youth was one that handicapped him for the greater part of his life. Definite enlargement and fusion of the joint into a partial bent configuration would account for a large measure of his lameness. It would seem that a quick removal of the penetrating arrow and a period of forced flight would have precluded a normal healing process.

Further damage was discovered to the muscle tissue of the upper right leg which penetrated as high as the hip bone on that side. This deformation then caused a compensatory misalignment of the backbone which was evident as far as the rib cage, forcing Timur to carry his left shoulder higher than his right.

The wounds sustained by Timur in the battle of the Seistan when he was just twenty-six years old were definitely confirmed. The arrow penetration into his right elbow seemed to easily be the more severe. Ossification of his joint at the elbow showed considerable enlargement, a factor in the near immobilization leading to a crooked configuration which persisted during his lifetime. As a result of this he gradually developed an oversized scapula where the articulation with his upper humerus (shoulder area) on the right side resulted from the need to compensate for the loss of muscle tone.

Timur's index finger showed a permanent crook which had resulted from continued use of his digits where they had been constricted after the damage to his elbow and the muscle fibers ranging downward. The area of the right wrist was also enlarged as a result of his activity during convalescence to counter any display of deficiency in front of his army. The pathological search of his remains also revealed that he had more than just an incipient case of tuberculosis. This alone could account for his gradual decline in robust health.

Other than this, no signs of debilitating sickness were evident. Although Timur's teeth were well worn, his broad shoulders and otherwise heavy frame bore out claims that attested to his rugged condition. His mouth was described by the scientific experts as full and wide with straight and well defined nostrils. His hair was not curly as described by a contemporary, and his fairly short triangular beard contrasted with a characteristic long drooping mustache. It was concluded that Timur's demise was probably brought about by a respiratory failure, possibly a variety of pneumonia. Treatment in those days was confined to little understood symptoms in the internal system.

# *Appendix B*

## *Mulfuzat — The Institutes of Timur*

Be it known to my fortunate Children, to my intelligent Ministers, to my faithful and zealous Nobles, that Almighty God, on account of the Twelve following Rules, which I have constantly practiced, hath conferred greatness on me, and hath made me Shepherd of his flock, and hath assisted me by pre-eminence of Sovereignty:

1st. Having taken in hand the Scales of Justice, I have neither increased nor decreased (the portion of any one) but weighed equally to all;

2nd. I have administered strict justice to mankind and endeavored to discriminate between truth and falsehood;

3rd. I paid obedience to the orders of God and respected his holy laws, and honored those whom he had honored;

4th. I had compassion on mankind and conferred benefits on all, and by these qualities, I gained the affections of God's creatures, nor did I ever vex a single heart by injustice, I never turned away a supplicant from my court, but whoever took refuge with me I assisted;

5th. I ever gave the affairs of religion precedence over worldly affairs. I first performed my duty towards God and then attended to my worldly concerns;

6th. I always spoke the truth, and ever listened to the truth, and with sincerity performed my religious and secular duties, and avoided the paths of crookedness. For I have heard that, when God created Adam, the Angels said to each other, "A creature has been formed whose posterity will be liars, breakers of their promise, and guilty of wickedness." The Lord said to the Angels, "I will send a Sword among them, which shall cut in pieces every perverse or unrighteous person it encounters," as I have heard that the Sword there meant is (the power of) Princes, it is therefore incumbent on every Monarch to speak and listen only to truth;

7th. I have always performed whatever I promised to any person, nor ever deviated from my agreement. I was never guilty of Tyranny nor Injustice, nor ever permitted myself to fall into vice or infamy, nor, on any occasion, did I cut the cord of affection due to my children, grand-children, relations, or connexions.

8th. I considered myself as the Treasurer of the property of God, and never expended any of his sacred property without the sanction of his deputies (the clergy). In collecting the revenues from his servants, I observed lenity and discretion, nor did I employ myself in accumulating riches or substance, but ever looked to the welfare and happiness of my soldiers and subjects: thus did I not touch the accumulations of my Father's nobles, nor was I covetous of the property of any person; for it is known to me, by experience, that Amir Hussein having cast the eyes of covetousness upon the property of his soldiers and subjects, and seized upon wealth of his Father's nobles, his prosperity was soon annihilated;

9th. I considered obedience to God as consisting in submission to his prophet, and therefore acted according to the Law of Muhammed, and did nothing contrary to that sacred code: I always considered the Descendants of Muhammed (on whom be the peace of God) and the companions of his Holiness as my friends, and performed to them the duties of affection;

10th. I gave currency to the faith of Islam through all my dominions, and supported religion, by which means I gave stability to my government; - for I had heard that Church and State are twins, and that every sovereignty that is not supported by religion soon loses all authority, and its orders are not obeyed, but that every person, worthy or unworthy, presumes to meddle therewith;

11th. I gave free admission to the Syeds*, to the learned, and to the prelates of religion, and always treated them with great respect, and never turned any of them away from my court, so that they constantly attended my assemblies, and induced the people to pray for my prosperity; I constantly associated with the learned and

* descendants of Muhammed, also called "seids"

religious, and heard from them many anecdotes, both of sacred and profane history;

Thus they related to me that the King of Constantinople, once invaded the dominions of the King of Ry, but having heard that his Court was attended by numbers of Syeds, and many learned and devout personages, he refrained from subduing his country, but wrote to the Ministers and Nobles, "I have read in the Heavenly books, that whatever Court is attended by learned, devout, and religious persons, that Government cannot be overturned, and having been informed that such is the case of your country, I am convinced it cannot be subdued." He also wrote to the King, "Whereas I have discovered that your disposition resembles that of our former just Monarchs, I have not injured your country, but having withdrawn my army, have ceased from attacking you. Farewell."

12th. I asked the blessings of the Hermits, of the other inspired and holy persons, and besought their prayers; I also protected the Anchorets and the Dervishes, I never vexed them, but captivated their hearts; I exerted myself in arranging the affairs of the Musulmans, and avoided killing any of their people; I paid particular respect to the descendants of the Prophet, and was cautious never to degrade or injure any of that noble race; I also shunned the discourse of the wicked and ungodly;

For I had heard that when God elects a person to the government of a country, and places in his hands the reins of authority over mankind, in order that he may rule them with justice, if he conducts himself with equity and propriety, his kingdom endures, but if on the contrary, he is guilty of injustice and tyranny, and commits unlawful actions, the Lord renders him childless, and takes away his Dominion and Sovereignty, to give them to another;

Wherefore in order to preserve my Sovereignty, I took Justice in one hand, and Equity in the other hand, and, by the light of these two lamps, I kept the palace of Royalty illuminated;

As I had heard that just Kings are the Shadow of God, and that the best King is he who imitates the disposition of the Lord, in forgiving sinners, I followed the examples of those just Kings, and forgave my enemies.

*Note:* The Institutes continued with twelve rules of conduct to correspond to the twelve signs of the zodiac. Following this were the twelve classes of people, with each given a prescribed method of treatment. Rules were listed for the establishment of courts, judges, and religious teaching.

An old book, found in Medina by Abu Talib-ul-Husaini, a native of the Khorassan, recorded the events of Timur's life from his seventh year to his last years of existence. It also detailed sundry rules of ordinance relating to king craft and strategy. (The original has never been produced, therefore, its contents were later altered to conform with the *Zafar Namah.*)

# Appendix C

## The Political and Military Institutes of Timur*

Selected briefs from the original text of the *Tuzukats:*

"People broken by oppression, though readily agreeing with an opposition may break their engagements."

"When a person aspiring to the throne is known among the people, they will look with observation at him. Therefore, he must please them. He must show royal generosity and 'ligerality.'"

"Unless it be quite necessary, a prince should not displease officers of his own promotion."

"History and politics should be studied by a prince; that he may know what had happened to royalties and realms, and wherefor how it happened."

"Not only good and great men are to be rewarded, but enemies and traitors on submission are to be pardoned and used as friends, till their suspicions are overcome and their hearts won. Especially if they are brave, wise and eminent."

"When those who are injured can be made friends, their injuries are not to be revenged, but forgot. If they still will be evil, they are to be left for a time. Else they are to be overcome with good."

"A prince should hear advice from everyone, but to attend to none as to make him equal or superior to his self in ruling."

---

* Written originally in the Mongol language translated by Major Davy, Oxford Clarendon Press, 1783.

---

# Appendix D

## The Military and Religious Edicts of Timur

"Councils tending to divide the soldiers are not to be hearkened to and the dictates of fear are not to be regarded."

"And I saw the duration of my power in this, that I should divide among my soldiers the treasures which I had gathered."

"It is known to me by experience that every empire, which is not established in morality and religion, shall pass away."

"I united myself with holy men and pious men; with those to whom the almighty had given wisdom. And I associated with them. And I heard from them the word of God. And I acquired knowledge of the blessings of a future state. And I saw them perform miracles and wonderful things. And I reaped delight from their conversation."

"And by experience it is known to me, that there are two kinds of counsel; that which proceedeth from the tongue, and that which proceedeth from the heart. I turned my ear to that which proceedeth from the tongue; but to the counsel of the heart, which I heard, I gave a place in the treasury of my soul."

"And in times of hostility I found counsel relative to peace and to war; and I studied the hearts of my chiefs, whither they were desirous of war or of peace. And if they advised peace, I compared the advantages of peace with the perils of war. And if they proposed war, I opposed the benefits and advantages thereof to the inconveniences and dangers that might follow from peace; and which ever appeared most profitable, that I preferred and approved."

Note: Known as Timur's Statement of Purpose from his *Tuzukats*

# Glossary

| | |
|---|---|
| Ak | white |
| Amir | ruler; prince |
| Atabeg | tutor; guardian |
| Bagh | garden |
| Bahaudur | valorous man |
| Beg | noble |
| Cadi | judge; scholar |
| Dagh | mountain |
| Darband | (pass) mountain |
| Darya | sea or river |
| Darugha | governor |
| Dervish | religious acetic |
| Elchi | official messenger |
| Gur | mausoleum |
| Gurgan | son-in-law |
| Ghazi | Islamic warrior |
| Jete | semi-nomad from Jettah |
| Kabil | chief |
| Kara | black |
| Karshi | palace |
| Khalif (Caliph) | Moslem ruler |
| Khan | king; prince |
| Khitay | Cathay |
| Khizr | Islamic immortal |
| Kibitka | round felt tent |
| Koran | "recitation" in Arabic |
| Kurgancha | fortress |
| Madrasa | school; college |
| Malik | king; prince |
| Mamluk | early slave class; later, ruling class in Egypt |
| Meerza | prince |

| | |
|---|---|
| Moghul | resident of Moghulstan |
| Mullah | teacher in the mosque |
| Musulman | one of Muslim faith |
| Noyon | noble; lord |
| Ordu | Mongol tribe |
| Qara | black |
| Qizil | red |
| Sarai | palace; government seat |
| Seid (Syed) | descendent of Muhammed |
| Sharaf | holy law of Islam |
| Tamga | official seal |
| Tugh | horsetail standard |
| Touman | ten thousand warriors |
| Ulus | tribal area |
| Vizier | court noble in charge of finance |
| Yam | posting station for horses |
| Yurt | apportioned grazing land |

# References

Alhussein, Abu Talib *Institutes, Political and Military,* translated from the Persian by Major Wm. Davy, Oxford Clarendon Press, 1783

Arabshah, Ahmed Ibn *Tamerlane, or Timur the Great Amir,* translated by J.H. Sanders, Luzac & Co. London, 1936

Barthold, V.V. *Four Studies on the History of Central Asia,* translated from the Russian by V. Minorsky, Leiden, E.J. Brill, 1962

Berezikov, Evgeny *The Great Timur,* translated by Marina Karpova, Tashkent, 1994

Davy, Major *Timur, Great Khan of the Mongols,* edited by Professor J. White, Oxford Press, 1783

de Clavijo, Ruy Gonzalez *Narrative of the Embassy to the Court of Timur at Samarkand,* A.D. 1403, translated by Clements R. Markham, Hakluyt Society, 1859

de la Croix, Petis *Histoire de Timur Bec, Empereur des Mogols et Tatary,* Vol. 1&2, 1723

Elliot, Sir H.M. *Tuzak/Timur,* Sind Sagar Academy, Lahore Pakistan 1974

Fischel, Walter J. *Ibn Khaldun and Tamerlane,* Univ. of California Press, Berkeley & Los Angeles, 1952

Ghyasaldin *Habeebussiyar (Life of Tamerlane),* Vol. V&VI, Bombay Univ., 1900

*Gourasri The Era, the Personality, the Deeds* (series of monographs), authors shown below: translated by Marina Karpova, Moscow, 1992
– Barthold, V. *On the Burial of Timur*
– Gerasimov, M. *The Portrait of Timur*
– Klavicho, G. *The History of Timur the Great*
– Lyangle, L. *The Life of Timur*
– Metsopsky, F. *Tamerlan*

- Mouminov, I. *The Role and Place of Timur in the History of the Middle Asia*
- Vambery, G. *Description of Timur*
- Yakubousky, A. *Timur*
- Zimin, J. *Details of Timur's Death*

Hookham, Hilda *Tamburlaine the Conqueror,* Hodder & Stoughton, London, 1962

Lamb, Harold *Tamerlane, the Earth Shaker,* Garden City Publishing Co., New York, 1928

LanePoole, Stanley *The Mohammedan Dynasties,* Oriental University Press, London, Revised ed. 1925

Malcolm, Col. Sir John *The History of Persia* Vol 1, Pahlavi Commemerative Series, April, 1976

Manz, Beatrice F. *The Rise and Rule of Tamerlane,* Cambridge Univ. Press, 1989

Marlowe Christopher *Tambourlaine the Great,* London, 1580

Nicolle, David *The Mongol Warlords,* Firebird Books, 1990

Nicolle, David *The Age of Tamerlane,* Ospry Publishing , Ltd. London, 1990

Price, Major David *Mahommedan History* Vol III, Part I, London, 1821

Rieu, Charles *The Persian Manuscripts,* British Library Vol I, 1879

Scrine, Francis S. & Ross, Edward D. *The Heart of Asia,* Arno Press, New York Times Co., New York, 1973

Sharaf-ud-din *Zafar Namah (Book of Victory),* Translated by John Darby, London, 1723

Sokol, Edward D. *Tamerlane,* Coronado Press, Lawrence, Kansas, 1977

Stewart, Major C. *Timur, Great Khan of the Mongols,* London, 1830

Storey, C.A. *Persian Literature,* Royal Asiatic Society of Great Britain and Ireland, Luzac & Co. Ltd., London, 1970

Sykes, Gen. Sir Percy *A History of Persia Vol II,* Barnes & Noble, New York, 1969

Telfer, Commander J.B. and Bruun, Prof. P. *The Bondage and Travels of Johann Schiltberger* (1396–1427), Burt Franklin, New York, 1859, reprinted 1970

Thomas, William *Travels to Tana and Persia,* translation for the Hakluyt Society, 1873

Vambery, Arminius *History of Bokhara,* Henry S. King & Co. London, 1873

Wepmen, Dennis *Tamerlane,* Chelsea House Publishers, New York, New Haven, Philadelphia, 1987

White, Edward *Tamburlaine, the Great,* printed for North Door of St. Paul, London, 1605

# Index

To order additional copies of

## *Tamerlane, The Ultimate Warrior*

Book: $16.95    Shipping/Handling $3.50

Contact: ***BookPartners, Inc.***
P.O. Box 922, Wilsonville, OR 97070
Fax: 503-682-8684
Phone 503-682-9821
Phone: 1-800-895-7323